What Is Philosophy?

As philosophy departments attempt to define their unique value amid program closures in the humanities and the rise of interdisciplinary research, metaphilosophy has become an increasingly important area of inquiry. Richard Fumerton here lays out a cogent answer to the question asked in the book's title, *What Is Philosophy?*. Against those who argue that philosophy is not sharply distinguishable from the sciences, Fumerton makes a case for philosophy as an autonomous discipline with its own distinct methodology.

Over the course of nine engaging and accessible chapters, he shows that answering fundamental philosophical questions requires one to take a radical first-person perspective that divorces the truth conditions of philosophical claims from the kind of contingent truths investigated by the empirical sciences. Along the way, Fumerton briefly discusses the historical controversies that have surrounded the nature of philosophy, situating his own argument within the larger conversation.

Key Features

- Illuminates the unique role of thought experiments and especially the "paradox of analysis" in understanding the purpose and value of philosophy.
- Shows that philosophy asks fundamental questions, unanswerable by the sciences, that are critical to thinking clearly and rationally about the world.
- Highlights the distinct character of philosophical questions in specific subject areas: philosophy of language, epistemology, ethics, philosophy of mind, and philosophy of science.
- Concludes by making a unique case for philosophy's contribution to cross-disciplinary work in ethics, politics, mathematics, and the empirical sciences.
- Written in a way to be engaging and accessible for advanced undergraduate readers.

Richard Fumerton is the F. Wendell Miller Professor of Philosophy at the University of Iowa. He is the author of, among other books, *Realism and the Correspondence Theory of Truth* (2002), *Epistemology* (2006), *Mill* (co-authored with Wendy Donner) (2009), *Knowledge, Thought and the Case for Dualism* (2013), and *A Consequentialist Defense of Libertarianism* (2021). With Diane Jeske, he has also edited *Philosophy Through Film* (2009), and *An Introduction to Political Philosophy* (2012).

What Is Philosophy?

A First-Person Perspective

Richard Fumerton

NEW YORK AND LONDON

First published 2023
by Routledge
605 Third Avenue, New York, NY 10158

and by Routledge
4 Park Square, Milton Park, Abingdon, Oxon, OX14 4RN

Routledge is an imprint of the Taylor & Francis Group, an informa business

© 2023 Taylor & Francis

The right of Richard Fumerton to be identified as author of this work has been asserted in accordance with sections 77 and 78 of the Copyright, Designs and Patents Act 1988.

All rights reserved. No part of this book may be reprinted or reproduced or utilised in any form or by any electronic, mechanical, or other means, now known or hereafter invented, including photocopying and recording, or in any information storage or retrieval system, without permission in writing from the publishers.

Trademark notice: Product or corporate names may be trademarks or registered trademarks, and are used only for identification and explanation without intent to infringe.

ISBN: 978-1-032-12205-2 (hbk)
ISBN: 978-1-032-12203-8 (pbk)
ISBN: 978-1-003-22356-6 (ebk)

DOI: 10.4324/9781003223566

Typeset in Bembo
by codeMantra

For Patti

Contents

Acknowledgments   xi
Preface   xiii

PART I
How to Approach Metaphilosophy   1

1 **Introduction**   3
    1.1 Philosophy as a Distinct Field 3
    1.2 Meta-Questions within Fields of Philosophy 5
      1.2.1 Ethics as an Example 5
      1.2.2 Epistemology as Another Example 7
      1.2.3 Metaphilosophy 8
    1.3 Some Examples of Paradigmatic Philosophical Questions 9
    1.4 Different Conceptions of Philosophy—A Very Brief Overview 13
      1.4.1 Philosophy as a Search for Fundamental
          Categories of Reality 14
      1.4.2 Conceptual Analysis 15
      1.4.3 The Linguistic Turn 16
      1.4.4 A Second Linguistic Turn—Content Externalism 18
    1.5 Doing Metaphilosophy without Begging Questions 20

2 **The Paradox of Analysis and Methodological Solipsism**   24
    2.1 The Paradox of Analysis 24
    2.2 Methodological Solipsism and a Master Argument 28

3 **What's Left?**   35
    3.1 Foundationalism and Phenomenology 35
      3.1.1 Phenomenology: The Starting Point of All
          Philosophical Reflection 40

3.2 Philosophical Analysis 45
   3.2.1 Stipulative Definition 47
   3.2.2 Beyond Stipulation 51
   3.2.3 More about Thought Experiments 53
   3.2.4 Wittgenstein and the Private Language Argument 56
3.3 Beyond Phenomenology and Analysis—"Internal" Relations among Properties 58
3.4 Summarizing 61

PART II
Illustrating the View—Mapping Clear Borders   67

4 Philosophy of Language   69
4.1 Externalism about Meaning 69
4.2 The Significance of the Content Internalism/Externalism Controversy for Understanding Philosophy 73
4.3 Rejecting Externalism 75

5 Epistemology and Metaepistemology   80
5.1 Knowledge 80
5.2 Epistemic Justification/Rationality 84
   5.2.1 Non-epistemic Reasons to Believe 84
   5.2.2 Propositional vs Doxastic Justification 84
   5.2.3 The Internalism/Externalism Controversy in Epistemology 85
5.3 The Implications of the Internalism/Externalism Controversy for What Else Should Be Included in Philosophical Epistemology 89

6 Ethics and Rationality/Metaethics and Meta-rationality   97
6.1 Rational Action 98
   6.1.1 Regress 102
6.2 Morality 102
   6.2.1 Intrinsic Value 103
   6.2.2 Right Action, Duties, Obligations, Virtues, and Supererogation 105
6.3 Summary 111

7 Philosophy of Mind   114
7.1 Meta-Questions in the Philosophy of Mind 115
   7.1.1 Phenomenology Again 115

7.1.2　Substance vs Property Dualism　116
　　　7.1.3　Applying Our Conception of Philosophy to the
　　　　　　Philosophy of Mind　118
　7.2　*Inappropriate Philosophical Intrusion into Empirical Matters*　124
　7.3　*Summary*　129

8　**Philosophy of Science and Metaphysics**　　　　　　　　　　131
　8.1　*Philosophy of Science—An Older Paradigm*　131
　8.2　*Causation and Explanation*　132
　8.3　*Space and Time*　136
　8.4　*Epistemology and the Philosophy of Science*　138
　　　8.4.1　Is There a Distinction between the Observable
　　　　　　and the Theoretical?　139
　　　8.4.2　How to Understand the Theoretical　141
　8.5　*From Philosophy of Science to Traditional Metaphysics*　142
　8.6　*Summary*　146

9　**The Relevance of Philosophy Proper**　　　　　　　　　　　150
　9.1　*Intellectual Curiosity*　151
　9.2　*Positioning Oneself Better to Answer Applied Questions*　152
　9.3　*For Whom Is This Book Written*　156

References　　　　　　　　　　　　　　　　　　　　　　　　159
Index　　　　　　　　　　　　　　　　　　　　　　　　　　167

Acknowledgments

I can't possibly list the many past and present colleagues and students to whom I owe gratitude for helpful discussions we have had about the nature of philosophy. I do want to specifically mention my teachers at Brown University who were so helpful to (and patient with) a graduate student who had far too much misplaced confidence in his philosophical views. I learned so much about philosophy from Rod Chisholm, Ernie Sosa, and James van Cleve (among others). When I first came to Iowa my early views about the nature of philosophy were challenged in instructive ways by Gustav Bergmann, Panayot Butchvarov, Laird Addis, and Phil Cummins. In more recent years, I have continued metaphilosophical discussion at Iowa with my colleagues Gregory Landini, Ali Hasan, David Stern, David Cunning, Asha Bhandary, Katarina Perovic, Jovana Davidovic, and Diane Jeske. Diane has been particularly helpful in reading drafts of some of this book's chapters. I also discussed parts of this manuscript with both undergraduates and graduate students in a seminar I taught in the Spring of 2022. Their questions and objections were very helpful to me in thinking through the issues I discuss in the book. I would also like to thank an anonymous reviewer for helpful comments on an earlier draft of this manuscript.

Work on this book was supported by generous financial support from the University of Iowa and its Board of Regents.

Preface

I have been a professional philosopher for half a century. It's not a bad time to collect thoughts about just what I've been doing all this time. Indeed, one might suppose that the metaphilosophical question of what makes a question philosophical is the *first* question a philosopher should ask. Doesn't it seem almost obvious that one should know what one is trying to do, before one tries to do it?[1]

Consider some analogies. Many philosophers argue that we need to investigate metaethical questions (questions about the *nature* of value) before we turn to applied ethical questions. Why? Because if we aren't clear about what would make a state of the world valuable or what would make an action right, we aren't in an ideal position to *find* value or *recognize* the right course of action to take. Similarly, some would argue that we shouldn't try to decide *what* we know or rationally believe until we answer the metaepistemological questions: "What is required for knowledge?" and "What would make a belief epistemically rational?" If the meta-questions have a kind of priority in various fields within philosophy, why wouldn't the analogous meta-question about philosophy as a discipline have that same sort of priority? The answer to this question isn't all that clear, nor is it obvious how a philosopher should investigate the question of what philosophy is. This book will address these questions.

The discussion of what philosophy is and what makes a question paradigmatically philosophical is particularly timely. Interdisciplinary research is all the rage today, and philosophy departments are urged by some to become more relevant by partnering with other disciplines (like psychology, neurology, cognitive science, physics, political science, linguistics, social science, gender studies, and law, to name but a few). But before one engages in interdisciplinary work, it is a good idea to get clear about just what makes individual disciplines distinct and what sort of contribution each discipline can make to interdisciplinary or cross-disciplinary research. Doing that requires one to engage in metaphilosophical thought—it requires one to think about the subject matter and methodology of philosophy.

Overview

This book will be divided into two main parts. Part I addresses in an abstract way the question of how to understand philosophy. In Chapter 1, I'll give examples of controversies that I take to be paradigmatically philosophical, and briefly discuss why it seems impossible to resolve these controversies through scientific investigation. I'll then go on to give a brief overview of some of the historically influential views about how to understand philosophy. The chapter will conclude with what amounts to a meta-metaphilosophical discussion in which I will explain how I plan to investigate the nature of philosophy without encountering a regress.

In Chapter 2, I'll argue for two constraints on any plausible conception of philosophy. I argue *first* that philosophy must account for what is sometimes called the paradox of analysis. It seems to be a *datum* that philosophy is hard and that rational philosophers disagree with each other, often dramatically, on how to answer paradigmatically philosophical questions. This is viewed by some as a paradox, or at least a puzzle (going back to Plato's *Meno*), because one might think that in order to be in a position to address a philosophical question (say a question about knowledge), one must already understand the question. But if one understands a question about the nature of knowledge, one already knows what knowledge is—one already has an answer to the metaepistemological question. One's conception of philosophy should resolve this puzzle.

Second, relying heavily on an analogy with a well-known (though highly controversial) approach to discovering the foundations of knowledge and justified belief, I will argue that one gains critical insight into the nature of philosophy by reflecting on the fact that the *truth* of philosophical positions and the ability to *discover* such truths are compatible with some *very* radical skeptical scenarios.

In Chapter 3, I re-examine *traditional* metaphilosophical views in light of the claim that there is a paradox of analysis and the claim that philosophical truths are compatible with radical skeptical scenarios. These two claims form the premises of what I call a "master argument" for the conclusion that the traditional conceptions of philosophy surveyed in Chapter 1 are inadequate. I explain my own conception of philosophy and compare and contrast it with other approaches. The conception of philosophy I defend includes the results of phenomenology and what I call philosophical analysis from the first-person perspective. The question of what *else* belongs in philosophy *proper* crucially depends on *what* we discover through first-person philosophical reflection.

Part II of the book tries to illustrate the conception of philosophy I endorse by looking at fundamental questions in some of the most important areas of philosophy. Through these examples, I try to explain how I think one can draw clear borders between philosophy *proper* and the kinds of questions that can only be answered through scientific investigation. Where the border lies, I argue, depends on what the answers *are* to the fundamental philosophical questions that arise in different areas of philosophy. I'll end the book by explaining how I think we should view the way in which philosophy *can* contribute to cross-disciplinary work in mathematics and the empirical sciences.

Note

1 I'll talk more about what makes a question a *meta*-question in the next chapter. Briefly a meta-question is a question about a question. A *meta*-meta-question is a question about a question about a question. And so on as we add more "meta" prefixes.

Part I
How to Approach Metaphilosophy

Chapter 1
Introduction

1.1 Philosophy as a Distinct Field

As I mentioned in the Preface, professional philosophers today are often encouraged to partner with academics in other fields to find answers they seek to the questions they ask. One might argue that this amounts to the suggestion that we *return* to what was the norm centuries and even millennia earlier. Many of the most influential intellectuals in the history of thought didn't explicitly carve up their inquiries into the academic fields we recognize today. Aristotle was as much interested in what we would call physics, astronomy, psychology, and biology as what we would call philosophy. Plato built much of his ethical and political philosophy around a science of human nature, and even famously speculated about the whereabouts of the fabled lost continent of Atlantis. Descartes thought of himself as a mathematician, physicist, and biologist (and often tried to get patronage by suggesting he was close to finding a "fountain of youth"). Hobbes was a mathematician, a metaphysician, and a political philosopher. Berkeley and Hume are two of the most influential empiricists. Although famous as an idealist (a philosopher committed to the view that everything that exists is either a mind or an idea), Berkeley also wrote a sophisticated work on the nature of vision. And the Scottish philosopher David Hume (who certainly *seemed* to be a fairly extreme skeptic)[1] also had views about human psychology, and wrote what was once considered to be the most definitive history of England. In the early twentieth century, many intellectuals like Mach and Russell straddled the fields of theoretical mathematics, theoretical physics, and what we would recognize as philosophy. So the suggestion that we focus more on interdisciplinary or cross-disciplinary work might just be the proposal that our future should look more like our past.

There were, however, reasons that intellectuals began to specialize, particularly beginning in the middle to the late twentieth century. On a purely pragmatic level, as venues for publication proliferated, it became exceedingly difficult to keep up with the literature in more than a very few fields. But another explanation, of more relevance to the present work, is the idea that over time we got better at distinguishing different sorts of controversies that need to be investigated in distinct ways. Plato and Aristotle may have asked all sorts of different questions, but the questions *were* different, and not just in terms of *specific* content, but in terms of important differences among the *kinds* of questions they were. Hume *qua historian* was interested in all of the salacious gossip and intrigue involving the royalty of England. *Qua* psychologist, he was interested in empirical questions about inferences (legitimate and illegitimate) that people make. But *qua* philosopher, he was trying to answer very different sorts of questions. Or so I will argue.

The turn to specialization occurred even within the fields that correspond to the different departments recognized in most research universities. So if you find yourself at an American Philosophical Association Meeting, you'll find some slightly strange looking people who, when they introduce themselves, often soon identify their areas of specialization within philosophy. The most traditional areas of philosophy include metaphysics (an investigation into the fundamental categories of existence), epistemology (the study of knowledge and justified belief), ethics (the study of value, right and wrong, duty, obligation, and virtue), and political philosophy (an area that might, controversially, be thought of as largely a branch of ethics—the study of duties and obligations that states have to their citizens, and citizens have to their states). But these fields are very broad, and at least most philosophers will argue that within metaphysics and epistemology we should single out the philosophy of mind and the philosophy of science. And within ethics and political philosophy, we should recognize a distinction between more theoretical questions and more applied questions. The more applied areas of ethics include feminist ethics, critical race theory, military ethics, ethics and biology, business ethics, agricultural ethics, and so on. One might also include in ethics at least some of the questions that arise in the philosophy of law.

The above *crude* characterizations of some of the different areas of philosophy are all very controversial. There are different ways of slicing the philosophical pie. Gustav Bergmann once suggested to me that *all* of philosophy is metaphysics.[2] Epistemology, for example, should be thought of as the metaphysics of the knowing situation, ethics, as the metaphysics of value. As we shall see I'm more than a bit sympathetic with Bergmann's idea. And as we'll also see there are conceptions of philosophy that won't recognize as *fundamentally* philosophical some of the questions that arise in various sub-disciplines within philosophy. We'll return to these matters throughout the book.

At the outset, I should stress that when I conclude that a given discipline does not fall within philosophy **proper**, I am **not** in any way disparaging the importance of answering the questions that arise within that discipline.

As I shall try to make clear, my primary goal is to find a way of distinguishing philosophy *proper* from both mathematics and the many critically important empirical sciences. And this might be an appropriate point at which to acknowledge the fundamentally important area within philosophy that is called the *history* of philosophy. Historians of philosophy (like all other philosophers) disagree about how to characterize what they are doing.[3] But superficially, it certainly seems as if the historian of philosophy is trying to figure out just *what* important and influential historical philosophers believed and *why* they believed it. They also try to place in some sort of helpful context the way in which those views and arguments evolved. I would be the first to argue that the best historians of philosophy are also excellent philosophers. The philosopher trying to come up with the most *charitable* interpretations of Aristotle, Plato, Descartes, Leibniz, Kant, Berkeley, Hume, Mill, Russell, Wittgenstein, or Quine (to take a few examples) needs to understand what a *plausible* view is and what a *plausible* argument for that view might be. But having said that, in this book I intend to treat the history of philosophy as a field that is in many respects more like history than it is like philosophy. Certainly, the "master" argument I will present for thinking of philosophy *proper* in a certain way will not recognize as *fundamentally* philosophical some of the most important claims made by historians of philosophy.

1.2 Meta-Questions within Fields of Philosophy

One of the oldest areas of philosophy is the field of metaphysics. The name for that field is created, of course, by adding the prefix "meta" to "physics." But physics is not recognized as a paradigmatic field of philosophy. And if we try to explain the way in which the prefix "meta" added to the description of a field changes the kind of questions we are asking in the meta-field we might beg some important questions by focusing first on metaphysics. Instead, I'll talk here about more recent creations of a kind of discipline within fields of philosophy through the use of the prefix "meta." I'll return to metaphysics in Chapter 8.

1.2.1 Ethics as an Example

As noted above philosophers often make a distinction between meta-questions and more applied questions in various fields of philosophy. The addition of the prefix "meta" to generate an area within a field of philosophy is perhaps most familiar in the field of ethics. So the philosopher in ethics might be trying to figure out what things or kinds of things are good or bad. After making a distinction between the things that are good/bad as a *means* (*instrumentally* good/bad, good/bad for their *consequences*) and things that are good/bad *in themselves* (*intrinsically* good/bad, good/bad just in virtue of what they are), the philosophers in ethics might *first* ask the question of what things (or more usually *kinds* of things) are intrinsically good/bad.

But ethics is also concerned with answering questions about how one ought to behave, what our duties or obligations are, which actions are morally impermissible, and so on. Ethicists might also be interested in the question of what kinds of people are virtuous (what character traits one ought to develop). All of these questions are obviously interesting and important. But, some ethicists would argue, they are not the most *fundamental* questions in the field of ethics. Before we answer *any* of the above ethical questions, we need to ask philosophical questions *about* ethical questions. Put another way, we need to engage in metaethics. The prefix "meta" when used by philosophers just indicates that we are moving up a level. Meta-questions are questions about first-level[4] questions. Meta-meta-questions are questions about questions about questions, and so on.[5]

Philosophers love to move up levels and often when they do controversies arise. Controversies arise as to how to even *state* the relevant meta-questions. So it won't be easy to give uncontroversial examples of metaethical questions. We might start with a formulation of such questions that seems to focus on *language*. Understood this way metaethical questions include the following: What does it *mean* to say of something that it is intrinsically good/bad?; What does it *mean* to say that the right thing for someone S to do is X, that someone S morally ought to do X, that S is morally obligated to do X, that S is morally permitted to do X, that S is virtuous?

As we indicated, and as we will discuss at some length later in this book, some philosophers would object to characterizing the distinction between metaethics and applied ethics[6] as questions about *meaning*. Some might prefer to understand metaethics as an investigation into *ideas* or *concepts*. On this way of characterizing metaethics, the metaethical questions might be rephrased as follows: What is the *idea* or *concept* of being intrinsically good/bad?; What is the *idea* or *concept* of an action's being right/wrong, obligatory, or permissible? What is the *idea* or *concept* of virtue?

Still, other philosophers would resist the suggestion that metaethical questions have anything to do with *either* language *or* concepts or ideas, at least if concepts or ideas are understood as something that is tied to the existence of conscious beings.[7] They might prefer the metaethical questions to be focused on ethical *properties*. So when they think about something's being intrinsically good, their statement of the metaethical question might be: What is the property or characteristic of being intrinsically good—the property or characteristic that makes the thing in question intrinsically good? If an action is the right action to take, what is this property or characteristic of being right that the action in question has (and that alternatives to that action lack)? If certain kinds of actions are at least *prima facie*[8] obligatory, what is this property of being *prima facie* obligatory that actions of this sort have.

The emphasis on ethical properties in metaethics is particularly problematic, however, given that some ethicists have endorsed metaethical *non-cognitivism*. Put simply, the non-cognitivist holds that ethical utterances are neither true nor false. It is, perhaps, an initially implausible view given that we don't seem to feel the slightest bit odd about asking someone what they *believe* we ought to do in a given situation. Nor would we think that there is anything odd about the question, "Do you think that it is *true* that we should legalize all abortion?" But non-cognitivists argue that they can make a compelling case for the view that the "surface grammar"[9] of ethical language is misleading. Despite the fact that at least some ethical statements look as if they are descriptions, they argue, we would do better to construe such utterances as having the same sort of meaning that an imperative has (a view sometimes called *prescriptivism*), or the same sort of meaning that an interjection has (a crude version of a view that is sometimes called *emotivism*). In any event, if we don't want to beg the question against the non-cognitivist's metaethical view, we cannot assume at the outset that there *are* moral properties (properties that are picked out by adjectives like "good" or "right."

Again, some of those who make the distinction between metaethics and applied ethics would argue that metaethical questions are more fundamental. As ideally rational agents, we aren't in a position to discover what is good or bad, right or wrong, and so on, until we *understand* fully the object of our search.

I.2.2 Epistemology as Another Example

A little reflection will convince us that the sort of distinction we make between metaethics and applied ethics can be made in other fields of philosophy. I described epistemology as the field of philosophy that investigates questions about knowledge and justified belief. But the meta-/applied-distinction is again important. We can ask *what* we know or are justified in believing (questions in applied epistemology), or, alternatively, we can ask what knowledge or justified belief *is*. And again, there will be controversies that arise concerning the most perspicuous way of framing the metaepistemological questions. We might put the questions in terms of meaning. On this sort of view the metaepistemological questions might take the form: What does it *mean* to say of someone S that S knows or justifiably believes that P. We might also understand the relevant meta-questions as questions about ideas or concepts: What is the idea or concept of knowledge and justified belief? Or one might insist that the metaepistemological inquiry is the search for the properties of knowing or justifiably believing.

Just as one might argue that metaethical questions need to be answered before we try to answer questions in applied ethics, so also one might argue that metaepistemological questions need to be answered before we try to answer questions in "applied" epistemology.

1.2.3 Metaphilosophy

We've talked about meta-questions that arise within various fields of philosophy, but we haven't said much about what makes a question philosophical. When we ask *that* question, we are asking a metaphilosophical question. And just as it is tempting to suppose that one should answer metaethical questions before one tries to answer ethical questions, and metaepistemological questions before one tries to answer epistemological questions, so also one might think that in order to do philosophy one should first do metaphilosophy.

In discussing very briefly controversies about how to ask metaethical questions or metaepistemological questions, we have already hinted at some of the controversies that arise concerning how to ask metaphilosophical questions. We could construe metaphilosophical questions as questions about the meaning of "philosophy," as questions about the concept or idea of philosophy, or as questions about the property of being philosophical. But how do we choose the right way to ask a metaphilosophical question without presupposing some understanding of philosophy? We certainly don't want to be seduced into thinking that we need to ask meta-metaphilosophical questions before we try to do metaphilosophy—we know where that will lead. We will be soaring endlessly into the increasingly rarified air of ever higher-level meta-questions.

One way to start is to consider briefly a few *paradigmatic* philosophical questions with an eye to discovering what those questions have in common. I am particularly interested in making an initially plausible case for the conclusion that none of these paradigmatically philosophical controversies can be settled by the empirical sciences. I won't pretend that I have no agendum in selecting what I call paradigms. There is a reason that the sub-title of this book is "A First-Person Perspective"! But in the concluding remarks of this chapter, I'll try to deflect the charge of begging metaphilosophical questions.

Of course, there is an even less subtle way of distinguishing philosophical questions from scientific questions. That is to stipulate at the outset that we will not count a scientific question as a philosophical question. That seems to be precisely what Ayer famously did in his classic *Language, Truth and Logic*. In the first chapter of that book he suggests that it really isn't that hard to discover the subject matter of philosophy. We just do it through a process of elimination. If a question is scientific, he seems to argue, then it obviously isn't philosophical. Ayer's thought also finds expression when Alston and Brandt (1967) in their introduction to an anthology say:

> Philosophy is an attempt to arrive at reasoned answers to important questions which by reason of their ultimacy and or generality are not treated by any of the more special disciplines.

They go on to explain the critical notion of ultimacy:

> By speaking of questions as ultimate, sometimes we mean that some answer to them is taken for granted by anyone who uses the methods of science.

Perhaps a somewhat more persuasive approach to distancing philosophy from science might begin by looking at specific philosophical questions that seem to fall outside any of the natural or social sciences.

1.3 Some Examples of Paradigmatic Philosophical Questions

Consider the following questions and ask yourself how we might go about answering them.

1. Can I know truths about my own current mental states in a way in which I can't know truths about anyone else's mental states? And can I know truths about my own current mental states in a way in which I can't know truths describing a mind-independent physical world?[10]
2. If I can be more certain of my own existence than the existence of anything physical, does that imply that I am not identical with anything physical?[11] (a variation of one well-known argument from Descartes's *Meditations*).[12]
3. Are objects distinct from the properties they have (e.g. When I become aware of a red, round shape in my visual field, am I aware of an object (a particular or a substance), that is *distinct* from its redness and roundness?[13]
4. When I am aware of two red round spots in my visual field, is the redness of the two spots numerically identical (not just very *similar*), or is the redness of the one distinct from the redness of the other?
5. Is Oedipus's having killed his father one and the same event as Oedipus's have killed the King of Thebes (in the myth Oedipus's father was the King of Thebes)? If only one event occurred, are there nevertheless two distinct *truths* (the truth that Oedipus killed his father and the truth that Oedipus killed the King of Thebes)? And if there

are two truths, is the *fact* that makes the first true distinct from the fact that makes the second true?
6. Are mental states identical with neural states? Are my mental states in some important respects like the files stored in my laptop? If they are, can we (in principle) copy those files and store them in another mind (the way we often save our files in more than one computer drive)? If my "files," in particular my memories were stored in more than one place, would there be more than one of me? Can we imagine a world in which we split (amoeba-like) into indefinitely many people, all of whom are identical with their common "ancestor"?
7. When we think of something X (the Eifel Tower, the "big bang," God, Sherlock Holmes) what makes it the case that the thought has the "object" it has?[14] When I think of X, is *thinking of* a relation that I stand in to X? If it is, when I think of something that doesn't exist am I committed to the "being" of things that don't exist?
8. Is there any inconsistency in the thought that time is *infinite*—that there always have been and always will be states of the world? Is there any inconsistency in the thought that time is *finite*? (And what precisely does it mean to say that time is finite/infinite?)
9. When something is intrinsically valuable (valuable just for what it is), is its having value identical with its being valued? If the value of X is identical with its being valued, *whose* subjective values make X valuable? Is the question ill-formed? Should we instead think that having intrinsic value is always a matter of having intrinsic value *for* S, where the value of X for S is a matter of *S's* valuing X for its own sake?
10. Is the fact that we ought to do X just identical with some version of the fact that X is the alternative that will have the best consequences?[15]
11. Can one know that something P is true without being in a position to know that one knows that P? Can one be justified in believing that P without being in a position to have justification for believing that one has a justified belief that P?
12. What is the difference between a true generalization that is in some sense a law of nature (e.g. metal expands when heated) and a true generalization that is in some sense "accidentally" true (e.g. presidents of the United states never have the first name "Leslie")?
13. Is there always at least some moral reason to obey the law of the country in which one lives (just because it is the law)? Does it depend on the way in which the government of that state was chosen? Does it depend on whether one has *agreed* to abide by the laws of the state in which one lives?

Philosophers have struggled to answer the above questions for hundreds, and, in some cases, thousands of years. It seems to me that *all* of the above questions have this in common. You are not going to get answers to these questions by turning to *any* of the empirical sciences. You are not even going to get any *help* from the empirical sciences when you try to answer these questions.

Of course you won't, my critic might reply. You *chose* philosophical questions that are least amenable to empirical research. You *chose* questions that highlight some of the most intractable problems in the history of philosophy. Indeed, the questions are so intractable, that perhaps we should wonder whether at least some of them are ill-formed—pseudo-questions whose very meaning might be problematic. A philosopher pushing the line that there are no sharp divisions between philosophy and the empirical sciences might offer another list of important philosophical questions that are superficially similar to the questions on the above list, but that could only be answered with help from the empirical sciences:

1e What are the causal processes that take internal and external stimuli and result in an organism's forming beliefs about their mental life and their external surroundings?
2e What states of the brain are the direct causes of pain, visual experience, tactile experience, fear, and so on?
3e What is the difference between the way in which red things reflect light and the way in which blue things reflect light?
4e Do all red things reflect light the same way?
5e Is heat molecular motion? Is lightning an electrical discharge? Is pain caused in the same way in all creatures who feel pain?
6e Just as we leave it to science to tell us what heat is and what lightning is, isn't it the job of science to tell us what pain is, what fear is, what visual experience is, what memory is?
7e Again, isn't it the job of science (psychology, neurology, or cognitive science) to tell us what thought is? Won't science at least tell us what the physical manifestations of thought are?
8e Has there always been some combination of matter and energy and will there always be some combination of the two?
9e Do your value judgments serve an evolutionary purpose, and if so what is it?
10e Is there an evolutionary advantage to acting in ways that do not maximize value?
11e Is there an evolutionary advantage for beings who evolve in such a way that they are always in a position to monitor and self-correct their epistemic states—beings who can always know when they know, justifiably believe that they have justified beliefs?
12e What are the fundamental laws of nature? What are examples of pseudo-laws?
13e Are we genetically programmed to do what people in positions of authority tell us to do?

A close examination of our two sets of questions suggests that many questions in the first set are more fundamental than the second, at least in the sense that one would ideally have answers to what I have called paradigmatic philosophical questions before one would try to answer questions on the second list. Just as importantly, a little reflection will suggest that one can't tell whether answers to questions in the second set are relevant to answering questions in the first set until one has answered questions in the first set.

Consider the claim about priority. Until one answers (5) and reaches conclusions about whether it is crucial to distinguish events, facts, and truths one might be overlooking important ambiguities one needs to keep in mind when one tries to answer (5e). Until one answers questions about the possibility of time extending infinitely into the past (8), one wouldn't be able to speculate intelligently about whether matter and energy have, in fact, always existed (the subject matter of (8e). Until one knows the answer to (12) and understands precisely what the difference is between a law of nature and a true general claim that does not describe a lawful regularity, one surely isn't ideally positioned to answer (12e), a question about what the fundamental laws of nature are.

That one needs to answer questions on the first list in order to assess the philosophical relevance of questions on our second list seems even more obvious. The answer to (1e) *might* be relevant to answering philosophical interesting question about knowledge or justified belief, but we will need to *understand* introspective knowledge before we are in a position to assess the relevance of the causal origin of a belief to its epistemic status. Similarly, the answer to (2e) may or may not be relevant to questions about the plausibility of dualism (the view that we can't identify mind with body/mental states with physical states). But we'll need to address the knowledge argument[16] before we can resolve that controversy. We do empirically investigate the answers to (3e) through (6e) but it is not clear whether any answers that we discover will give us the *philosophical* understanding that we seek. Put another way, the answer to (7e) is "No." The identity claims about heat and lightning do seem to be empirical discoveries of science. Questions about the *causal* origin of pain in different creatures are also empirical questions, but it is not clear that the answers to these empirical questions will tell us what pain *is*. Of course, we do need a philosophically plausible account of how to distinguish identity claims that are within the purview of science, and those that resist empirical investigation. An affirmative answer to (8e) entails that time is infinite (in some sense), but a negative answer to (8e) doesn't by itself settle questions about the *possibility* of time extending infinitely in both directions. (9e) and (10e) are interesting questions, but we need to answer more fundamental ethical questions in order to decide whether these empirical questions bear on our understanding of value judgments. Similarly, (11e) may or may not be relevant to philosophical questions in epistemology, but we can't determine the relevancy of those questions without answers to questions about the nature of knowledge and justified belief. The answer to (12e) doesn't tell us what a law of nature *is*. The answer to 13e) doesn't tell us how we should *understand* political authority.

1.4 Different Conceptions of Philosophy—A Very Brief Overview

I'm going to argue for a very specific metaphilosophical view, one that many will find highly idiosyncratic. Before I do, however, it might be useful to provide some initial context by summarizing very briefly a few historically influential positions on how to understand philosophy. The views I discuss all fall within what is sometimes called *analytic* philosophy. Analytic philosophy is often contrasted with continental philosophy, but I've never run across a very illuminating attempt to mark a clear contrast between analytic and continental philosophy.[17] It often seems that the distinction, if one really exists, is more a matter of style than substance. Analytic philosophers sometimes seem to take pride in their ability to state clearly and answer clearly the questions that interest them. Continental philosophers sometimes seem to revel in almost poetic statements of problems and solutions to which one can only gesture. But those in the continental tradition will be insulted by what I just said, and, in any event, there are plenty of self-proclaimed analytic philosophers who are anything but clear and who indulge in their own poetic flights of fancy.

It might be a bit more helpful to stress the "analytic" in analytic philosophy. At least many analytic philosophers do sometimes describe themselves as engaged in analyzing various interesting properties, concepts, ideas, meanings, or facts. As we very briefly noted earlier, many of those who think of themselves as in the business of analyzing *something* don't agree with each other on what the objects of their analyses are. But a prevailing theme, one to which we shall return, is that we can make philosophical progress by breaking something complex down into its simpler parts. On some versions of that view, the goal of analysis is to break the complex down into *unanalyzable* parts (philosophical "atoms") out of which the complex that is the target of analysis is "built." Of course, the goal of physics is often thought of in a similar way. From the ancient Greeks to modern science, the search was on for the ultimate constituents out of which all of reality is constructed. These constituents often seem to be always just out of reach. We think that different kinds of things have as constituents different kinds of molecules, and different kinds of molecules have as constituents different kinds of atoms. Despite the optimism conveyed by the use of the term "atom," atoms themselves seem to consist of still finer and finer grained entities or fields, and the search for the ultimate building blocks of physical reality continues. Philosophers aren't physicists though, and presumably their search for *philosophically* important "atoms" is to be understood as a quite different sort of investigation from that carried out by the physicist.

1.4.1 Philosophy as a Search for Fundamental Categories of Reality

On one very old view, philosophical analyses make claims about the ultimate *categories* of reality. On this view, the philosopher is searching for fundamental *kinds* of things out of which all other kinds are to be understood. This talk of kinds was famously discussed by Plato in terms of "forms" in which things "participate," but among philosophers sympathetic to the Platonic approach, talk of forms was often replaced with talk of properties. So to illustrate with a relatively trivial sort of example, we distinguish various shapes that two-dimensional (plane) figures have. We distinguish, among infinitely many others, squares, triangles, and circles. And we can ask, for example, the question: In virtue what is something a square? What do squares all have in common in virtue of which they are squares? As a first stab, we might try talking about lines. A square is a figure closed by straight lines. But so is a hexagon, a rhombus, and a triangle. So we need to say more. A square is a figure closed by four *straight* lines. But so is a rhombus, and so are quadrilaterals that aren't squares. A square is a figure closed by four straight lines that are *equal* in length. But so is a rhombus. OK, so a square is a figure closed by four straight lines that are equal in length and where the interior angles are all 90 degrees. Done. Well sort of done. We have appealed to the notion of a line, a straight line, and angles of various degrees. Don't we need to say what makes something a straight line? Probably, but as we keep asking questions, we'll end up in the land of philosophy.

When I was in high school, I wasn't happy when I was told that a line has length, but no width. And I was even less happy when I was told that lines are composed of points (infinitely many points), none of which have either width or length. Being a *straight* line was supposed to have something to do with being composed of points in such a way that the resulting line was the shortest distance between the points at either end of the line segment. Claims like these inevitably lead one to difficult questions in the philosophy of space and time. And they also invite questions about what should be explained in terms of what. Is our conceptual geometric building block the idea of being a point? Or do we have a better grasp of what makes something a line, and should we be trying to understand an extensionless point in terms of the intersection of lines? Perhaps our concept of a line without width is itself better explained in terms of our idea of an edge (between say a patch of red and a patch of green).

I advertised our search for the correct analysis of being a square as a relatively superficial example of analysis. But we can see that even with an example this simple things can quickly get complicated. The example might nevertheless have been instructive. Just as we can get interested in what it is about a figure that makes it a square, so also we can get interested in what state of a conscious being constitutes knowledge, what relations constitute causation, what feature of an action makes it obligatory.

Understanding philosopher as a search for the ultimate categories of reality still leaves unexplained the difference between philosophy and science. We leave it to the scientist to tell us what water is made of, what the distinctions are among different sorts of cancer, and what magnetic fields are. Why shouldn't science tell us what knowledge is, what causation is, what perception is, and even what value is?

1.4.2 Conceptual Analysis

Those philosophers who turn their attention to concepts or ideas might seem to go some way toward distancing the subject matter of philosophy from the subject matter of science. The attempt to get clear about the concepts or ideas of knowledge, justice, goodness, causation, the self, perception, and the like is arguably as old as the search for the fundamental categories of reality. In *The Republic*, Plato can be viewed as trying to say what constitutes a just life, or he could be interpreted as trying to get clear about what the *concept* or *idea* of justice is. In the *Theaetetus* Plato might be trying to say what knowledge is or he might be trying to get clear about the concept or idea of knowledge.

Whether there even is a sharp distinction between analyses of properties, say, and analyses of concepts or ideas depends on how one understands talk of ideas. When he wrote *Principia Ethica*, Moore was the paradigm of a philosopher who thought that analysis is crucially important to philosophy. But Moore seemed to talk about both analyzing or defining the *property* of being good and analyzing or defining the *idea* of goodness. For Moore, it didn't make much of a difference for according to him the *idea* of a property is just the property "in" or "before" mind.[18] To get clear about the idea of goodness is just to get clear about that property of goodness that is before the mind. As we shall see below, in the late twentieth century there has been a revolution in the philosophy of mind that locates the content of (at least some) mental ideas in objects that are *external* to the mind of a person—objects that cause certain internal states but whose intrinsic character might be quite unknown to the person who has the relevant idea. As we shall see, on these views, science might regain a foothold in the philosophical search to get clear about concepts or ideas.[19]

For those who think of philosophical analysis as conceptual analysis, the project is often thought of as finding "conceptual atoms" out of which all other concepts or ideas are built. Moore is again one paradigm of a philosopher who thought of analysis this way. Famously, he argued that the idea of goodness, more specifically the idea of intrinsic goodness, is one of the many *simple* ideas out of which complex ideas are built. For Moore (1903), we can define instrumental goodness, the distinction between right and wrong, virtue and vice appealing to the idea of intrinsic goodness and various sorts of causal facts about what would or would tend to maximize intrinsic value. It is in virtue of its simplicity, Moore argued, that the idea of intrinsic goodness is indefinable.

1.4.3 The Linguistic Turn

When we briefly discussed metaethics, we noted that some philosophers framed the relevant metaethical questions as questions about the *meaning* of ethical expressions (like "good," "right," "virtue"). More generally, philosophers who embrace analysis as a key part of philosophy sometimes seem to embrace the view that analysis is performed on the meaning of expressions or the meaning of sentences. Even Moore *sometimes* described the metaethical task as one of getting clear about the meaning of "good." But he was quick to argue that the task of the philosopher is distinct from the less lofty task of the lexicographer. It's never been clear to me just what empirical research *does* go into writing a dictionary, but it is obvious that philosophers haven't been trained in the relevant empirical research.[20] If philosophers are practicing lexicography, they are practicing without a license.[21]

In trying to explain how *his* search for meaning is different from the lexicographer's search for meaning Moore (1903, Chapter, 1, sec. 6) says the following:

> What, then, is good? How is good to be defined? Now, it may be thought that this is a verbal question. A definition does indeed often mean the expressing of one word's meaning in other words. But this is not the sort of definition I am asking for. Such a definition can never be of ultimate importance in any study except lexicography. If I wanted that kind of definition I should have to consider in the first place how people generally used the word 'good'; but my business is not with its proper usage, as established by custom. I should, indeed, be foolish, if I tried to use it for something which it did not usually denote: if, for instance, I were to announce that, whenever I used the word 'good,' I must be understood to be thinking of that object which is usually denoted by the word 'table.' I shall, therefore, use the word in the sense in which I think it is ordinarily used; but at the same time I am not anxious to discuss whether I am right in thinking that it is so used. My business is solely with that object or idea, which I hold,

rightly or wrongly, that the word is generally used to stand for. What I want to discover is the nature of that object or idea, and about this I am extremely anxious to arrive at an agreement.

I quote the passage at length because I will defend a conception of analysis that is at least inspired by it. But ordinary language philosophy certainly doesn't take its inspiration from Moore. Indeed, it usually *does* make claims about how "we" use words, what "we" would say about this, that, or the other situation.

J. L. Austin, Gilbert Ryle, Paul Grice, and the later Wittgenstein, to take but a few examples, all called our attention to various alleged facts about what we would or wouldn't *say* about certain hypothetical situations. Their point in doing so was usually an effort to "dissolve" various philosophical puzzles by pointing out subtle facts about how we use language. But even philosophers who *wouldn't* classify themselves as ordinary language philosophers also often talk about what we would or wouldn't say in talking about knowledge, right and wrong, causation, and so on. In what is probably the most famous two-page article in the history of philosophy, Edmund Gettier tried to convince philosophers that they were wrong in thinking that knowledge is justified true belief by describing certain justified true beliefs that *we* would *not describe* as knowledge. Critics of the idea that causation can be understood in terms of regularities in nature call our attention to the fact that we wouldn't *describe* the barometer's falling as the cause of the storm even though there are non-accidental correlations between what happens to barometers and changes in the weather.[22]

Again, the history of such discussion raises the question of how philosophers are supposed to *know* what "we" would say about various hypothetical situations. To be sure, philosophers often do talk to their academic colleagues about what they would say, but the sample is small and unlikely to be representative of people in general. Philosophers think about such odd hypothetical situations that their "ear" has often been seriously compromised when it comes to what seems natural or unnatural to say. Linguists often face the same problem when they ask each other whether certain odd sentences violate the rules of syntax. After you have thought about enough odd sentences, odd sentences don't seem so odd to you.

A philosopher who thinks of philosophy as meaning analysis faces a number of formidable objections. Most obviously, philosophers rarely couch their philosophical theses in such a way that they seem to be talking about language. The view about knowledge that Gettier was attacking is the view that knowledge just is justified true belief. It was almost never stated as the view that "knows" has the same meaning as "has a justified true belief." When we *want* to talk about words, we have a perfectly clear way of doing so—we use quotation marks. Dogs are mammals, but "Dogs" is a word. "Dogs" begins with the letter "d," but it isn't even clear what it would mean to assert that dogs being with the letter "d." So on the face of it, when philosophers ask questions about knowledge, or causation, or value, for examples, they aren't asking questions about words. If they are discussing the meaning of words, they are doing it in a very roundabout way.

The above concern about treating philosophical questions as questions that are at least in part about the meaning of language is hardly decisive. As we briefly noted in our earlier discussion of metaethical controversies, philosophers are often quick to point out that the "surface" grammar of a sentence can disguise its subject matter. The sentence "Sherlock Holmes was a detective who lived on Baker Street" is in some sense true. And it might appear to describe the address of a person in precisely the same way that someone might describe my address. But, many would argue, the *true* sentences we use to describe Sherlock Holmes are best construed as descriptions of the stories—descriptions of various meaningful sentences that appear in the fiction (and what can reasonably be inferred from those descriptions). Or consider what one does when one introduces oneself at a party. One might say "Hi, I'm Richard." Alternatively, one might say "Hi, my name is 'Richard'." The latter includes specific reference to a word; the former doesn't. But it is not clear to me that the *content* of the two sentences is different. More ambiguously, perhaps, the two sentences are certainly used to accomplish the same end. Finally, consider one more example. Think about how we use expressions like "now" or "later." It is at least prima plausible to argue that when I say that the party will start now, I am saying that the party will begin simultaneously with my use of the word "now." And when I say I'll do the yardwork later, I might be reasonably interpreted as saying that I'll start the work after the statement I am currently making.[23] None of these examples are decisive. It is not clear when a sentence involves self-reference. But it seems equally obvious to me that the interpretations of the examples that I suggested are at least initially plausible.

I will be arguing in the rest of this book that analysis is an important *part* of philosophy *and* that we can't divorce analysis from language. The trick will be to reconcile that truth with the desideratum that we not reduce this part of philosophy to an *empirical* study of natural language.

1.4.4 A Second Linguistic Turn—Content Externalism

I mentioned earlier that the later twentieth century brought with it a highly influential *externalism* about the content of mental states. On one such view, what I am thinking *of* is partly a function of the causal history of my current mental life. There is an analogous view about the meaning of linguistic expressions. Perhaps the most fundamental question in the philosophy of language is the question of what makes a word (a sound, a mark) *signify* a thing, kind of thing, or a property. Crudely put, the externalist suggests two answers. One is that we associate with a word what philosophers call a *definite description*. A definite description is just a phrase that begins with the definite article "the" and purports to pick out something in virtue of its uniquely exemplifying some property or properties. I can use the definite description "the world's tallest man" in a sentence to assert that the world's tallest man is taller than I am. There is no guarantee that a definite description will succeed in picking something out. After all, for all I know, there might be three or four people who share a height that is taller than anyone else's. I might try to pick out some being using the definite description "the conscious being causally responsible for the creation of all matter and energy" and fail because it turns out that there is no such being. That we can use definite descriptions seems relatively unproblematic. The externalist, however, argues that we can use a definite description to "fix the reference" of an expression without taking the definite description to be *synonymous* with the expression. On this sort of view, the meaning of the expression introduced this way *is* just whatever is picked out by the definite description.[24]

But reference-fixing definite descriptions are only one way that the externalist thinks one can succeed in breathing life into language. Many of us can succeed in referring to a thing, a kind of thing, or a property without being able to come up with *any* definite description that does the relevant work (or so the argument goes). A *very* long time ago I took a course on Egyptian history. We studied the pharaohs and I'm pretty sure that one of them was Khafre. If asked to name someone who built a pyramid, I might hazard the guess that Khafre built a pyramid, and, as it turns out, I would be right. But how did I succeed in talking about that guy? I wasn't thinking of *the* guy who built a pyramid because I know that there were a number of Egyptians who built pyramids. I wasn't even thinking of *the* guy named "Khafre" who built a pyramid because if I didn't think that Khafre built a pyramid, I would still have been relatively confident that Khafre was an Egyptian. And I'm not thinking of Khafre as the Egyptian named "Khafre" as I have no idea how many Egyptians might have shared that name. So how *do* I successfully use the term "Khafre" to refer to that long dead Egyptian? The basic idea of one version of externalism is that my use of "Khafre" stands at the end of a very, very long causal chain that has as its first crucial link someone's "baptizing" an Egyptian with either the name "Khafre" (or some other name that over time morphed into "Khafre").

I illustrated the basic idea behind the view by talking about our use of names. But proponents of the view believe that one can understand in a similar way our successful talk about *kinds* of things (water, heat, positrons, quarks) and *properties* (having a positive charge, having Legionnaire's disease, being autistic). I'll talk much more about content and linguistic externalism in Chapter 4. Here I'll just note that *if* one thinks that philosophy investigates meanings *and* that meanings should be understood in the way sketched above, then it looks as if philosophy in its search for meanings might give way to science. On this sort of view, science tells you that when you use the term "water" you mean (and always have meant) by "water" stuff with molecular structure H₂O. Science tells you that when you use the term "lightning" you have been talking about a certain sort of electrical discharge.[25] If science can tell you what you mean by "water" and "lightning," why can't science tell you what you mean by "knowledge," "causation," "thought," and "value"? This view (content externalism) is, however, a *philosophical* view and *it* won't be decided by science. Moreover, it is a false philosophical view, and, as I shall argue, we won't need to worry about philosophy being forced to cede the search for successful philosophical analyses to science.

1.5 Doing Metaphilosophy without Begging Questions

We sketched ever so briefly *some* of the ways in which philosophers have understood philosophy. There is a great deal of disagreement. How should we try to decide who is right? The problem is that when we ask the metaphilosophical question "What is philosophy?" we need to approach the question without begging any questions as to what philosophy is. So if you understand the metaphilosophical question as a question about the meaning of "philosophy," you will immediately lose the philosophers who don't think that philosophical questions are questions about meaning. If I understand the question as one about the property of being philosophical, I will lose the philosophers who don't think that philosophical analysis is concerned with properties.

Long ago Strawson (1959) made a distinction between *descriptive* and *prescriptive* metaphysical analysis. Roughly, the idea is that when one is engaged in the descriptive analysis of something like knowledge or virtue one is committed to capturing the ordinary way in which people actually talk about knowledge and virtue. When engaged in prescriptive analysis, one feels free to "clean up" the ordinary way we talk in part by stipulating the meaning of some of the expressions we use. The goal of such stipulation is to enable us to say what we want to say, but to do so in a way that is clear. In his classic discussion about the meaning of "good," Stevenson (1937, p. 14) made clear at the outset that his goal was not to capture the ordinary use of the term "good." Instead, he says he wants to *substitute* a clear definition:

> In order to help answer the question "Is X good?" we must substitute for it a question which is free from ambiguity and confusion. It is

obvious that in substituting a clearer question we must not introduce some utterly different kind of question. It won't do (to take an extreme instance of a prevalent fallacy) to substitute for "Is X good?" the question "Is X pink with yellow trimmings?" and then point out how easy the question really is. This would beg the original question, not help answer it. On the other hand, we must not expect the substituted question to be strictly "identical" with the original one. The original question may embody hypostatization, anthropomorphism, vagueness, and all the other ills to which our ordinary discourse is subject. If our substituted question is to be clearer, it must remove these ills. …
Just how, then, must the substituted question be related to the original. 1 answer that it must be relevant. A defined meaning will be called "relevant" to the original meaning under these circumstances: Those who have understood the definition must be able to say all that they then want to say by using the term in the defined way. They must never have occasion to use the term in the old, unclear sense.

I'm going to try to do for "philosophy" what Stevenson tried to do for "good." I won't pretend that what I call philosophy *proper* captures everything that people have called philosophy. Indeed, many will reject my conception of philosophy proper as outrageously narrow. But I'm not trying to be outrageous for the sake of being outrageous. My goal is to understand philosophy in such a way that it is distinct from empirical sciences and mathematics. In the next chapter, I'll suggest two data that any conception of philosophy should respect. If accepted these data will tell against a number of the conceptions of philosophy sketched above.

Notes

1 There are alternative readings of Hume these days, but I'm quite convinced that he was serious about his commitment to skepticism.
2 See also Bergmann (1964) and (1967).
3 Some argue that the relevant task is to discover what views and arguments were advanced by various influential historical figures. Others argue that the project is "rational *reconstruction*." On this view we should be primarily interested in figuring out what a given philosopher of interest should have believed given their commitment to various premises. Still others adopt the more extreme view that historical texts should be studied primarily for the way in which they cause us to think of issues and arguments (without much regard for what these historical figures actually thought themselves).
4 For our purposes we can say that a first-level question is a question that is *not* a question about questions.
5 The distinction between first-level questions and second-level questions about those question can be raised with respect to just about any sort of question. For example, one might raise a mundane question about the color of a shirt, a house, or a cat. Philosophers, however, sometimes ask questions about what it means to say of some object that it has a certain color. That's a meta-question

about the meaning of first-level questions about color. And as we shall see, there isn't much agreement among philosophers about how to *understand* first-level assertions about color.

6 The expression "normative" ethics is often used to mark the contrast between metaethical questions and other sort of ethical questions. It is not clear to me, however, that the expression "normative ethics" is used univocally. Sometimes normative questions in ethics seem to be understood as applied ethics but where the ethical concepts are still applied at a very general level (e.g. What *kinds* of things are good/bad? What *kinds* of actions are at least prima facie obligatory?) By contrast, applied ethical questions are thought of as applying ethical concepts to more specific ethical controversies (e.g. Should we abolish capital punishment? Should we reduce inequality of wealth?).

7 There are philosophers—Frege (1892), for example—who use the term concept to refer to something non-mental.

8 The rough idea is that a *prima facie* obligation to do X is a reason to do X, but one that might be overridden by other reasons to not do X. So on one view, if I promise you that I'll do X, that creates a prima facie obligation for me to do X. But I might have prima facie obligations not to hurt other people and if doing X hurts other people I have conflicting prima facie obligations. Ultima facie obligations are what one is obligated to do all things considered.

9 The distinction between surface grammar and deeper structure did not originate with, but is most closely associated with Chomsky (1975).

10 See Armstrong (1963 and 1968) who will try to convince you that I am wrong in suggesting that science won't address this question. See also Churchland (1989), Conee (1994), Bigelow and Pargetter (1990), Fumerton (2003 and 2006b), Feldman (2004), Dowell (2006), Reed (2006), and Gertler (2011) for samples of philosophical discussion of issues that arise in addressing this question. Ludlow and Martin (1998) edited an excellent anthology discussing a number of controversies concerning the nature of self-knowledge. Nagel's (1974) discussion of how hard it would be to know what it is like to be a bat vividly raised questions about whether one can know the character of experience without actually having had the experience.

11 A crude version of a famous argument associated with Descartes argument for dualism (the view that mind and body are radically distinct kinds of things (he called them substances).

12 The subject of intensive philosophical debate over thousands of years. To my way of thinking, some of the best discussion of this general question includes Broad (1925).

13 See Addis (1967) for a good overview of the issues that arise when trying to answer this question.

14 "Object" is in scare quotes to underscore the fact that sometimes we seem to think about things that don't exist. We seem to be able to think about unicorns, Aphrodite, the fountain of youth, and so on. Again, see Addis (1989) and Searle (1983) for examples of excellent discussions of this question.

15 As we shall see later, more sophisticated versions of this view insist that we can identify what one ought to do with facts about consequences, but those facts are decidedly complex—possible consequences are relevant we need to adjust their value (positive and negative) for the probability of their occurring.

16 Again, the knowledge argument proceeds from the observation that we know truths about our existence and our mental life in a quite different sort of way from the way in which we know truths about the physical world. Jackson (1982 and 2004), Lewis (2004), Nida-Rümelin (2004), Churchland (1989), and Chalmers (1995, 1996, 2003 and 2004). Dennett (1991) and Conee (1994)

all evaluate various forms of the knowledge argument, and argument most famously associated with Frank Jackson. On my view earlier versions of the argument can be found scattered throughout the history of philosophy. See particularly Leibniz (1714), Broad (1925), and Nagel (1974). For a terrific collections of papers (including many listed in this footnote) critically evaluating versions of the knowledge argument see Ludlow, Nagasawa, and Stoljar (2004).

17 It is also contrasted with Buddhist and Indian philosophies, African philosophy, the philosophies of Indigenous people, and so on. As with continental philosophy (where the continent refers to Europe), the philosophies are identified in the first instance with places or cultures. The interesting questions, however, concern differences (and similarities) that one can find in the philosophies themselves. So Duerlinger (2012) for example understands various Indian philosophers struggling with at least some of the same questions about the self that Hume was trying to answer.
18 Russell (1967, Chapter IX) seemed to hold the same view.
19 We'll talk much more about this later.
20 Apparently, trained philosophers (and linguistics) are seldom hired by lexicographers. As I argue later linguistics and philosophers might have lost their "ear" for how ordinary people use language.
21 In fairness there has been an increasing interest in what is sometimes called experimental philosophy (X-Phi for short). As part of that movement at least some philosophers do conduct surveys or interview people about what they would say about certain hypothetical situations. The methods usually seem to me a bit suspect. For fear of biasing the subjects, the questioner typically doesn't add much detail about the hypothetical situations invoked. And without the detail, it is not clear that the subjects even understand fully the question that is asked. Employing the method, the experimental philosophers sometimes purport to discover that other philosophers have often misrepresented the extent to which there is consensus on how to describe hypothetical situations (like the famous Gettier thought experiments discussed below—see Weinberg et al. 2001). In any event, if the arguments I give later in this book are sound, X-Phi is not plausibly regarded as an improvement on ordinary language philosophy.
22 The dialectic is, of course, much more complicated.
23 Even more controversially, one might argue that all tensed verbs involve a kind of self-reference. When I say that the game is on now, perhaps I can plausibly be construed as asserting that the game *is* taking place at the same time as I am uttering the words. When I tell you that Caesar *was* assassinated, I am implicitly asserting that the assignation too place before the utterance describing the event.
24 My colleague Evan Fales suggested to me that the definite description is like an arrow one shoots from one's bow. One doesn't know what the arrow will hit, but whatever target it finds becomes the meaning of the expression.
25 The example is from J. J. C. Smart (1959).

Chapter 2
The Paradox of Analysis and Methodological Solipsism

We are searching for data that can guide our conception of philosophy. In this chapter I'll offer two. The first is relatively uncontroversial. It emphasizes the fact that philosophy is difficult. The second is much more controversial. It suggests that the truth of philosophical claims and knowledge of philosophical claims is compatible with massive error with respect to the nature of *empirical* reality.

2.1 The Paradox of Analysis

Philosophy is difficult. Philosophers looking for the correct analyses of knowledge, value, causation, perception, and philosophy itself often disagree dramatically with each other concerning what the correct analyses are. This I take to be a *datum* that all conceptions of philosophy should respect. But for reasons that will become obvious later, I don't want the evidence for this claim to rely primarily on the observation of widespread disagreement among philosophers.[1] After all, perhaps at least some of the disagreement among philosophers might be merely apparent. At least some disagreement might be merely verbal. Or perhaps philosophers don't really *believe* many of the claims they make. In philosophy, we often "run" with positions to see how far we can get defending them (see Fumerton 2010). Before we know it, we have built a career on defending certain views even when we never were that sure that the views are correct.

It is primarily *introspective* data upon which I'm relying in making the claim that philosophy is difficult. When I ask *myself* what knowledge is, what causation is, what makes a belief justified, what makes something intrinsically valuable, or what makes a question philosophical, the answers to these questions usually don't seem *at all* obvious to me. I try out a view often to discover later compelling reasons to reject the view. And I have simply given up trying to answer some philosophical questions—I can't figure out how to answer them.

The fact that philosophy is difficult gives rise to a puzzle, a puzzle that is sometimes called the paradox of analysis.[2] On at least some conceptions

DOI: 10.4324/9781003223566-3

of philosophy, it would be hard to understand *why* philosophy is difficult. Consider, for example, the philosopher who disdains interest in language, recommending instead that we perform our analysis on properties that our words signify. You want to get clear about what knowledge is? Don't worry about the word "know" and its cognates. Just hold before your mind the property of knowing something to be true. You want to get clear about what causation is? Don't worry about the word "cause" and its cognates. Just hold before your mind that relation that we are talking about when in English we say that X caused Y. And, in general, whenever you ask a question of the form "What is X," follow that same advice. Get the relevant X before your mind and try to break it down into its simplest parts.

But how, exactly, is one supposed to follow this advice? And if we *could* follow the advice, why would we find it so difficult to characterize the property that we are holding before our minds? When Hume tries to find that *objective* property of value that some things have and some things lack, why does he find nothing that is even a remotely plausible candidate for the property? And when G. E. Moore does the same thing, why does he succeed in finding a simple, objective (non-natural) property of being good?[3] When Hume tries to find the relation of causation holding between singular events, why does he find nothing? Why does Davidson (1967), by contrast, seems to find that very relation that was eluding Hume?

OK, so maybe it's a bit more complicated than leaving language behind and holding before your mind the property that is the target of your philosophical search. Instead, what you need to do is hold before your mind some *instance* of the property for which you are looking. If you are looking for causation, for example, think of a paradigmatic case of one thing's causing another. If you are looking for the property of being intrinsically valuable hold before your mind a paradigmatic case of something's being intrinsically valuable. And so on. If you *succeed* in choosing a genuine case of causal connection, the causation should be present and you can go about looking for it. If you choose wisely an example of something that is intrinsically valuable, the value you are looking for should be present in the example waiting to be found.

There are two problems with the above suggestion. The most obvious concerns your choice of a paradigm. If you haven't yet figured out what causation is, for example, how can you be sure that your putative example of one thing's causing another is a *genuine* instance of causation? Second, even if you have located an example of causation, how are you supposed to recognize among the indefinitely many properties present in the example the causal connection? Suppose my example of causal connection is a white billiard ball hitting a red billiard ball causing it to move. Is the whiteness or redness at all relevant to the causation? Presumably not. Is the roundness of each ball a relevant part of the causal story? Is the fact that the collision took place on a Sunday? We're obviously going to need more than one example of causation to answer these questions. We'll want to vary the conditions in many paradigms of causal connection to find "common denominators." But now we need to be able to recognize the distinction between genuine and spurious causal connections, all without yet knowing what causal connection is.

There might seem to be a similar problem facing those who think that analysis is performed upon *concepts* or *ideas*. Again, we are invited to leave language, and just hold before our mind the idea of whatever we are interested in analyzing. Staying with our example of causation, we are invited to hold before our mind the idea of causal connection (not worrying about what *language* we use to convey that idea). But what happens when you try to leave language behind and just think of causation? You might form the idea of one billiard ball striking another, the idea of heating a piece of metal as it expands, or the idea of flipping a light switch just before the light goes on, but these are all complex ideas that have all sorts of "parts." Which part of the idea is the idea of causal connection? And how are you supposed to isolate that part of the complex idea that is the idea of causal connection without already knowing what it is that you are looking for? But if you do already know what you are looking for, what's the problem? Why is it so difficult to figure out what that idea of causation is all about?

A version of the puzzle *seems* also to arise when one thinks of philosophy as an investigation into the meaning of language. Obviously, if you don't *understand* the question "What is knowledge?" you can't even begin to answer it. But if you do understand the question, then you already know what "knows" means. How can it be difficult to answer a philosophical question about knowledge if we understand that question as a question about the meaning of "knows?"

This time there is available an answer, one that we will rely upon later in advocating for a view of philosophy that does *not* divorce philosophical analysis *entirely* from meaning. There is an ambiguity in the notion of knowing the meaning of an expression. In one sense, one knows the meaning of a term when one can use the term meaningfully. One understands an expression when one knows *how* to use the expression. But, in general, one's knowing *how* to do something doesn't entail that one knows *what* it is that one is doing. I had a friend who was a very good golfer. He knew how to hit his drive a long distance. But in his quest for even more length, he decided that he would film his golf swing to discover precisely what he was doing with his swing. Not only did he fail in his effort to hit a longer drive, but he almost destroyed his swing completely.

What has an anecdote about golf got to do with discovering how one is using a given linguistic expression? Knowing how to use a word is a bit like knowing how to hit a golf ball. One can use language competently without knowing *that* one is using the language in such and such a way.

Put somewhat differently, one can *follow* semantic rules that govern the meaning of an expression without knowing what those rules are.

Still, that is puzzling, isn't it? How could one follow a rule unless one knows what the rule is that one is following? Wouldn't it be like trying to follow the directions on a map without being able to understand the conventions governing the map's representations? But consider yet another analogy. At a relatively early age many children learn how to speak, and, indeed, some speak very *well*. They follow rather complex rules of syntax (rules of grammar). But as anyone who was taught how to diagram a sentence knows, *following* grammatical rules is a far cry from knowing what those rules are that one follows. Linguists write books trying to reach conclusions about the underlying structures of natural language.

All of this suggests that there are different senses in which one can follow rules. In one sort of case, it really is hard to see how one could follow rules without knowing what the rules are. At least some games might be like this. I only know *how* to play chess if I know *that* the various pieces in the game may only move in certain ways. But knowing how to speak grammatically doesn't seem to involve knowing that certain words can only occupy certain places in a sentence. It's more like knowing how to swim, something that doesn't seem to involve propositional knowledge (e.g. knowledge *that* such and such movements will keep one afloat).[4] Following grammatical rules might best be construed as having complex dispositions to use language in various ways. Following semantic rules (meaning rules) might similarly be construed as having complex dispositions to use language.[5]

Recognizing that it might be difficult to discover the meaning of terms we use undercuts a famous and oddly influential argument in the history of ethics. Moore (1903) famously argued against what he called naturalistic accounts of intrinsic goodness by using what has become known as the open question argument. Moore offered a kind of instruction on how to refute any such account of the meaning of "(intrinsically) good." Suppose, for example, that I am considering the view that "good as an end" just means "desired as an end by most people." Now think about the question "Is everything that is desired an end by most people intrinsically good?" The question, Moore argued, is obviously *significant*. It is an "open" question the answer to which certainly isn't obvious. But notice that if "good" just means "desired by most people," then the significant question should be equivalent in meaning to the question of whether everything that is desired by most people, is desired by most people. But the latter question is utterly trivial, the answer to which is obvious. Red things are red, round things are round, and what is desired by most people is desired by most people. A significant question can't be equivalent to a trivial question, so the proposed analysis of what "good" means is absurd. If one reflects on how the argument works to refute this proposed view about the meaning of "good," one should see that it will work against any other proposed analysis of good. And that should soften you up for Moore's own view that "good" is indefinable.

There is much that can be said about the presupposition underlying Moore's open question argument.[6] One should probably look at any argument that powerful (it refutes thousands of years of philosophers proposing definitions of "good") with healthy skepticism. As Langford (1942) pointed out, if the argument works against proposed analyses of "good," it will work against proposed analyses of anything. And that's not a conclusion Moore himself would welcome (he was the paradigm of an analytic philosopher who thought that there were important and illuminating analyses of *some* concepts). The explanation of how the open question argument goes wrong, I would suggest, lies in reflecting carefully on the fact that we can use language meaningfully without knowing just how we are using that language. Two statements can be equivalent in meaning even if we don't realize that they are. And two questions can have distinct meanings even if we think that they are synonymous.

So construing philosophical analysis as meaning analysis *might* explain why it isn't easy to find correct philosophical analyses. It might explain why philosophers often disagree with each other on the semantic rules we follow when using a given expression. But it would still leave us struggling to explain the distinction between philosophical analysis and lexicography.[7] We can get insight into that distinction after we look more closely at the importance of what we might call methodological solipsism.

2.2 Methodological Solipsism and a Master Argument

There is another way in which we might try to find a datum upon which we can rely in trying to understand philosophy. We might reflect on what the necessary conditions are for the adequacy of philosophical analyses. I'll explain what I have in mind by relying on an *analogy* from epistemology.

What is the justification we have for believing what we do about the physical world? As Descartes suggested, we might begin answering that question by thinking about the most straightforward beliefs we form about our immediate physical surroundings—perceptually-based beliefs formed in what we take to be ideal conditions of perception. When we ask ourselves what reason we have for thinking that there is a table in front of us, or, perhaps less ambitiously, a physical object that is brown and rectangular,[8] our first instinct might be to suggest that we just *see* it. On one view, inspired by this response, in visual experience we are directly aware of the physical object's existence. But there is a famous, highly influential, and, I believe, correct argument against this sort of direct or "naïve" realism— the argument from the possibility of hallucination. No matter how vivid our visual experience might be, can't we at least make sense of the possibility that we are having an experience with that character even though the object we take to be its cause isn't there? As Descartes argued, can't we make sense of the possibility that we are dreaming or are being deceived by some evil demon with telepathic powers to induce massive and vivid hallucination?[9]

Contemporary versions of such "skeptical scenarios" include the idea that we might be brains in a vat hooked up to artificial devices that produce the same neuronal patterns that are the immediate cause of experience (if the world is as we think it is). Once we concede that these skeptical scenarios are *intelligible*, the question is then asked: Wouldn't the justification you would have for believing what you do about the physical world (falsely as it turns out) in the skeptical scenarios be just the *same* as the justification you have should the experience be veridical (should the experience be caused in the way you think it is)?[10] A great many philosophers think that the answer to this question is "Yes."

While still powerful, the above argument against epistemological direct (naïve) realism is hardly uncontroversial. *Disjunctivists* think that the justification available to you when you are in the "good" case (veridical perception) is different, perhaps even *radically* different, from the justification available to you in the "bad" case (one of the non-veridical skeptical scenarios). They will, of course, concede that it *seems* to you that your justification is the same—after all that's why you are fooled. But from the fact that you don't, or even can't, *notice* a difference between A and B, it doesn't *follow* that A and B aren't different. In the good case, the disjunctivist insists, we are directly aware of at least some physical objects and their properties; in the bad case, we *think* we are in the good case, but we are not. There are different versions of this view. Some disjunctivists try to develop an account of perception that would *explain* how a nonveridical experience might be very like a veridical experience (Johnston 2004); others just rely on the aforementioned general premise that failure to notice a difference doesn't entail that the difference doesn't exist.

One can write an entire book on the metaphysics and epistemology of perception (I have 1985), but here I am only appealing to the undeniable force of the claim that the available justification for beliefs about one's physical surroundings is compatible with those beliefs being false. And if that is so, we can't think of the relevant justification as involving anything like direct awareness of physical objects or their properties. After all, one isn't directly aware of external physical objects when dreaming or hallucinating, and if the justification we have in non-veridical perception is the same as the justification we have in veridical experience, such justification isn't *constituted* by direct awareness of physical objects in the veridical case either.

Just as the truth of claims about my justification for believing what I do about the physical world is compatible with *all* of my beliefs about the physical world being false, so also, I will argue, the truth of fundamental philosophical claims is also compatible with radical skeptical scenarios. When I ask *myself* what knowledge is, what properties are, what causation is, what value is, what perception is, what a physical object is, and what mental states are, I am often not sure what the answers are to the questions. But I can't see how answering correctly the questions that interest me *requires* my having true beliefs about the existence of other people (let alone their linguistic habits), the physical world, the past, or the future. If any of the radical skeptical scenarios are true, I would be bereft of friends, family, people who love me, people who hate me, my publications, my actually having had five holes-in-one, my (long ago) Johnson County doubles tennis championships—the truth of skeptical scenarios would rob me of all these. But I could still take comfort in the possibility that I have whiled away my life discovering interesting philosophical truths. Evil demons, computer-generated matrix-like worlds, my being a brain-in-a-vat, *none* of these possibilities, if actual, would stop me from practicing philosophy, nor would they stop me from arriving at satisfying philosophical truth.

The above claim may strike some as preposterous. If we accept the claim, we will relegate much of what passes today as philosophy to the realm of "non-fundamental" philosophy. It is worth underscoring again, however, that the view I will be developing is a view about what should count as *fundamental* philosophy (what I'll also call philosophy *proper*). I am in no way interested in denigrating the importance of questions raised in areas that fall outside of philosophy. I have also earlier acknowledged that I am carving out the history of philosophy as an important part of philosophy, but one that is distinct from philosophy proper, the history of which it studies.

But surely philosophers also study human nature, they critically evaluate different sorts of societies and the laws that govern them. We include in philosophy business ethics (a field that at least includes the causal impact of actual business practices), environmental ethics (a field that at least includes the causal impact of actual agricultural policies), applied ethics (a field that at least includes empirical facts about the effects of various social practices and policies), critical race theory (a branch of ethics that explores among others things the impact of various past and present social and legal practices on various racial groups), feminist ethics (a branch of ethics that does the same sort of thing in terms of impact on gender and sex), social epistemology (a branch of epistemology that explores the way in which testimony and other pragmatic considerations impact knowledge and justification). Conclusions reached in these perfectly respectable philosophical fields are surely *incompatible* with the truth of radical skeptical scenarios. As we shall see below, however, there might be a way of returning such fields to the kind of philosophy that is compatible with skeptical scenarios *if* one is willing to restrict the relevant philosophical theses to *conditional* claims (more about this below).

As we shall see, what counts as fundamental philosophy on my view will depend critically on what the correct philosophical answers *are* to certain paradigmatically fundamental philosophical questions. It also depends on precisely *how* conclusions in these areas of philosophy are couched. In Part II, I will try to convince you of this by illustrating the metaphilosophical view I defend by seeing how it would apply to various areas of philosophy. For now, however, it is worth remembering a number of obvious truths.

First, on one standard philosophical reading, *general* claims about kinds of things have no existential import.[11] It can be true that Xs are Ys even if there are no Xs. The proposition that everyone who is 12 feet tall is taller than I am is true. And it is true even if there is no one who is over 12 feet tall. It can be true that all bodies in motion upon which no forces are acting continue in motion, and it can be true even if there are no bodies in motion upon which no forces are acting. Philosophers make general claims about knowledge, veridical perception, mind-independent physical reality, justice, lawful connection, causation, and many more sorts of things. But it is not clear that *any* of those claims entail that there is knowledge, veridical perception, mind-independent physical reality, lawful connection, veridical perception, or justice.

A closely related observation is that a conditional can be true even if the antecedent of the conditional (the part following the "if" and preceding the "then") is false. We'll talk more about this later, but much discussed counterexamples that are supposed to present difficulties for various philosophical views are not intended to be descriptions of *actual* situations. Rather, the counterexamples involve descriptions of *hypothetical* or *possible* situations. In *The Republic* when Plato had Socrates object to the view that a just person always tells the truth and returns what is borrowed, Socrates asks the participants in the dialogue whether a just person would return a borrowed weapon to a person who has gone mad. The participants in the discussion quickly agree that such behavior would *not* be dictated by justice. Socrates wasn't talking about some particular weapon borrowed from some actual person who subsequently went mad. The argument involved what philosophers call a *thought experiment*. If we can imagine the situation in question, that is enough to convince us that we aren't getting at what is key to being just by talking about repaying debts. In his comedy *The Clouds* Aristophanes had some fun at the expense of philosophers by describing a group of philosophers who ended up entertaining the position that there is no more to being human than being a featherless biped. Eager to provide a refutation, a member of the group left and returned with a plucked chicken. It is supposed to be funny in part because that was a lot of needless effort that went into refuting a philosophical position. The wag should just have asked the philosophers to *think* of a chicken-like creature without feathers—that would be enough to remind everyone that they weren't on the right track in their efforts to *understand* humanity. The above considerations hardly establish that we can, in principle, evaluate philosophical views without turning to empirical facts about the actual world. The dialogues in question were after all *dialogues*. They involved a number of people arguing with each other about the nature of justice or the nature of humanity. But I'll try to convince you later that even the existence of other people isn't conceptually *required* to critically evaluate philosophical views.

As I implied above, the conditional statement can be the philosopher's best friend. By turning to conditionals philosophers can often find a necessary truth knowable *a priori*.[12] The conditional can replace an unconditional assertion that is clearly knowable only by employing the methods of empirical sciences. So if I am a political philosopher discussing the importance of freedom of expression, I might make unconditional claims about the many ways in which society will be better off in the long run by encouraging the free exchange of ideas. But causal claims, particularly those that involve a huge range of variables involving people and what motivates them to behave in various ways, are notoriously difficult to establish. We can, however, profitably debate questions about what we ought to do *if* certain causal connections obtain. If I were a philosopher of mind who argues for a functionalist account of intentional states,[13] I might make the claim that it is certain patterns of neurons firing that play the relevant functional role, but since I'm not a neurologist (or even a cognitive scientist), I might be content to claim that *if* those neurons firing have a certain typical cause and have a certain typical effect, *then* the firing of those neurons would play the relevant functional role. I might also be interested in philosophical questions concerning free will and I might claim that no one ever acts freely because everything has a cause. Alternatively, I might be content *qua philosopher* to argue just for the incompatibilist thesis—the thesis that *if* everything has a cause, *then* no one ever acts freely. The former claim requires empirical evidence that everything has a cause.[14] The latter claim may not.

Notes

1 If we ignore various sorts of skeptical possibilities and assume that the world is the way we think it is, then this is obviously evidence that philosophy is extremely difficult. I'll say more below, however, way I don't want to rely on *this* sort of observation about disagreement to reach the conclusion that philosophy is difficult. As I will keep emphasizing, I need to *start* with what I know about myself. See Feldman and Warfield (2010) for a discussion of the epistemic significance of disagreement.
2 I first put forth my take on the paradox in Fumerton (1983).

3 Butchvarov (1982) does try to offer an explanation. Siding with Moore, he argued that Hume was "blinded" to objective value by methodological commitments that prevented him from looking "in the right way" for intrinsic value.
4 There are interesting debates on what precisely the connections are between knowing how and knowing that. The correct view might again be one that recognizes ambiguity. A great tennis coach might retain extensive propositional knowledge about how to play tennis well—what strategies to use, how to put various sorts of spin on the ball and so on—all while ruefully admitting that she no longer knows how to play tennis well. She doesn't know how to play in the sense that she no longer has the ability to follow the instructions that she gives her students.
5 Wittengstein (1953) is probably the philosopher most famously associated with the slogan that "meaning is use." But like most slogans, the idea would need considerable development. When say to use "The roads are icy" as you leave my party, it seems obvious that in some sense I am *warning* you to walk and drive carefully. But that use doesn't seem to require us to construe the sentence as anything but a description of the state of the roads. In discussing the different uses to which we put words, C. L. Stevenson (1937) makes an important distinction between the use of a word and its meaning. He thinks that the latter is related to the former, but is, by definition, stable in a way that use need not be.
6 See Fumerton (2007).
7 Ayer in *Language, Truth and Logic* embraced the view that philosophy deals with meaning. But he was also concerned to distinguish philosophy from lexicography. He drew a distinction between what he called explicit definitions (dictionary definitions) and what he called *definitions in use* (28). About the latter he said:

> We define a symbol in use, not by saying that it is synonymous with some other symbol, but by showing how the sentence in which it significantly occurs can be translated into equivalent sentences which contain neither the definiendum itself, nor any of its synonyms.

It is not clear to me that this makes the needed distinction, however. Dictionaries often explain the synonymy of expressions by giving examples of alternative sentences in which the terms occur·
8 Less ambitiously because the concept of a table is actually very complicated. Tables are artifacts defined in part by what they were designed to do.
9 A staple of the plots of novels (like *The Martian Chronicles*), movies (like *Total Recall* or *The Matrix*), and TV shows (like the pilot episode of *Star Trek*).
10 We need to be careful in how we understand this claim. Trivially, if we the experience is veridical, our justification will be justification that we have when we are having veridical experience. If the experience is nonveridical our justification will be justification that we have when we are having nonveridical experience. When we say that the justification is the same, however, we are talking about the intrinsic (non-relational) character of that experience.
11 This is just a fancy way of saying that a claim of the form that all F's are G's does not imply that there any F's.
12 For now, we'll just understand what is known a priori as what is known independently of sense experience and "introspection" of one's own mental states·
13 Really crudely, a functionalist understands a mental state in terms of whatever it is that plays a certain causal role. Think about your understanding of what it

is for a computer program to spell check a document. If you are like I am, you understand that in terms of whatever is going on as a result of a spell-check command, and that results in the highlighting of misspelled words.

14 There is precious little that is uncontroversial in philosophy. That includes the claim one can only discover empirically that everything has a cause (if, in fact, everything does have a cause). Kant (1929) famously argued that the thesis is a necessary truth knowable *a priori*. But his arguments for that claim aren't very plausible.

Chapter 3
What's Left?

Let's suppose for a moment that the truths discovered by fundamental philosophy are compatible with well-known skeptical scenarios—that there is no physical world, that all sense experience is non-veridical, that there is no past, that the future will be radically different from the past, that the theoretical posits of physics are all false. What kind of truths would be left as objects of philosophical investigation?

3.1 Foundationalism and Phenomenology

In Part II, when illustrating the conception of philosophy I defend, I'll look more carefully at the field of epistemology. For the moment I want to suggest, without much argument, that there is *foundational* knowledge, and there are *foundationally* justified beliefs. I'll focus on the foundationalist's view about justified belief. What is said about justified belief will apply *mutatis mutandis* to knowledge.[1]

The foundationalist distinguishes two ways in which a belief might be justified. Often (probably usually) we have justification for believing something P only in virtue of the fact that we can legitimately infer P from something else E1. If I have no first-hand acquaintance with George Washington or the times in which he lived, then the justification I have for believing that Washington was the first President of the United States is based only on what I take to be reliable written and oral testimony. If I have justification for beliefs about the molecular structure of water, it is again only because I can legitimately *infer* what I believe from what I have been told by people I take to be experts in physics. The foundationalist is convinced, however, that if we are to have any justification for believing anything whatsoever, there must be a kind of justification (noninferential justification) that doesn't involve inference, and that is the source (the *foundation*) of all other justification.

There are two *regress* arguments for the foundationalist's view about the structure of knowledge and justified belief. The more familiar is what I call the epistemic regress argument. The argument starts with the claim that we can arrive at a justified belief that P by *inferring* it from something else E1 only if there is justification for us to believe that E1. A more controversial view (a view that I call *inferential* internalism) also insists that someone's inference from E1 to P would yield justified belief only if that person had justification to believe that E1 makes probable P.[2] But even if we rely only on the very plausible claim that one needs justification for believing one's premises before one can justifiably believe a conclusion based on those premises, it looks as if we couldn't justifiably believe *anything* if *all* justification were inferential. If all justification were inferential then our justified belief that P based on E1 would require an additional justified belief in E1 based on something else E2. And that belief would require inference from yet another justified belief in something else E3, and so on *ad infinitum*. Finite beings aren't capable of completing an infinitely long chain of reasoning. Arguably, *infinite* beings couldn't do it either (consider the fact that having an infinite amount of time at your disposal wouldn't enable you to *finish* counting the natural numbers).

The conceptual regress argument has a stronger conclusion. The proponent of this argument claims that the very idea of justified belief is parasitic upon an understanding of noninferential justification. That's because the principle that a justified belief in P based on E requires a justified belief in E is true *by definition*. Inferential justification needs to be *defined* in terms of noninferential justification in just the same way that being good as a means needs to be defined in terms of being good in itself (being good just for what it is).[3]

I have argued elsewhere for foundationalism and have defended the view against alternative accounts of justification. A foundationalist needs to give more than an abstract argument for the need to choose between embracing the idea that there is noninferential justification and surrendering to a radical skepticism. The foundationalist also needs an account of what would render a belief noninferentially justified. And there are radical differences among foundationalists when it comes to answering that question. I'll sketch here the view that I take to be correct. But I won't argue in detail for that view or attempt to respond to the many objections have been raised against it. Again, I have done that elsewhere (1996).

The version of foundationalism I defend is most closely associated with a view defended by Bertrand Russell (1910). But, I would argue, similar views have been implicitly accepted throughout the history of philosophy. The fundamental idea is that the search for justification of a belief ends when we find ourselves *directly acquainted* with (directly aware of) the truth maker for our belief and the "fit" or correspondence between our thought and the fact that makes it true.

There are a lot of presuppositions embedded in this acquaintance theory of foundational justification. One is the so-called correspondence theory of truth. Painting with a very broad stroke, the correspondence theorist believes that thoughts are the kinds of things that are most fundamentally true or false. Sentences in a natural language are also true or false, but only because they express thoughts. Thoughts are representations of how things are. True thoughts are representations that correspond to how things are. False thoughts fail to correspond.[4] How should we understand all this talk of representation? That's one of the most fundamental questions in the philosophy of mind? Some of the British empiricist's seemed to suggest that at least simple thought is a kind of "copy" of what it is a thought of. I've argued, by contrast, that both representation and thought defy any sort of illuminating analysis. Still, other philosophers seek to "naturalize" the mind and might like to model mental representation on the sense in which a photograph represents what it is a photograph of. No matter how bad my photograph is of you, no matter how little it resembles you, it is still a photograph of *you* in virtue of the critical *causal* role you play in producing the image that appears on the paper.[5]

I haven't said much of anything about how to understand direct acquaintance with some aspects of the world. Like representation and correspondence I think it defies any sort of analysis. The best one can do is "point" to the relation. Think about severe pain and your awareness of it. Imagine being distracted by a conversation or some other experience. During the distraction you momentarily no longer notice the pain. Direct acquaintance is the relation you *had* to the pain, a relation that temporarily ceased, and that begins again when you are no longer distracted.[6]

What are the objects of direct acquaintance? In the last chapter, when discussing methodological solipsism, we talked briefly about skeptical scenarios. There we argued that in our search for noninferentially justified belief we would need to reject beliefs about the physical world. Traditional foundationalists identify noninferentially justified beliefs with beliefs based on direct awareness of the "fit" between a belief and that aspect of reality that makes true the belief. So that sort of foundationalist will use the skeptical scenarios as a way of deciding with what we are directly acquainted. You might initially think that you are directly acquainted with at least some features of the physical world, but when you reflect on the fact that the character of your experience is compatible with your suffering massive hallucination, you might ultimately conclude that even in a veridical experience you don't stand in a *relation* of acquaintance to physical objects or any of their properties. The relevant physical objects exemplifying their properties aren't *there* to be the objects of acquaintance in hallucination. No matter how close attention you pay to what you are directly aware of in experience, you wouldn't be able to distinguish veridical perception from its vivid hallucinatory counterpart. The most plausible explanation of this fact is that whatever you are directly aware of in experience, it *isn't* a perceiver-independent physical world.

Similar considerations seem to mitigate against your being directly aware of what has happened in your past. At least some philosophers have convinced themselves that there is a "thick" present of which you can be directly aware—thick in the sense that it has some temporal extension. But even if that is true, it is hardly the case that we can be directly aware of experiences that we had a decade ago, a week ago, a day ago, or even a few hours ago. When you get to be my age, you don't need an argument to convince yourself that you can have vivid apparent memories of what didn't happen. But even younger people understand that seeming to remember having had a given experience doesn't guarantee that you did indeed have the experience.[7]

If ordinary "macro" physical objects and even subjective experiences in your past elude the light shone by direct acquaintance, it is even more obvious that we are not directly acquainted with truthmakers for the theoretical posits of science. And experiences in your future are still less plausibly viewed as objects of current direct acquaintance. There may be such things as accurate premonitions, but the *experience* we call premonition won't guarantee that the future experience occurs, any more than vividly seeming to remember some past experience guarantees that the experience in question occurred.

I have said quite a bit about what *eludes* direct acquaintance. What is left? Well, none of the skeptical scenarios discussed above seem to undermine the possibility of our knowing truths about our subjective experience. Even when hallucinating the existence of a cat in front of me, it still *appears* to me as if there is a cat there. In his classic book *Perceiving* Chisholm (1957) has what is still one of the best discussions of different uses of the expression "appears." When we say it appears as if X, sometimes we just mean to express the tentative belief that X is the case. Call this the *doxastic* use of "appears."[8] Sometimes when we say that it appears as if X, we mean that we are having an experience of a kind that would under normal conditions be caused by X's being the case.[9] Call this the *comparative* use of "appears." To know how things appear in this sense one would need to know truths about physical objects and how they generally appear—a kind of knowledge you wouldn't have if the radical skeptical scenarios obtain. But, Chisholm argues, there is *that kind* of experience, that way of looking, with which we are familiar (which we associate rightly or wrongly with what we take to be the presence of physical objects in what we take to be normal conditions), and it would be good to have a way of describing the occurrence of experiences of that intrinsic kind (whatever their cause). To that end, we can *stipulate* that when we say it appears as if X, we are just trying to characterize a certain kind of experience—we all know what that kind of experience is even if we can't define it.[10] Chisholm calls this the *noncomparative* use of "appears."[11]

So evil demons inducing hallucination, mad scientists manipulating our brains, powerful drugs that distort experience, none of these would seem to preclude our knowing truths about our current mental states—pains, visual, tactile, olfactory, auditory, gustatory, and kinesthetic (experiences as of movement) experiences. Or at least that was the conclusion of many classic foundationalists.

Our mental life goes beyond experiences of this sort. What about more complex mental states common to humans and probably some higher-order mammals? Descartes seemed to think that our knowledge of at least some *thoughts* can survive even the most radical of skeptical scenarios.[12] Was he right? The question is complicated. The mental states we are discussing now are sometimes called *intentional* states.[13] Intentional states are mental states that are "directed at" some object. Or put more linguistically, they are described by sentences in which the verb is transitive and the sentence requires some sort of object term (singular noun or a noun clause) to be meaningful. So, for example, I can't just believe, I can only believe *that* such and such is the case. (Or I might derivatively be said to believe *you*, but where that will likely translate into something like my believing *that* what you say is true.) I can't just want, there must be something that I want—I want peace and quiet, I want to be rich, I want it to be the case that X is elected president. I can't just fear, there must be something that I fear—I fear getting old, I fear snakes, I fear that race relations will get worse. Famously, Brentano (1874) argued that intentionality is the *mark* of the mental. He was suggesting that *all* mental states are intentional, even those states described above as sensations. And there are philosophers who think that visual experiences, for example, represent the world as being a certain way. So do the other five senses. Even pain, some suggest, represents something like damage to the body. By contrast, there are also philosophers who suspect that there can be such mental states as generalized anxiety even when one would have difficulty identifying precisely about what one is anxious.

One must be careful in characterizing intentional states as mental states that have objects. The reason that it might be better to use the linguistic characterization suggested above is that it seems that the "objects" of intentional states don't need to exist. I can want world peace even if there never has been, is not now, and never will be world peace. I can be afraid of hell even if there is no hell. I can believe that there are unicorns even when the noun clause doesn't pick out anything—there are no unicorns. This apparent fact about intentional states leads to intense debate about how to understand intentionality. Some philosophers (Meinong famously) decided that there must be at least two sorts of objects—those that have being but don't *exist*, and those that do exist.[14] Still, other philosophers warn that we shouldn't be misled by the noun clauses that complete descriptions of intentional states. The so-called adverbial theorist takes the noun clauses to be characterizing the kind of belief, fear, desire, thought, etc. we are discussing. It's called the adverbial theory because according to its proponents the object terms are really functioning more the way adverbs function. Here are two quick analogies to make the point (one from Chisholm). We say that John is dancing a jig. Our confused audience might interject: I see the dancing but where is the jig? The question is, of course, confused. The noun "jig" just tells you what sort of dancing is being described. Or consider what it is to feel pain. When we say that S feels pain, the sentence grammatically looks as if it describes a *relation* between you and pain. But again it strikes many as entirely plausible to suppose that the noun "pain" is functioning more like an adverb to describe the kind of feeling you have. You can develop adverbial theories about all sorts of descriptions of mental states that at first blush look as if they have objects, and one strong reason for doing so is that one can avoid commitment to such "weird" entities as objects that don't exist.

We are not going to settle here fundamental questions in the philosophy of mind about the nature of sensations and intentional states. For our present purposes, I am going to proceed on the assumption that even if any of the exotic skeptical scenarios were to actually obtain, it wouldn't stop me from having experiences and other intentional states.[15] Nor would it stop me from knowing that (or at the very least having justified beliefs that) I am in those states.

Lastly, I want to suggest that although it may take more effort, we can become aware not only of our own thoughts, but also of *relations* that hold between thoughts. I can think of something's being red and think of something's being pink and realize that the thought of red is the thought of a darker color than the thought of pink. I can think of being a square and think about having interior angles that are all 90-degree angles and realize that the former thought is, in some sense, inextricably involved with the latter.[16] I'll discuss this last point in more detail in Part II of the book.

So if I have convinced myself both that I can do philosophy even if skeptical scenarios obtain, *and* I can arrive at correct philosophical positions even if skeptical scenarios obtain, then how should I understand both the methods of philosophy and the contents of those philosophical theses that are supposed to be so isolated from empirical reality?

3.1.1 Phenomenology: The Starting Point of All Philosophical Reflection

The above discussion suggests that philosophy begins with *phenomenology*. Talk of employing the method of phenomenology is just a kind of pretentious way of talking about paying close introspective attention to the character of one's experience. Philosophers sometimes debate the wisdom of adopting the *first-person perspective* when doing philosophy. They sometimes talk about this as if there is some alternative. *There isn't*. You and I can only approach the world we are interested in discovering by beginning with our own experiences and the thoughts to which those experiences give rise. The most fundamental question in metaphysics is the question of what exists. *Direct acquaintance* gives you knowledge that you and your current experiences exist. It doesn't give you knowledge of the experiences of anyone else. It doesn't even seem to give you knowledge of your past existence.

We have talked about direct acquaintance as the source of all foundational knowledge. There is an even more controversial view about the role of direct acquaintance, one that can be traced to the radical British empiricists. Consider, as an example, David Hume, who argued that all ideas are "copies" of prior impressions. The thesis as stated is wildly implausible, but Hume immediately made clear that he was prepared to restrict the claim to "simple" ideas. We can create the idea of a mermaid or the idea of a unicorn by combining various ideas (like the ideas of the torso of a woman and the tail of a fish, or the ideas of a horse and a horn). But while we can "mix and match" ideas to create complex ideas to which nothing corresponds, we won't find a *simple* idea that doesn't correspond to a past impression (Hume's term for experience). Hume seemed prepared to modify even further his claim when he allowed that one might "fill in the gap" of experiences of colors along a color continuum of experiences to create the simple idea of a "missing" shade of blue. But he didn't seem to think that this admission created much of a problem for his general thesis about the origin of ideas. Presumably, he was prepared to modify his original claim to one that holds that all simple ideas are copies of prior impressions or something that is "pretty close" to being a copy of a prior impression.

It is ironic that Hume made this thesis about the origins of ideas a cornerstone of his empiricism. In his famous *A Treatise of Human Nature*, he made other controversial claims. He argued for the following conclusions about causation: (a) Causation is nothing but certain regularities in nature; (b) All causal claims are contingent and known only through past experience of correlations; (c) It isn't *necessarily* the case that everything that happens has a cause. Hume is also famous for his skepticism about inductive reasoning. Put crudely he doesn't see how it is *rational* to infer that correlations between kinds of properties/events exist in the *unobserved* past, the *unobserved* present, and the future just because the correlations have always obtained in the *observed* past. But if you put all this together, Hume seems committed to the view that he hasn't got any reason *at all* to believe his thesis about the origin of ideas (again the cornerstone of his empiricism). After all, his only reason to believe that all simple ideas correspond to prior simple impressions is presumably that when he surveys his own simple ideas, he always seems to remember that they correspond to a prior simple impression. But this is inductive reasoning (and inductive reasoning based on a limited sample to boot). Even if *he* never did have a simple idea that failed to correspond to a former simple impression, he must allow that someone else might have had such an idea. He must also allow for the *possibility* that tomorrow he will have simple ideas that pop into existence without any sort of cause.

Even if Hume faced difficulties reconciling his empiricism with his other views, the claim about simple ideas might strike many as plausible. With a variation on a number of similar arguments in the history of philosophy, Frank Jackson (1982) convinced many that those who are color-deprived since birth would never be able to *understand* what it is to experience color.[17] He used that claim to argue for the view that a physicalist world-view leaves something out of the complete story of what exists (for the color-deprived would still be able to understand all of the claims of *physics*). Again, one might not want to go so far as to conclude that we *couldn't* conceive of the color-deprived person having the idea of color. But still many of us are inclined to think that such a person *wouldn't*, in fact, form the idea of color. Like Hume, I'm not sure that I ever do form complex thoughts without building those thoughts out of "atoms" that are simple thoughts of data that I seem to remember having experienced. But I'm also not sure how to argue for that conclusion other than by employing an argument from my own personal experience (or at least experiences that I seem to remember having had).

In deciding questions about the foundations of thought it is important to make a distinction between what we think of *directly* and what we think of only *indirectly*. Some things—perhaps even most things—we think of only by thinking of *other* things. As I indicated earlier, I can, in some sense, think of the tallest person in the world today. I even have beliefs that are, in some sense, about the tallest person. I believe, for example, that the tallest person in the world is taller than I am. In more technical language, the belief in question involves quantified thought. Quantifiers include "There exists," "all," "most," "there is just one." Arguably, my belief that the tallest person is the world is taller than I am is no more than the belief that there is just one person who is taller than everyone else and who is taller than I am.[18] While my belief is, in some sense, about the tallest person, it is also true of me that I don't in fact know *who* the tallest person is. My thought of that person is indirect in that I can think of height, I can think of people, I can think of the relation of being taller than, and because I can also think of there being just one …, I can form the complex thought of the one person who is taller than everyone else. My thought *might* not correspond to anyone. There might be no person taller than everyone else. There might be a tie between one, two, or many people all of whom are tall and where there are no people taller than any of them.

It is an interesting, important, and controversial question as to what thoughts are indirect in the sense described above. My thought of Jack the Ripper seems to me indirect. I can think of that person but only as *whoever* was responsible for a series of horrific murders at the turn of the last century. More controversially, I can think of George Washington but only as *whoever* it is that was the first president of the United States, who led the continental army, and so on. But on some rather plausible (though *very* controversial) views, *all* of my thought about the physical world is indirect in just the way we have been discussing. On such a view I can think of perceiver-independent physical objects but only as *whatever* it is that occupies a certain potential causal role in producing networks of sensations of various sorts.[19] In the same sense, perhaps my thought of other people is similarly indirect. I can think of you but only as the mind causally responsible for movements of your body (including, of course, sounds and marks made by that body).

We'll see later on that the way I have described this supposed distinction between direct and indirect thought is more than just a bit controversial. There was a highly influential "revolution" in the late twentieth century that rejected so-called descriptivist interpretations of names and common nouns for individuals and "kinds."[20] The alternative theory was sometimes called a direct-reference theory. On that view, the idea is that I can think of all sorts of properties, kinds of things, and individuals *directly*. I don't need to think of those things in terms of what various descriptions uniquely pick out. There is a *sense* in which I don't even need to know what I am thinking of directly in order to think of it directly. I'll argue later that this "direct reference" theory is incorrect. But I will also concede that important metaphilosophical and methodological controversies hang in the balance.

What do *I* take to be the plausible foundations of thought—the conceptual atoms out of which we can build more complex ideas? Well, we can obviously "bring to mind" the specific qualitative character of the sensations we have had (or seem to remember having had)—pain, euphoria, visual, tactile, auditory, olfactory, and gustatory sensations. Or at least we can *with effort*. Contemporary philosophers have often complained that the radical empiricists implausibly over-intellectualized what goes on both when we *perceive* and *think* about the physical world. The appearances presented by the physical world are in *constant* flux, but even at a very early age, we start thinking about the world in terms of "stereotypical" appearance—some standardized appearance associated with shape, texture, color, smell, and taste. To *notice* that visual appearance, for example, is constantly changing, and to notice *how* it is changing involves a kind of skill—the skill that a good painter acquires. There is a reason your young child's artwork is displayed only on *your* refrigerator. The rectangular table is usually drawn as a two-dimensional rectangle with four straight lines underneath. Even ancient Egyptian "professional" artists charged with decorating the tombs and monuments of pharaohs seem to have had a terrible time understanding perspective and producing images that capture the way ordinary objects look.[21] But from the fact that we don't notice the constant change of experience as our relation to objects shift, it doesn't follow, of course, that the change doesn't occur. Nor does it follow that we aren't *capable* of focusing our attention in such a way that we notice and think about the subtle changes in experience.

We must be careful not to *overstate* what belongs in the foundations of thought. There is another problem discussed in great detail by the British empiricists—the problem of *abstract* ideas. I can think about *particular* shades of red, *particular* shapes, *particular* textures, *particular* sensations of pain, but such thoughts don't by themselves answer the question of what makes something red, round, rough, or painful. Consider the last. There are *many* differences between kinds of pain. Sharp piercing pain, dull throbbing pain, mild headaches, persistent back pain, and painful lectures are all painful experiences. But what do they all have in *common*? What is it in virtue of which all of these are pains? This is a question that isn't decided by introspection. This is a question about the *analysis* of pain. And analysis, I shall argue, is a question that cannot be completely divorced from language.

Earlier I argued that it is a datum of philosophy that philosophical questions are difficult to answer. There is a view that the objects of acquaintance include not just *determinate* properties, but *generic* properties (also sometimes called *determinable* properties). And acquaintance with determinables, according to this view, gives rise to thought about determinables. So what is supposed to be this difference between a determinate property and a determinable property? Well think of the paint chips you look at in the paint store. Each chip has a particular color and the paint store typically invents a name to refer to just that *way* of being blue, say.[22] Until you face the bewildering choice of colors to paint a room, you might have had no idea that there were hundreds, if not thousands, of different ways of being blue. But they are all *ways* of being blue (or so the paint store says). In addition to being this or that particular shade of blue, there is being light blue, being dark blue, being light-greenish blue, being light-greyish blue, and of course just being blue. These properties are called determinables because it seems that something has the more *general* property of being blue, for example, only in virtue of its having one or another of those *determinate* shades of blue. The blueness of this shirt is determined (in some sense that requires explanation) by that very particular shade of blue that is so specific it probably can't be described using language other than by using demonstratives (*that* shade of blue). Again, one might suppose that just as we can experience a particular shade of blue and think of that very shade in its absence, so also we can simultaneously experience and think about the many more abstract properties that are determined by that particular shade of blue.

Are there both determinate and determinable properties, are we directly acquainted with determinable properties, and can we think directly of determinables? These questions are difficult. I have at least some sympathy with the radical empiricist's view that the world as experienced is actually perfectly determinate in its character. There is, however, abstract *thought*. Thinking about what it is to be blue is different from thinking about what it is to be some perfectly determinate shade of blue. Thinking of being triangular is different from thinking of some particular triangular shape. But this almost obvious truth doesn't answer the question of what abstract thought is. On one dialectically attractive view, one might claim that the ability to abstract something common to all the different shades of blue, for example, is simply unanalyzable. There is an abstract thought of blue and all the different shades of blue correspond to that abstract thought. Alternatively, one might think of an abstract thought as a *disjunctive*[23] thought. To think of being blue is to think of being either this color or this color, or this color ..., where the "this color" picks out a specific way of being blue. Such a view makes the thought of being blue decidedly complex. Remember our paint store with the four pages full of samples of specific shades of blue. Furthermore, it is doubtful that any of us have succeeded in thinking of all of the different shades of blue. That, however, would be perfectly compatible with the fact that we have a linguistic *disposition* to use the word "blue" to describe indefinitely many determinate ways of being blue (many of which we haven't yet experienced). A closely related view takes abstract thought to be something like a constantly morphing thought. If I ask you to think of being blue, and emphasize that I don't want you to think only of some particular shade of blue, you may form a thought that "shifts" (or at least has the potential to shift) along a continuum, perhaps a continuum with "fuzzy" borders. Lastly, there may be nothing more to your possession of the concept of being blue than your being disposed to regard various particular shades of color as all correctly described as "blue."

One might worry that this last view is just a version of the view that philosophical analysis should be understood as an investigation into language. But, I argue, it is crucial to emphasize that on the view I defend, it is still *thought* that breathes life into language. Without the ability to think of features of the world (even if only determinate features of the world), there wouldn't be the ability to represent linguistically the world we inhabit. It is thought experiments that allow to discover how we use the language that we find philosophically interesting.

3.2 Philosophical Analysis

So philosophy begins with phenomenology. Direct awareness gives us foundationally justified beliefs that are the premises from which we can draw inferences. But philosophy doesn't *end* with phenomenology. And while our justification for believing *all* truths begins with our introspective knowledge, it certainly doesn't follow from this fact alone that the philosophical truths in which we are interested don't make assertions about a world of facts that extends well beyond our selves. In the analytic tradition, we also try to arrive at analyses of fundamental concepts that we deploy in asking questions. We want analyses of knowledge, causation, value, perception, mental states, properties, space, and time. We even want an analysis of analysis. The questions that require analysis are often framed as questions about what some kind of thing *is*. What *is* knowledge? What *is* causation? What *is* it for something to be valuable or for an action to be rational or morally correct? What *is* it to perceive some object? What *is* it to think, to feel, to sense? What *is* it for something to have a property or characteristic? And, of course, there is the metaphilosophical question: What *is* it to arrive at a correct view about what some kind of thing is?

I have suggested two criteria for understanding analysis. The first isn't very controversial. It is just the observation that it isn't easy to answer philosophical questions. Even after we arrive at a *tentative* view about what knowledge is, what causation is, or what perception is, we often discover to our dismay that our proposed analysis was incorrect. The Gettier (1963) thought experiment convinced almost everyone that knowledge isn't fully analyzed as justified true belief. Some of us found Hume's "regularity" theory of causation seductive only to be frustrated by our inability to develop in a plausible way the distinction between "accidental" and lawful regularity.[24]

Our second suggested datum to guide our conception of philosophy, however, is decidedly more controversial. It involves the claim that the truth of our philosophical analyses is consistent with even extreme skeptical scenarios. Whether I am right or wrong about the nature of knowledge doesn't depend on the existence of a physical world or other minds, and, *a fortiori*, doesn't depend on any facts about a *public* language.

I argued earlier that the first datum makes problematic the idea that when we seek a philosophical analysis we simply hold before our minds a property or concept. Being able to hold before our minds either the idea of, or the property of being intrinsically good, being the right course of action to take, the relation of causation, temporal and spatial properties, meanings, or perceiving, for example, is, at best, the *result* of successful analysis. It isn't something that happens at the outset. Again, if it happened at the outset, philosophical analysis wouldn't be as difficult as it is. We wouldn't be in the all-too-familiar situation of realizing that the idea or property we were searching for wasn't at all what we thought it was.

When we briefly discussed meanings earlier, I acknowledged that if we distinguish our using language meaningfully from our knowing that we mean such-and-such by the terms we use, it wouldn't be at all surprising that we often have difficulty discovering what semantic rules we follow when we use language. If philosophical analysis were construed as meaning analysis, we *would* have an explanation of how it is often difficult to arrive at correct philosophical analyses. But our second, more controversial datum might seem to stand in the way of construing philosophical analysis as meaning analysis.

Our second datum is that the success of philosophy proper is not held hostage to empirical facts about the world around us. Put another way, the success of philosophy proper is not dependent on the supposition that radical skeptical hypotheses are false. But on the most natural understanding of linguistic meaning, the meaning of terms in a *natural* language is a function of facts about how people in general are disposed to use language. The meaning of words (at least in *one* familiar sense of meaning) is not determined by *my* use of those words. My use of language might be highly idiosyncratic. I might not have learned how to use a word correctly. If my parents were unusually cruel, they might have played an elaborate practical joke on me, deliberately teaching me to use words in a way that is divorced from ordinary usage.

The above seems obviously true. But there is a very old distinction between the ordinary meaning of an expression and the *speaker's* meaning. In an interesting exchange with Alice, Humpty Dumpty said the following about the meaning of a word:

> "When *I* use a word," Humpty Dumpty said, in rather a scornful tone, "it means just what I choose it to mean—neither more nor less."
>
> "The question is," said Alice, "whether you *can* make words mean so many different things."
>
> "The question is," said Humpty Dumpty, "which is to be master—that's all."

In the sense of meaning we were discussing above, Humpty Dumpty obviously had it wrong. *I* can decide to use "red" to mean "round" but that won't determine the *ordinary* meaning of "red." Still, we as individuals can introduce *technical* expressions for a host of good reasons. Further, it is at least possible that we *find* ourselves using words in a way that is idiosyncratic.

3.2.1 Stipulative Definition

When philosophers talk about the meaning of a term like "knowledge," "good," or "causation," to take a few examples, they are not typically interested in *stipulating* a meaning for the relevant of expressions. They typically think of themselves as *discovering* correct analyses. Still, as a philosopher, I do sometimes *stipulate* the meaning of an expression I use. I often do this in a philosophy class hoping to make a *clear* distinction that I will employ in discussing a given controversy. For example, it is useful to define the internalism/externalism debate in epistemology so that the distinction is clear and interesting (we'll do that later). Often we quickly realize that there isn't just one controversy we need to define, but a number of related though importantly different controversies. In ethics, it is useful to define the debate(s) between cognitivists and noncognitivists or the debate(s) between absolutists and relativists. In contemporary political philosophy, it is now sometimes useful to define a distinction (or distinctions) between ideal and non-ideal political theories.[25]

Introducing technical vocabulary to define *abstract* philosophical controversies (and philosophical movements or schools of thought) is hardly the *only* reason for introducing technical philosophical terminology whose meaning is, in a way stipulated. Philosophers will often argue that it is useful to introduce technical terminology to capture other important distinctions that will facilitate clear discussion of interesting and important questions. Sometimes the technical terms are introduced to eliminate ambiguity. Sometimes the technical terms are introduced to mark distinctions that are either overlooked or obscured by language as it is ordinarily used.

Consider again our discussion of phenomenology above. I tried to introduce the expression "direct awareness" to describe a special sort of relation that I bear to features of my own mental life, a relation in which I don't stand to physical objects or the mental lives of other people. And in trying to say more about that mental life to which I have a special access, I talked about a very traditional distinction between subjective appearance and mind-independent reality. If there is a distinction to be made, we also need a way of talking about those fleeting and subjective appearances.

In his classic attempt to dissolve what has come to be known as "the problem of perception," J. L. Austin tried to underscore what he took to be disastrous wrong turns made by philosophers such as H. H. Price and A. J. Ayer, mistakes that Austin thought were often the result of paying insufficient attention to the nuances of ordinary language. Austin quite correctly pointed out that in ordinary language we don't describe ourselves as indirectly perceiving material objects (at least under normal conditions of perception). Indeed, as he pointed out with a touch of irony, we don't normally talk about perceiving *material objects* at all. In developing the traditional problem of perception, philosophers often talked about the senses deceiving us, and offered various "illusions" as examples of such deception. Again, Austin was probably right that philosophers often play fast and loose with both the terms "illusion" and "deception." It is a gross misuse of language to talk as if the round coin creates an *illusion* of being elliptical when seen from an angle, or that a road creates an illusion of disappearing into a far-off horizon. And Austin (followed years later by Sellars 1956) was also quite right to urge caution when turning to the use of words like "looks" and "appears" in an effort to characterize the "inner" experience to which the radical empiricists thought we have privileged access.

But, as we noted earlier, it is precisely because words like "looks" and "appears" have so many uses in ordinary language that a philosopher would be well advised to *introduce* a technical vocabulary to say what needs to be said. Consider, for example, the various uses of "looks." "He looks like a lawyer" I might say gesturing toward someone in a courtroom. "He always looks angry" I might say of someone (even if I don't think that the person is usually angry). "When I wear these rose-tinted sunglasses, the snow looks red," I might say having just put the glasses on. In the first example, I might be expressing a tentative judgment that the person is a lawyer. Alternatively, I might just be commenting on the fact that the person is dressed the way stereotypical lawyers dress. When I say of someone that they look angry, but also don't want to assert that they *are* angry, I might again be saying that they have the kind of expression that people often have when they are angry. Similarly, when wearing the glasses and observing that the snow looks red, I am hardly indicating a tentative conclusion that the snow suddenly changed its color from white to red. Again, I am probably *comparing* the way the snow looks to me now with the way that red things look under "standard" conditions.[26]

None of these familiar uses of the expression "looks" gets at the appearance that the traditional epistemologist wants to describe. We get *close* if we look at the "comparative" use of "looks" and focus on *the way of looking* to which it appeals. When we talk about the way something looks it is more than a bit tempting to suppose that there *is* such a way of looking.[27] That might, however, only get us a *relation* that an object bears to a subject—the looking red "relation." But, as we did when discussing phenomenology, it is tempting, though much more controversial, to suppose that the way of looking we are discussing can occur even in the context of a vivid dream or hallucination. And if we convince ourselves that there is such an experience common to both veridical experience and radical hallucination we need a way of talking about that common denominator. Unless we create hallucinatory "objects" to stand in relations of appearing to us, we might want a way of describing appearance that doesn't presuppose that we are talking about a *relation*. Chisholm suggests we introduce a non-comparative use of "appears" to do just that. We might talk about "being appeared to red-ly" to make sure that our audience knows we are talking in a very technical way about this alleged common element to both veridical experience and hallucination.

A philosopher like Austin wouldn't be happy with our inventing these odd expressions. At the very least, he would argue that you better have a really good reason for torturing language in this way. But, of course, the empiricists did think that they had a really good reason for calling our attention to a state of mind that can occur whether or not the physical reality we take to be its cause is present. They were convinced (rightly or wrongly) that the most plausible account of what justifies us in believing what we do about ordinary objects around us are facts about subjective experiences. As Austin caustically observed, normal people don't talk about their *evidence* for thinking that a pig is in front of them when the animal comes into plain view. They don't, but they can get talked into thinking that they would have the very same justification for believing that the pig is there even if they were suffering some bizarre vivid hallucination. Like the disjunctivists we discussed earlier, Austin isn't at all sure why we would be quick to describe the justification in the case of vivid hallucination as the same, but *that* is the point of contention between Austin and the philosophers he is criticizing. And we are only confusing the key issue by focusing exclusively on how people ordinarily talk.

Just as there are good reasons to introduce technical language in epistemology, so also there are reasons to introduce technical vocabulary in almost all areas of philosophy. The ancient distinction between a thing being intrinsically good and its being only instrumentally good isn't all *that* technical a distinction. There are contexts in which the importance of recognizing the distinction comes out even in ordinary conversations. But it's not obvious that ordinary people mark the distinction *clearly* or *consistently*.

Or consider another example from ethics. When people talk about whether someone ought to have acted the way they did, it seems to me obvious that we sometimes take up different perspectives. Sometimes we ask the question taking up the epistemic perspective of the actor in question. Sometimes we adopt *our* epistemic perspective. Sometimes we take up the perspective of a kind of "ideal" observer. If this is so, we would be well-advised to mark the distinctions so we don't end up taking at cross-purposes when we debate something like the wisdom of having gone to war with Iraq.

In the philosophy of mind we almost certainly want to make a distinction between different ways of reporting beliefs, a distinction we might mark by talking about *de re* reports and *de dicto* reports of beliefs.[28] When I say that when he entered it, Henry Hudson believed that Hudson's Bay was a passage to the Orient, I am presumably not saying that Hudson was dumb enough to think that a bay was a passage, nor am I suggesting that he had a premonition that the body of water in question would someday be named after him. Rather, I am picking out Hudson's Bay, and I am saying that Hudson believed that *it* was a passage to the Orient. More controversially, I am saying that Hudson believed some proposition whose subject term picked out that body of water. This would be an example of a *de re* report of Hudson's belief. Sometimes, however, when I describe someone's belief I intend everything following the "believed that" to be an accurate description of the content of the belief (we can call that a *de dicto* report of belief). We could devote chapters of a book discussing *de re/de dicto* distinctions. My only purpose here is to give another example of how a distinction might be important to mark with technical terminology—important because making the distinction can prevent no end of needless confusion.

3.2.2 Beyond Stipulation

We talked above about various ways in which one might find it important and useful to stipulate the meaning of various expressions to make and to mark distinctions. But we also noted that the kind of meaning in which philosophy is interested goes well beyond stipulation. In commenting on Humpty Dumpty's exchange with Alice we noted that even if we are, in some sense, the masters of the words whose meaning we introduce through stipulation, it is hardly plausible to suppose that we as individuals are masters of the meanings of words used in a *natural* language. The meaning of such words, one might suppose, surely has something to do with their ordinary use by members of a linguistic community. There is certainly a sense in which that is true. But beyond mere stipulation, and more importantly for our present purpose, we should acknowledge that there can be facts about how *I* use an expression even if those facts don't make true any claim about how most people use an expression. Again, we can appeal to our skeptical scenarios to make the point. According to some traditional epistemologists, I can make sense of the hypothesis (solipsism) that I am the only conscious being who ever has or ever will exist. If such a hypothesis makes sense, it seems almost obvious to me that it wouldn't alter the fact that I use words and that those words have meaning. Since there are no other conscious beings, it wouldn't be facts about anyone else's linguistic dispositions that make it true that the words I use have the meaning they have. It would, instead, be facts about *my* linguistic dispositions.

As we noted earlier, it would be a mistake to suppose that if I am interested in discovering how I use a given word, that investigation would involve nothing more complicated than introspection. Still, if Humpty were right, and I am the *master* of what my words mean, then whatever I say or think goes. But he *isn't* right. Facts about the semantic rules *I* follow when using words are no more plausibly viewed as *transparent* to me than are facts about the semantic rules other people follow when using words. I might initially think that I use "knowledge" to characterize all and only justified true belief. A thought experiment then convinces me that I was mistaken.[29] And the same is true of any other philosophically interesting word I use.

But what are these dispositions that constitute the meanings of my words? We could construe the relevant dispositions as dispositions to respond linguistically to confronting certain circumstances in the world. So perhaps what I mean by "red" is a function of what sorts of things I would describe using the expression "red." But if we continue to rely on the datum that philosophical analysis is not held hostage to empirical facts about an external world, we need to tread carefully. If I am in one of the skeptical scenarios, I'm not responding to *any* mind-independent reality when I use language. The obvious solution, it seems to me, is that we construe the relevant dispositions as disposition to use language to describe the world as *thought* of by me in various ways.

Consider a relatively straightforward example. If I am interested in the philosophy of religion, I might ask myself whether there is a God. In thinking about that question, I might naturally ask myself precisely what I mean by "God." I can't answer that question by asking myself what *actual* beings I describe as "God." If I am considering whether to be a theist, an atheist, or an agnostic, I have not yet made up my mind concerning the existence of God, and perhaps I haven't responded to any *actual* being using the name "God." But I can still employ *thought* experiments. I can *think* of various sorts of beings, and I can discover whether or not I would describe those hypothetical beings as Gods. Would I describe a being who caused the existence of matter and energy, but who isn't omnipotent, omniscient, or omnibenevolent as a God? Would I describe a being who isn't perfect but who is more powerful, more knowledgeable, and kinder than any other being as a God? Would I describe a being who is omniscient, but not omnipotent or omnibenevolent as a God? I can ask myself these questions in an attempt to find out just how I am using the expression "God." Or consider an even more straightforward example. Suppose I'm not the brightest star in the sky and I am trying to figure out how I use the expression "square" (and assume for present purposes that I am thinking about plane/two-dimensional figures). I think being a square has something to do with being a quadrilateral and having equal sides. I picture a quadrilateral with equal sides. The picture I form is of a quadrilateral with equal sides and right angles, but I don't "notice" the angles. Instead, I reach the tentative conclusion that I use the word "square" to describe all and only those things that are quadrilaterals with equal sides. I think of another quadrilateral with equal sides, a blue parrallelogram without interior angles of 90 degrees.

I immediately realize that my first thought about how I use the term "square" was incorrect. I have found a *counterexample* to that view. I wouldn't call anything a square unless it were a quadrilateral with equal sides. But there *could be* quadrilaterals with equal sides that I wouldn't describe as squares. The counterexample above, of course, involved, a blue quadrilateral, and, if I were really dim, I might suppose for a moment that not being blue is also critical to being a square. But I can disabuse myself of that idea with additional thought experiments. I can easily think of a blue square. In the real world, counterexamples are often suggested by one's colleagues, but philosophers thinking carefully about their tentative conclusions will also try to come up with their own counterexamples to those views.

When considering more philosophically interesting examples, it may well be true that many people would not, in fact, come up with counterexamples without the help of other people. In the real world, philosophical conversation is invaluable. But, our datum about what is *necessary* for the correctness of our philosophical analyses is not a datum about what is *causally* necessary to answer correctly the philosophical questions that interest us. Without other philosophers, I almost certainly wouldn't hold many of the philosophical views I do. If I hadn't studied philosophy as an undergraduate in Victoria College at the University of Toronto, I probably wouldn't hold many of the philosophical views I do. If I hadn't done my graduate studies in philosophy at Brown University, I probably wouldn't have held many of the philosophical views I do. For all I know, the *order* in which I have read various philosophical works strongly influenced my philosophical views. But when we are just talking about causal connections, it is also true that if my great-grandparents hadn't met, I wouldn't have existed and *a fortiori* wouldn't have formed any of the philosophical views I have. The question I raised earlier is what is *conceptually* necessary for me to rationally and correctly answer the philosophical questions that interest me. It is a question about whether we can make *sense* of my successfully answering the philosophical questions that interest me *were* I to live in one of the radical skeptical scenarios. And it still seems to me that satisfying my philosophical curiosity is not held hostage, in this way, to any *scientific* discoveries about the world around me.

3.2.3 More about Thought Experiments

I've talked about the critical role of thought experiments in the philosopher's search for analyses of value, knowledge, causation, and the like. One thinks that one uses "know" to characterize all and only situations in which certain features are present. One then tries to think of a situation in which one knows but those features are not present, or a situation in which those features are present but one doesn't know.

In his well-known work on metaphilosophy, Williamson (2007) also acknowledges that thought experiments are crucial to philosophy. But he argues that there is no sharp line dividing certain empirical truths we discover through thought experiments, and traditional philosophical analyses discovered (in part) through thought experiments. He gives the following sort of an example. Consider the question of whether a tarantula or an ant is larger. How would you answer that question? Well, arguably, you would not need to put on your ornithologist's hat and go out in the "field" to study insects. Nor would you even need to go on to *Wikipedia* to see what is said about ants and tarantulas. You would probably just think about an ant, think about a tarantula, and compare "in thought" the one to the other. Tarantulas are larger than ants, you will conclude. When you are playing pool and planning out your next shot, you use thought experiments. As vividly as you can, you imagine the cue ball hitting the target ball at such and such an angle, think of the ensuing direction the target ball will move, and think about where the cue ball will end up in relation to the other balls. There is clearly a sense in which all of this is a complex thought experiment employed to arrive at critical truths relevant to the successful execution of a shot. But they are not, I would argue, the same sort of thought experiments that the philosopher employs in searching for meanings.

What is the difference? It seems to me that the examples Williamson relies upon to expand the role of thought experiments and, in doing so, expand what we should call *a priori* knowledge (knowledge that is independent of sense experience) are more plausibly viewed as what I shall call "generic" memory. To explain this idea I need to distinguish veridical memory from apparent memory. Let's begin with some relatively straightforward distinctions. Most uses of "remember" and its cognates are what Williamson calls *factive*. The rough idea is that when the transitive verb "remember" takes a noun or a noun clause as its object, the memory claim can only be true if the noun succeeds in referring or the noun clause is true. So, for example, you can't remember your mother's brother if she didn't have one. You can't remember that you played the piano in third grade if you didn't. But most (not all) philosophers[30] would argue that there are always counterparts to veridical memory in which you are *internally* in the same sort of mental state, but where what you seem to remember didn't exist or didn't happen. If such a view is true, then we'll need a way of talking about that "common denominator," and following many other philosophers I'll again talk about what "seems" to be the case. So I can *seem* to remember interacting with my mother's brother (even if she doesn't have one), and I can seem to remember playing the piano in third grade (even though I didn't).

Philosophers and cognitive scientists who study memory also distinguish different sorts of memory. One sort is episodic. In episodic memory, the mind "re-creates" with a great deal of specificity a prior experience. Again, a non-veridical episodic memory would be just like that, but the cause of the apparent memory would be something other than what is represented by the mind. We also have what one might call *propositional* memory. We remember that both Caesar and Antony had affairs with Cleopatra. We remember that Columbus sailed the ocean blue in 1492. Again, this sort of memory isn't an attempt to recreate our experiences of Caesar, Antony, and Cleopatra, or our experiences of sailing the ocean blue. These memories also differ with respect to propositional detail. I can remember that Caesar was assassinated without remembering who assassinated him or without remembering when or where he was assassinated. I can remember that Columbus sailed to the new world without remembering where or when he did that. I can remember that I was taught by a very tall history teacher in seventh grade without remembering very much detail about what he looked like or sounded like.

Once we make these distinctions, it is tempting to think that some of the thoughts Williamson says that we rely on to reach empirical conclusions are nothing more than what one might call generic apparent memories. There are very real epistemological problems that arise concerning reliance on apparent memory to reach conclusions about the past, but setting those aside, one can rely on apparent memory to reach not only specific conclusions about the past but general truths about the past. One source of such knowledge is what I have called generic memory. I seem to remember that tarantulas are larger than ants. Do I seem to remember some particular tarantulas being larger than some particular ants? Probably not. I'm not sure I've ever even seen a tarantula in "real" life (though I do seem to remember having seen pictures of tarantula crawling on people's arms (in magazines and movies). I also seem to remember having seen ants crawling on an arm. Again, if apparent (episodic, propositional, particular, or generic) memory can justify beliefs about the past, we can indeed get justified beliefs of the sort Williamson talks about relying only on a kind of thought—the kind of thought that we call *memory*. But beliefs about the past based on apparent memory have always been a paradigm of *empirical* knowledge (not *a priori* knowledge).

Williamson suggests that both conclusions about the empirical world that rely on "armchair" thought experiments, and conclusions regarding various philosophical theses that also employ thought experiments are best stated in terms of subjunctive conditionals. I'm trying to figure out what shot to take at pool. What I'm interested in discovering is what precisely would happen if I hit the seven ball at such and such an angle with such and such force. When I try to discover "counterexamples" to some philosophical view about what knowledge is, I am hoping to think of some possible situation where the proposed conditions that are supposed to constitute knowledge would be present, but there wouldn't be knowledge (or vice versa). Consider, for example, what Williamson says about Gettier's familiar objection to the metaepistemological view that knowledge just is justified true belief.

In that really short paper we talked about earlier, Gettier described a couple of possible scenarios in which someone would indeed have a justified true belief, but wouldn't know. There are all sorts of Gettier-style counterexample, but I'll just focus on one that actually pre-dated significantly Gettier. Russell (1948) asked us to think about a person who looks at a clock that indicates that it is 3 p.m. and who, naturally enough, concludes that it is 3 p.m. As it turns out, unbeknownst to the person, the clock was actually broken. Still, as the old saying goes, even a broken clock is right twice a day.[31] Our hypothetical person would have a justified true belief, but wouldn't know, or so the argument goes. Williamson considers the idea that we should put our conclusion in terms of the following sort of generalization: Necessarily, whenever one is a situation like the one just described, one would have a justified true belief without knowing. He worries, however, that such a generalization might be false. After all, isn't it possible that we are looking at a broken clock without knowing that the clock is broken, and that some benign deity has arranged the world in such a way that whenever one looks at broken clocks some other reliable mechanism kicks in that causes us to believe the truth about the time?[32] In any event, all one needs to refute the view that knowledge is nothing more than justified true belief is the true subjunctive conditional: if one were in that *particular* situation (with the world being as it typically is) we wouldn't know.

This move to counterfactual reasoning is important for Williamson, because, as we noted earlier, that's how he tries to blur the line between the results of thought experiments that involve contingent truths about the world, and thought experiments that purport to reveal truths that philosophers have typically taken to be necessary. As I indicated above, the distinction still seems to me clear. A Gettier thought experiment doesn't rely on apparent memory in the way in which thought experiments about contingent features of the world do. To be sure, a philosophical thought experiment may be cryptic. The hypothetical situation described might take for granted a great many features that aren't specifically mentioned. But when one is in doubt about what those further features are, one can remove the doubt just by stipulating the character of your hypothetical situation. As Bob Ross used to remark, when you are painting, your imagination is your own; you make your "world" however you want your world to be. The same is true of philosophers constructing thought experiments.

3.2.4 Wittgenstein and the Private Language Argument

I have suggested that we cannot divorce completely philosophical analysis from language. Nor can we divorce philosophical analysis from thought. As philosophers the language that guides our search for a philosophical analysis is our own language. We are trying to discover what semantic rules govern our dispositions to use words to describe hypothetical situations—situations *thought of* in various ways. The thoughts in questions are often of particular or determinate states of the world. The mind may be capable of forming general or abstract thoughts. But general thoughts are the result of successful analysis. They don't precede analysis.

It would be irresponsible to make these remarks about the intelligibility of semantic rules governing an *individual's* use of language, without discussing Wittgenstein's famous objections to the intelligibility of a *private* language. In the *Investigations*, Wittgenstein appears to argue that one can't make sense of meaning unless there is a framework provided by a *community* of language users. The heart of the argument seems to have something to do with whether one can make sense of correct and *incorrect* use of language without the language's being public.

I'll begin this very brief discussion of Wittgenstein's argument by confessing that I have never talked to a self-proclaimed Wittgensteinian who would embrace *any* proposed interpretation of the private language argument. Their response to such interpretations is usually a wry smile at the proposal's failure to capture the depth of Wittgenstein's insight. But acknowledging in advance that Wittgensteinians probably aren't going to like what I say, I'll offer both an interpretation of the private language argument and my response to it.

Wittgenstein's complaint about the intelligibility of a private language seems to have arisen primarily in the context of criticizing elements of the radical empiricism that I have endorsed above. On that view, you will recall, the foundations of a person's knowledge consist, in part, of that person's knowledge of truths about the character of their own subjective experience—truths to which they have a privileged access. This version of foundationalism insists that I know the contents of my own mind in a way that no one else can. Furthermore, I have a way of thinking about and describing that subjective experience that doesn't depend for its accuracy on the existence of other people and their linguistic habits. But while the context of Wittgenstein's discussion was this idea that there are mental states to which each person has a privileged access, I'll argue below that there is no plausible version of the private language argument that, if legitimate, wouldn't tell equally against the possibility of a *solitary* linguist (a person who has a language despite the fact that there are no other people).

So what is supposed to be the problem with a person's having a private language? The best sense I can make of the argument is something like the following. You can't make sense of the *successful* use of language unless you can also make sense of *unsuccessful* use of that language. When it comes to a natural language, your use of an expression can be compared to the usual use of that expression. If your use of a word diverges from ordinary use, then your use of the word can be appropriately viewed as incorrect. But if the language is yours, and yours alone, then there is no distinction that can be defined between correct and incorrect use of the language. If you are the sole arbiter, for example, of whether something is red, and you face a borderline case, then there is nothing to overrule whatever decision you make. What you say goes. But if that's the case, then nothing could make your decision incorrect.

One can understand Wittgenstein's concern. Imagine Adam (before Eve) assigning names to the various animals he discovers. Suppose that he introduces the term "fish" to categorize what we would call salmon, perch, sharks, trout, seabass, and so on. One day he notices what we would call a seal and is deciding whether or not to extend the term "fish" to include *that* sort of creature. It might seem to Adam just that—a *decision*. And since the decision is his and his alone, in what sense could he make the wrong the decision? The next day he notices what we would call a whale, and decides that the creature is just a really big fish.[33] Again, it is his decision. In what sense could he be wrong? No incorrect use; no correct use. There is no sense to made of the private linguist's language.

There is an answer to the question of how Adam can make lingusitic errors. Even if the semantic rules one follows are one's own, one can still fail to follow those rules correctly. And one can still fail to *know* what those rules are that one is following. The more complete story of why this is so needs further discussion.

As I indicated earlier, if something like the above is a plausible interpretation of Wittgenstein's worry, then it is hard to see why a solitary linguist would be any less problematic than a person using words to describe subjective experience to which only that person has privileged access. If the problem is that we need other users of a language to give sense to the distinction between correct and incorrect use of language, then we shouldn't be able to make sense of language unless there is a *community* of language users. But is that a plausible position? However difficult it might be in the real world, can't we make *sense* of an "Adam" who is the only creature capable of higher-order consciousness in the universe and who whiles away his lonely existence naming the kinds of things that he notices in his environment? Setting aside skeptical worries about whether one can be aware of physical objects in one's environment, imagine Adam running across various sorts of creatures to which he gives names. Deciding whether we can make sense of such a "solitary" linguist will require us to consider questions about meaning more carefully. This we will do in Part II, Chapter 4.

3.3 Beyond Phenomenology and Analysis— "Internal" Relations among Properties

Philosophy may not end with phenomenology and analysis. It is tempting to suppose that there are truths made true by relations among properties, and that truths of this sort remain within the purview of philosophy proper.

As was suggested above, philosophical analyses are answers to questions of the form "What is X?" (What is knowledge?; What is perception?; What is causation?; What is value?"). Sometimes philosophers refer to correct answers to such questions as analytic truths. It isn't easy to define the analytic/synthetic distinction. Analytic truths are sometimes described as true *soley* in virtue of the meanings of the terms that express such truths. For those who think that it is something like thoughts that are the primary bearers of truth value, analytic truths have sometimes been described as true *soley* in virtue of relations among the concepts that in combination constitute the relevant thought. More technically, one might define an analytic truth as expressed by a sentence that can be reduced to a formal tautology through substitution of synonymous expressions. Such a definition obviously requires us to define what a formal tautology is and what synonymy is. Formal tautologies (as the term implies) are necessary truths whose truth can be discovered solely by inspecting the *form* of the sentence that expresses them. Consider some examples: Everything that is *red*, is *red*. Either there are *horses* or it is not the case that there are *horses*. Everything that is *red* and that is *round*, is *red*. If this is *red* then it is not the case that it is not, not *red*. The italicized terms can be replaced by any expression that is the same part of speech and the statement will remain true. Arguably, we don't even need to reflect on the meaning of the italicized expressions to realize that the statement that contains them is true. I don't know much about what it means to say of a quark that it has charm, but I do know that all quarks that have charm have charm.[34]

There are other statements that are necessarily true whose truth can't be discovered solely by looking at their form. If we allow, however, that we can substitute in a statement synonymous expressions, one for another, without altering the meaning of the whole statement, perhaps we can define analytic truths as truths that can be reduced to formal tautologies through such substitutions. So to consider an example we discussed above, as I use the expressions, the statement that all squares are quadrilaterals seems to be necessarily true. But if "square" just means "quadrilateral with equal sides and right angles," then the sentence "All squares are quadrilaterals" is equivalent in meaning to the formal tautology "Everything that is a quadrilateral and has equal sides and right angles is a quadrilateral."[35]

One can make a strong case that not all necessary truths are formal tautologies or reducible to such through substitution of synonymous expressions. Consider first truths of logic themselves. The same proposition cannot be both true and false. A proposition is either true or false. If it is true that if p then q, and also true that not-q, then it is true that not-P. This last truth will count as an analytic truth since it is a formal tautology. We can prove such propositions to be true using truth tables. The truth table proofs rely on truth table definitions of "connectives" like "and" and "if ... then ..." and "not." So, for example, (P and Q) is true just when P is true and Q is true and it is false for all other combinations of truth value (it is false when P is false and Q is true and when Q is true and P is false and when they are both false). "Not" has a simple truth table definition. Not-P is true when P is false and it is false when P is true. But logic has axioms. When we think about possible combinations of truth value, we don't consider the possibility that P is both true and false. We don't need to consider P's being both true and false because that isn't a real possibility. It is necessarily false that P is both true and false. The *philosophy* of logic, a field that should be thought of as more fundamental than logic, needs to answer questions about the nature of truth and the truth-makers for the axioms of logic. It needs to explain entailment and the relata of entailment.[36]

There are other truths that are good candidates for necessary truths even if they are not analytic. Consider the claim that equilateral triangles are equiangular triangles. There is obviously an intimate connection between the property of being an equiangular triangle and the property of being an equilateral triangle. In some sense, a figure can't have the one property without having the other. But is it plausible to argue that "equilateral triangle" and "equiangular triangle" are *synonymous*? The meaning of "equilateral" seems tied to lines being of equal *length*. The meaning of "equiangular" seems tied to the equality of *angles*. If *that* example from geometry doesn't convince you, consider the complicated statement that all right-angled triangles are such that if you were to draw a square on the hypotenuse of such a triangle its area would be equal to the sum of the areas of squares were you to draw them on the other two sides. It seems wildly implausible that "right-angled triangle" is *synonymous* with that complicated description of triangles and the relation of the areas of hypothetical squares drawn on their sides. Nevertheless, just as one can discover analytic truths by thinking carefully and correctly about meanings, so also one can *in principle* discover the above necessary truths (let's call them *synthetic* necessary truths) of geometry just by thinking carefully about the *properties* about which the statements make claims.

Now it might seem that we have taken a wrong turn if we try to understand *philosophy* proper in such a way that it includes within its purview the truths of *geometry*. It is a controversial question as to whether the truths of arithmetic are best construed as analytic or are more like the truths of geometry discussed above. But either way, even if there are close connections between philosophy and mathematics, mathematics shouldn't be viewed as a field within philosophy. I am ultimately not sure about how to distinguish philosophy from mathematics and geometry. *Philosophy* of mathematics and *philosophy* of geometry (space), however, *begins* with answers to the "What is …?" questions. What is a number? What is a line? What is a point? Frankly, I wouldn't trust those in mathematics *at all* to answer those questions. I think that would be as foolish as asking my plumber for insight into answering the question of how to understand the distinction between appearance and objective reality. To be sure, nothing I say in this book precludes the possibility of someone's becoming both an excellent philosopher and an excellent mathematician. And the same is true of virtually every other field of which one might think. Physicists interested in the most *abstract* empirical questions about the nature of space and time will naturally become interested in philosophical questions about the nature of space and time. They may or may not be good philosophers. The skills necessary to discover philosophical truths are not the same as the skills one employs in discovering empirical truths. I'll talk much more about the philosophy of science in Chapter 8 of this book.

Still, mathematics (as opposed to meta-metamathematics) is very close to some of the issues that might be included in philosophy proper. This conclusion is particularly plausible if one concedes that there are indefinitely many truths like the truths of geometry. When some philosophers claimed that all necessary truths are analytic truths, they faced a wide range of objections that went well beyond the truths of geometry described above. Consider the following: Whatever is red is colored; Whatever is red (all over) is not blue (all over); Middle C on the piano is lower than middle E on the piano; Pain is intrinsically bad. All of these are candidates for being necessary truths. Moreover, one might plausibly claim that all of these necessary truths can be known simply by reflecting on the relevant properties.

As we shall see in Chapter 4, many philosophers became convinced in the latter part of the twentieth century that there are examples of synthetic (non-analytic) necessary truths that *cannot* be known simply through reflection. Kripke and Putnam (among others) convinced many that it is not only true, but necessarily true, that water is H_2O, that heat is molecular motion, that (on the assumption that there is a Morning Star and an Evening Star) the Morning Star (also known as Phosphorus) is the Evening Star (also known as Phosphorus) (to take but a few examples). Yet it seems almost obvious that such truths could be discovered only through a kind of investigation that cannot be conducted "from the armchair." I won't say anything about this view now. I will discuss it in more detail when we consider the theories of meaning (I believe *mistaken* theories of meaning) that led philosophers to embrace the above view.

For now, I want to suggest that many would argue that there are at least some necessary truths that can be known simply by reflecting on the nature of certain properties, and that discovery of such truths should be included within the purview of philosophy. But, as we shall see in Part II, the question of what should be allowed as part of philosophy proper will often depend on the plausibility of various controversial claims about the correct analyses of the *meanings* in which we are interested.

3.4 Summarizing

I have suggested two criteria to guide our understanding of philosophy proper. The first is the relatively uncontroversial claim that philosophy is difficult. The second is the much more controversial claim that the successful employment of philosophical method to arrive at philosophical truth is, in principle, consistent with even the radical skeptical scenarios that played such an important role for traditional foundationalists in their search for plausible foundations for knowledge and justified belief.

Our first criterion, while relatively innocuous, casts serious doubt on the idea that philosophy should begin by leaving language behind to focus instead on the properties or concepts associated with meaningful language. If you could hold before your mind properties or concepts like knowledge, causation, meaning, and value, it just wouldn't be that hard to discover what those properties and concepts are. I distinguished forming thoughts about general properties from forming thoughts about particular states of the world. Without the latter, I don't see how philosophy could get a foothold. The lifeblood of philosophical analysis is the thought experiment. We think about some particular state of affairs and ask ourselves whether we would characterize it as a case of knowledge, causation, one thing's meaning another, or something's having value. But just because it is a state of affairs *in all of its particularity*, we may not know what about it prompts our linguistic use. Our thought experiment about the *particular* might not reveal to us what semantic rules we are following in using the language in question. Again, that might seem strange, particularly if we are imagining a solitary linguist. How can I start using a language in accordance with a rule if I don't know what the rule is? Good question—answer to follow.

Our second criterion is powerful. It precludes thinking of philosophy in a number of historically influential ways. Like most powerful criteria for delineating a subject matter, it is decidedly controversial. I've convinced myself that, *in principle*, I could successfully discover fundamental philosophical truths whether or not anybody else actually exists, whether or not there is an external world, and whether or not there is a substantial past. Of course, I don't *believe* that I am the only conscious being that exists. I don't *believe* that there is no physical world, and I don't *believe* that there has been no substantial past. I don't believe that *I* am the author of all of the many thought experiments that have led me to accept or reject philosophical views. But even if I *were* inhabiting one of the exotic skeptical scenarios that have so fascinated epistemologists, I don't think that it would affect my ability to satisfy my philosophical curiosity. If I were the victim of Descartes's evil demon, if I were a brain in a vat, or if I were the only conscious being who exists, I could still know the same truths about *my* mental life that currently form the foundations of all of my knowledge and justified belief. Moreover, I could still wonder what would make something valuable, what would make an action right, what would make a regularity lawful, what would make a thought mean what it does, what must be added to true belief in order for it to be knowledge, and a host of other traditional philosophical questions. But if this is so, then my questions about, value, right action, lawful regularity, meaning, and knowledge are not questions about the ordinary uses of various terms in a natural language. And this should be a welcome conclusion. As we noted earlier, we surely want to be on board with Moore's idea that we must distinguish philosophy from lexicography.

When we looked briefly at which metaphilosophical views are left standing after deploying our two criteria, I suggested that traditional *phenomenology* would be untouched by even the most radical of skeptical scenarios. I also suggested that even if ordinary linguistic usage is ruled out as the subject matter of analysis, it doesn't follow that philosophical analysis should be divorced from language. In fact, when I try to figure out what value, right action, causation, meaning, and perception are (to take a few examples), I find myself asking myself how *I* use various expressions. The data with which I work are facts about what *I* would regard as the correct ways to describe the world *as I think of it*.

As Moore suggested in *Principia Ethica*, we work on the *assumption* that our use of language isn't idiosyncratic. I believe that others use words the way I do. But it is just that—an assumption. Qua *philosopher*, I don't argue for that assumption. And qua *philosopher*, I recognize that the presupposition might be false. Indeed, perhaps at least some philosophical debates among philosophers *do* reflect the fact that people don't always use language the same way.

This egocentric conception of analysis needs to be developed in more detail. I am arguing for a view about what is essential to fundamental philosophy—a view about what makes a philosophical question distinctively philosophical. I'll try to illustrate the idea with respect to specific examples. I'll also try to illustrate the idea that one's philosophical analyses will dictate what *else* belongs in philosophy proper. I'll begin in Chapter 4 with a controversy in the philosophy of language that has the potential to limit philosophical analysis to just one controversy in the philosophy of language. Fortunately for those of us whose areas of philosophical interest go beyond the philosophy of language, the right view in the philosophy of language will allow us to explore philosophical analyses of other concepts critical to our thinking clearly about the world.

Notes

1 Such a claim is natural given some version of what is sometimes called the "traditional" account of knowledge as justified true belief, where the belief's being true is not a result of problematic "luck." That account of knowledge is hardly uncontroversial, however. A number of philosophers influenced by Williamson (2000) are convinced that one should understand justified belief in terms of knowledge—a view diametrically opposed to the traditional approach. The really crude idea is that we should identify evidence with

knowledge, and understand justified belief as belief supported by evidence (supported by what we know).
2 Where E's guaranteeing (entailing) P is the upper limit of making probable.
3 The more technical way of saying this is that inferential justification needs to be defined recursively. A paradigm of a recursive definition is the way in which we would define being an ancestor of X. We start with the notion of being a parent of X, and then we understand being an ancestor of X in terms of being a parent of X or a parent of a parent of X or a parent of a parent of a parent of X or ... and so on ad infinitum. The recursive analysis of justified belief would go something like this: A belief is justified if it is noninferentially justified or is inferred legitimately from a noninferentially justified belief or is inferred legitimately from a belief that is inferred legitimately from a noninferentially justified belief, or ..., and so on.
4 Though they are the kinds of things that *could* correspond. Rocks and trees fail to correspond to anything but they aren't false because they are not the kinds of things that could correspond to reality. Even this isn't quite right because there are thoughts that are necessarily false, and there is a sense in which a thought couldn't correspond to reality. Arguably, though, such thoughts have as constitutes ideas that can successfully correspond to reality. So my thought that there are round squares has as constituents the ideas of a thing being round and a thing being a square.
5 Of course, there are many causal links in the chain that leads to the image appearing on paper, and it is not an easy task for the causal theorist of representation to come up with criteria for which of the relevant causal factors is represented (pictured) by the image.
6 A critic might argue that acquaintance isn't necessary to explain the phenomenon. Why not say only that the distraction caused the pain to stop for a while. But think also about the fact that our sense experience is enormously complex and we notice at most a fraction of all of that wondrous detail.
7 Just as science fiction often trades on the possibility of vivid hallucination, so also it often trades on the intelligibility of memory "implants" that mislead one about one's real past—think about the plot of *Blade Runner* and its sequel.
8 "Doxastic" is just a technical way of talking about what pertains to belief.
9 So if I say of a shirt that I know is white that it appears red (perhaps because there is red light shining on the shirt), I might be construed as saying that it looks the way a white shirt looks under "normal" conditions. That "normal conditions" qualification isn't easy to define clearly.
10 Just as almost everyone knows what searing pain is even if it is impossible to define. (The exception might be those with a rare disorder that prevents them from ever feeling pain—a real and potentially deadly disorder.)
11 To say that we all know what kind of experience it is is not to say that we always know when we are having an experience of that kind. See Chisholm (1942).
12 Although he sent mixed messages. In what some take to be a catastrophic mistake he seemed to suggest that if there were an evil demon bent on deception, that being could cause us to believe falsely even simple arithmetic truths. But once that concession is made, once one rejects as a candidate for secure foundations, even beliefs about our own thoughts, it is unclear what would be left upon which to build. The interpretation of Descartes is, however, complicated. See Cunning (2010) for one of the best discussions of Descartes's project.
13 Here I'm contrasting intentional states with sensations. But as we will see below a great many philosophers would argue that sensations are themselves intentional states representing the existence and character of physical objects.

14 See Bergmann (1967) for the development of an intricate theory of mind that incorporates at least some elements of both Brentano's and Meinong's views about intentional mental states.
15 A classic challenge to this view is Putnam (1981). Externalist's who are tempted to rely on something like the way a photograph represents to understand how thought represents try hard to reduce representation to something that at least involves a causal process.
16 In *some* sense. This is tricky. I do think that one can believe that a figure is a square without believing anything about the interior angles of the figure. But if one is capable of forming a thought about interior angles, one can, in principle, discover the relevant connection between being a square and having interior angles that are 90 degrees, and one can do so without leaving the realm of thought.
17 He changed his mind (2004).
18 This is the view famously defended by Russell (1905).
19 We'll return to this idea in Chapter 8. For a detailed defense of this kind of view, see Fumerton (1985). Historically, this might be a way of making sense of Kant's distinction between things in themselves, and things as they appear. Ramsey (1929) had a sophisticated view of how to "translate" things that we can't observe into things that we can observe. But he didn't seem to have in mind the distinction between objective reality and appearance.
20 So examples of "kinds" are water, gold, atom, mind. I think that all of this talk of kinds of things can be translated into talk about properties, but in the literature many think that there is an important distinction between "natural" kinds and artificial kinds. Natural kinds (so the argument goes) figure into lawful explanations—they involve nature's cuts at the "joints."
21 So I know that this claim is controversial. Some argue that these artists *chose* not to represent objects "realistically." But given that there are *no* successful attempts at capturing perspective I find this claim suspect.
22 So I am discussing the example as though we are concerned with the color of physical objects. It is easier to talk that way. I'm really more interested in the different visual experiences produced by the paint chips.
23 A disjunction is a complex statement formed out of two or more statements by joining them with "or."
24 See Armstrong (1983) for a penetrating criticism of the regularity theory of causation and law.
25 With all of these examples, it is by no means easy to capture a clear distinction about which philosophers can then take positions. Technical terms are often introduced by philosophers to explain their views, but, as we shall see, one shouldn't presuppose that the terminology has a clear sense. I'm not sure, for example, precisely how to understand the debate between ideal and non-ideal theorists. The latter seem to stress the importance of taking the world as it is (and as it has been shaped) and emphasizing steps we might take to make it better or more just. Their opponent is sometimes conceived by them as more concerned with what an ideal world might look like, taking people and circumstances not as they are, but as they might be.
26 It is by no means easy to flesh out this notion of standard conditions. It is tempting to think that it has something to do with (statistically) normal conditions, but that's not quite right. It's dark almost half the time and white snow doesn't look white (in one sense of looks white) when there is no or little light).
27 Sellars (1956) thought this would be a terrible mistake. J. J. C. Smart thought the same thing (1959).

28 Some philosophers think that there are two sorts of beliefs—beliefs *de re* and beliefs de dicto. That view is far more controversial than the view that there is a distinction in how we *describe* beliefs.
29 I'll discuss this in more detail in Chapter 6.
30 We talked about the disjunctivist approach to the distinction between veridical and non-veridical sense experience. The classic empiricist thinks that there is a mental state common to both the veridical and the non-veridical case, and it is the qualitative sameness of this common denominator that can make it impossible to distinguish the "good" case from the "bad" case.
31 Not quite true. A clock can be broken in such a way that it doesn't correspond to the actual time, but also in such a way that it *always* misses the actual time.
32 One would probably need to add a great many more details before one decides whether in such a situation one still knows. What the right thing to say might also depend on metaepistemological theories that we will be discussing later in the book.
33 As did Melville in *Moby Dick*.
34 All of this is much more complicated. What I said presupposes that the relevant terms have the same meaning as they recur in a sentence. And that's not always true. When John Wayne says "Not all men are men" he wasn't contracting himself. The second use of "men" carries with it all sorts of value-related meaning.
35 This attempt to define analytic truth relies on an understanding of meaning and synonymy. Quine (1951) famously argued that we have no unproblematic understanding of meaning and, for that reason, have no unproblematic understanding of analytic truth.
36 I'll talk later about "internal" relations. A relation R between X and Y is internal when the very natures of X and Y guarantee that the relation obtains. Being darker than is a plausible example of an internal relation that obtains between being red and being pink. Being partially constituted by is an example of an internal relation that obtains between being a square and being a quadrilateral. And entailment is best thought of as an internal relation holding between the primary bearers of truth value.

Part II

Illustrating the View—Mapping Clear Borders

Chapter 4

Philosophy of Language

I have argued that philosophy proper includes phenomenology, philosophical analysis from a first-person perspective, and the discovery of synthetic necessary truths knowable a priori (knowable by thinking about the content of thought and *relations* between those contents). When I briefly discussed meaning, I talked about semantic rules that one follows when using words. I also suggested that following a semantic rule for the use of a term should be identified with dispositions to regard that term as the correct way to describe hypothetical situations. Only after settling controversies about various analyses can one rationally address the question of what else might be included within the purview of philosophy.

There are presuppositions of my approach to understanding meaning that are decidedly controversial. I've characterized the meaning of a person's language in terms of that person's linguistic dispositions. Although it is a matter of some philosophical controversy, A's having a disposition to do X in circumstances C seems to have something to do with the truth of the subjunctive conditional, if A *were* in C then it *would* do X.[1] So for example, the solubility of sugar seems to have something to do with the fact that sugar would dissolve under "normal" conditions in a liquid solution. But dispositions have grounds. The ground of a disposition is some feature of the thing that has the disposition, a feature that would lawfully explain the relevant behavior when it occurs.[2] To use the same example, the disposition of sugar to dissolve has something to do with the chemical constitution of sugar. There is some feature of the sugar that causally explains the fact that the sugar dissolves. As I characterized speaker's meaning, the dispositions that constitute the meaning of that person's words have grounds in the person who has such dispositions.

4.1 Externalism about Meaning

Hilarly Putnam (1975) colorfully defends the view that "meaning ain't in the head." The *traditional* view about meaning makes the meaning of language parasitic about upon thought. Language represents the world as being a certain way only because *by convention* sounds and marks go proxy for thoughts that represent the world as being a certain way. Sophisticated versions of the traditional view will allow, of course, that the conventions in question will have causal explanations. Onomatopoeia (the use of a word that sounds a bit like what it describes, e.g. "sizzle" and "cough") is a phenomenon that may well sometimes be explained by the fact that people might have originally tried to signify something by making a sound that reminds one of that kind of thing. Hieroglyphics, as we know, was an early language that, at least in part, used pictures to represent things (or parts of things), pictures that remind us of the things represented. But many words (marks and sounds) mean what they do only because people arbitrarily selected them to represent the world as being a certain way. We are, as Humpty suggested, masters of our words—we *make* the words mean what we *want* them to mean.

Hilary Putnam and another very influential philosopher, Saul Kripke, aren't having anything of Humpty's picture and they offer us a quite different account of meaning. On their view, what words mean is not determined by what goes on inside the minds/brains[3] of the speaker. Rather, at least in a host of cases, the meaning of a term is what the term refers to in the world, and that is often just a function of the causal history of one's use of the term. The theory is sometimes called a direct reference theory. John Stuart Mill is sometimes alleged to have endorsed such a view of ordinary proper names (though I don't think such views are consistent with what Mill actually said).[4] But the label "direct" reference theory is misleading for reasons discussed below.

As I indicated, Kripke and Putnam are the two most influential figures in the development of externalist theories about the meanings of names and expressions that refer to *kinds* of things. Both theorists allow that we can "inherit" the meanings of words as used by other people when we are caused (in the right way) to use the same words that they used. Putnam called this a division of linguistic labor. I succeed in talking about quarks when I use the expression "quark." But I haven't got much of an idea of what a quark is. I think of quarks as *really* small, and I think of them as discovered in the twentieth century, but I wouldn't even bet my life on the latter claim (unless I looked it up on *Wikipedia* and, even then, I wouldn't bet my life on what I read being true). But the experts who theorize about such matters have a much better idea than I do of what quarks are, and I can "piggyback" on their expertise by "borrowing" the term they use *with the understanding that* I'll be talking about whatever it is that they are talking about.[5]

The thought that we can end up successfully using language by inheriting the language from others who successfully use that language raises the specter of problematic regress. It can't be the case that *everyone* uses language meaningfully only because they are caused to use that language by others who successfully use the terms. We need an account of how language gets off the ground. I'll talk more about Kripke here without worrying what fine differences there might be between Putnam and Kripke.

The idea of a division of linguistic labor falls out of Putnam and Kripke's account of meaning and reference. One could write an entire book on externalist theories of meaning and reference. The following is painting with a *very* broad stroke. Kripke himself always admitted that he doesn't have a *complete* theory of meaning. And that's because he often appeals to the idea of an unanalyzed "baptismal" ceremony during which a term is affixed to an individual or kind of thing. But with that notion in hand, he suggests what is sometimes called a *causal* theory of reference. My use of the term "X" refers to something Y just insofar as my use of the term is the end product of a long causal chain that *begins* with someone's use of the term X (or some variation of X) referring to Y, and *ends* with *my* use of the term in some utterance. Causal theories of anything always face the problem of so-called deviant causal chains. To save the theory its proponent almost always starts talking about the fact that the causal chain needs to be the right *sort* of causal chain. But set that issue aside for the moment. As I indicated earlier, the basic idea behind the view is that we should understand representation rather like the way in which a photograph represents. I might be a very bad photographer. I might have moved the camera as I tried to take a picture of you, and the light might have had a distorting effect, but the resulting photograph is a photograph of *you* because *you* played the right sort of causal role in producing the image on the film. The externalist argues that language and thought represent in the same way that photographs represent. To find out what my use of a term represents or to find out what something going on in my mind represents, look to the causal history of the use of that term or the occurrence of that mental state.

The claim that the causal history of language use and thought can determine what language and thought represent is only one part of Kripke's picture of how language and mental states can come to represent objects and properties in the world. The other part invokes the technical notion of *referencing-fixing* definite descriptions. The theory is complicated and a full evaluation of it would take us far afield. But the basic idea is that one can introduce a name for a thing or person, or a name for a *kind* of thing by using a definite description. As we talked about earlier in distinguishing direct and indirect thought, a definite description is just a description that employs the definite article "the." The description attempts to pick something out as the *one* thing that has such and such a property. The following are all defined descriptions that can be used in making assertions:

1 The tallest person alive today.
2 The person who just finished typing this sentence.
3 The bird responsible for the sound I just heard.

4 The first president of the United States.
5 The capital of Wyoming.
6 The person who was named "Arthur" and who lived in Camelot.
7 The conscious being who created matter and energy.
8 The cause of high blood pressure.
9 The properties of physical objects that cause them to reflect or absorb light waves of various wavelengths.
10 The common link in the causal chain that results in both this kind of visual experience and that kind of tactile experience.
11 The genetic cause of Alzheimer's disease.
12 The neural correlate of pain.
13 The microstructure of metal.
14 The condition that must be added to true belief in order to get knowledge.
15 The difference between lawful regularities and regularities that are not lawful.
16 The property that makes something intrinsically good.
17 The feature of an action that makes it the right action to take.

Some of these definite descriptions pick out people, places, properties, relations, or states of the world. Some of the descriptions *fail* to pick anything out because nothing satisfies the description, or there isn't just *one* thing that satisfies the description. "The Canadian who is my sister" doesn't pick anyone out, because there isn't just one Canadian who is my sister. Some definite descriptions are arguably too vague to do the job of singling something out. Or perhaps their use requires additional presuppositions to get the job done. So whenever we talk about *the* cause of some state of the world, it is hard to see how we will secure reference. Most effects result from very complex chains of causes and effects, no one link of which can be said to be the *sole* cause of the relevant effect.[6] What was *the* cause of the French Revolution? There doesn't seem to be just one. There were a plethora of things going badly in Paris, each one of which contributed to pushing the French citizens toward revolution.

The idea that we can assign a word the *meaning* of a definite description itself seems relatively unproblematic. Why can't I introduce the locution "Jack the Ripper" announcing that I will be using it as shorthand for "the person who brutally killed four prostitutes in London at the turn of the century?" The reference-fixers' revolutionary idea, however, is that one can use a definite description to single out some person, thing, kind of thing, property (just about anything) and introduce a word using that definite description *without* regarding the word as being *synonymous* with the expression whose reference is "fixed" with the definite description.

Descriptivists (as they are sometimes called) reject the idea that one can identify the meaning of an expression with its reference or extension (think of the extension as the *class* of things the expression picks out).[7] Why should one think that one *can* use a definite description as a kind of magical wand that one waves over a sound or shape to turn that sound or shape into a word with meaning—a meaning *divorced* from the meaning of the definite description?

The revolt against descriptivism has at least two sources. One is the relatively straightforward claim that we often successfully use names (like "Aristotle," "Constantinople," "Djedefre") and common nouns (like "water," "gold," "quark," "electromagnetic field") without having *in mind* some definite description associated with the name. And at least sometimes (the claim is made), even with effort, we can't find a definite description that would do the relevant descriptivist work. Just as we often use proper names to succeed in referring despite not having available a definite description, so also we can use common nouns to pick out kinds of things without having a definite description (or for that matter much of *any* sort of description) that we associate with the noun. Above, I gave the example of my use of the expression "quark." As I said, I'm pretty sure that quarks are really small and have been discovered within the last one hundred years, but there are lots of really small things that have only recently been discovered. Am I able to find a *definite* description that picks out all and only the kind of things called "quarks?"

The other argument is much harder to summarize. It involves what philosophers call *modal* claims. A modal claim is a claim about what is possible or what is necessary. So to use an example from Kripke, we might be relatively confident that Benjamin Franklin was the inventor of bifocals, but we wouldn't claim that is *necessarily* the case that Franklin was the inventor of bifocals.[8] We don't think it is part of the meaning of "Franklin" that he invented bifocals, as we can acknowledge without inconsistency that it *might* be the case that he didn't. Perhaps it is folklore or a false claim put out by Franklin himself to enhance his reputation. We illustrated the point with a particular definite description, but the idea is supposed to be that we would have the same sort of problem with any other candidate for a definite description that is supposed to capture the meaning of "Benjamin Franklin."[9]

4.2 The Significance of the Content Internalism/ Externalism Controversy for Understanding Philosophy

The above debate about meaning has enormous implications for a conception of philosophy that emphasizes the importance of philosophical analysis as involving some kind of meaning analysis. If the meaning of an expression has something to do with contingent facts about the causal origin of that use of the expression, or contingent facts about what is denoted by a definite description, then meanings might seem to be outside of the purview of philosophy.

Consider the following example often used by externalists to illustrate their view. Water is H_2O. According to the externalists, the meaning of "water" is the stuff with that molecular content. That is either because we fixed the reference (extension) of water using a definite description like "the stuff with the microstructure causally responsible for that familiar look/feel/taste," or because someone else used such a definite description to fix the reference of "water" and we "inherited" our use of the expression from that person. As I indicated above, it is an empirical question appropriately left to science to figure out what kind of stuff is picked out by that definite description. The relevant sciences assure us that the microstructure picked out is, in fact, that combination of hydrogen and oxygen molecules. Most of us know that truth about the molecular structure of water, but, of course, the term "water" (or some term synonymous with "water") has been used for many thousands of years before anyone had any idea about molecular theory. And many today still use the expression "water" without knowing anything about molecular theory. Still, the externalist assures us, "water" and its synonyms have *always* meant that stuff with molecular structure H_2Os. It's just that all sorts of people didn't know that that's what "water" meant. If one can model the meaning of "knowledge," "value," "self," "survival," "causation," "mind," "perception," "space," "time," and other topics of philosophical interest on the meaning of "water" (as understood by the externalist), then the armchair philosopher might seem to be out of business.[10] Just as one can't discover the molecular structure of water through thought experiments, so also, one shouldn't assume that one can discover the meaning of any of these other terms employing thought experiments.

What *would* be left for philosophers? Arguably, philosophical debates about analysis would begin and *end* with debates about the meaning of "meaning." Both internalists and externalists about meaning *do* seem to employ traditional methods of philosophy in arguing about the meaning of "meaning." The causal theorist comes up with a causal theory of meaning and critics try to imagine situations in which there is the relevant causal history but we wouldn't describe the causal origin of the expression as determining the meaning of the expression. Perhaps the philosopher arguing for externalism *shouldn't* play by the rules of this game, but they *do*. And they do, because there wouldn't be any dialectical alternative. The critic obviously won't agree to search for the meaning of "meaning" by looking at the causal history of our use of the word "meaning." Nor will the critic agree that we "fix the reference" of the expression by using a definite description.

Fortunately, we don't need to worry about the prospects of philosophical analysis beginning and ending with a debate about the meaning of "meaning." We do need to have the debate. But the externalist will lose the argument.

4.3 Rejecting Externalism

There is an enormous literature on the internalism/externalism debates about meaning. I've argued against both the causal theory of reference and the idea of reference fixing elsewhere (1989), and I won't repeat in detail all of those arguments here. Critics of the causal theory of reference often rely on counterexamples—thought experiments of the sort we have discussed earlier. As we noted, causal theories of just about anything face the problem of "deviant" causal chains.

Even our crude example of what makes a photograph a photograph of X rather than Y isn't straightforward. Suppose, for example, I point the camera at you, a powerful being intervenes in the usual causal process and causes the image to appear on the film. That being, however, uses you as a model relying on memory to "copy" your features onto the film. Is it still a photograph of you? You *are* part of the cause of why the photograph looks the way it does, but the causal chain isn't the usual sort of causal chain that results in a photograph. In the same way, the causal theorist will face problems with complicated and unusual causal chains that result in the use of a word. You probably know that the question of whether the legendary Arthur was a real person has received quite a bit of discussion. There are a number of candidates for historical figures that might have figured in one way or another in the causal explanation of stories about Arthur. But it isn't clear if the causal connection is of the right sort to secure a reference for "Arthur." And similar questions arise concerning the reference of nouns purporting to refer to kinds.

Fortunately for the descriptivist, there is a recipe for "stealing" whatever is plausible in the causal theory of reference. It is also a recipe for "finding" a definite description that can be viewed as synonymous with ordinary names, nouns, and adjectives that might *initially* seem to resist the descriptivist's approach. Furthermore, the "theft" will give the descriptivist immunity from whatever force the modal arguments might initially seem to have.

The recipe is just this. Ask the causal theorists for their theory. In stating their theory they will need to give you a definite description that picks out what they take to be the critical link in the causal chain leading to your use of an expression, a link that is supposed to determine the referent of your use of that expression. So, for example, the causal theorist might argue that your use of the expression "Aristotle" picks out that guy who was named X (probably "Aristoteles") and whose being named X is the first link in a causal chain that results in your use of "Aristotle." The theory is either a good theory or a bad theory. (In all likelihood it is an incomplete theory that needs to be fleshed out.[11] The theory either survives counterexamples (can deal with thought experiments) or it can't. If it seems to the descriptivist a plausible theory, then the descriptivists can just take the definite description generously provided by the causal theorist and triumphantly proclaim that they have found the definite description that is equivalent in meaning to "Aristotle."

The causal theorists might object to the descriptivist's "theft" of a theory that is supposed to be an alternative to descriptivism. They might object, for example, to the idea that ordinary people have *in mind* anything as complicated as the causal theorist's definite description when they use ordinary expressions. But we have already anticipated this sort of objection. The semantic rules we follow when using an expression might be decidedly complex. It might be very difficult for us to *discover* what rules we follow when using words. At least sometimes, perhaps we do use a name like "Aristotle" or a common noun like "quark" meaning only to pick out the thing or kind of thing that someone else successfully singled out and that resulted in our use of the words. If the causal theorist is convincing enough, we might conclude that the theory has stumbled upon the semantic rule we actually follow (even if we never *realized* it until we heard about the causal theory of reference).

There is also a technical problem that a descriptivist counterpart to a causal theory faces. I'm thinking about the referent of my use of "Aristotle" in a sentence as whoever the guy is that plays the right sort of causal role in my use of "Aristotle" in the sentence. But notice that I couldn't replace "Aristotle" in "Aristotle was a Greek" with "The guy responsible for my use of 'Aristotle' in this sentence was a Greek. Doing so would eliminate my *use* of "Aristotle." To be sure I am *mentioning* the word "Aristotle" with the word "'Aristotle,'" but mentioning a word isn't the same thing as using it.[12] I'm not sure that this constitutes a formidable objection, however, to the view. Rather, it just seems a counterexample to the claim that if an expression "X" means the same as an expression "Y" then it is always possible to replace "X" with "Y" without changing the meaning of the sentence. There are other potential counterexamples to the principle as well. When I say that the concert is happening now, it is at least initially plausible to claim that by "now" I mean the time cotemporaneous with my use of "now." But again, I couldn't replace "now" with the description "the time cotemporaneous with my use of 'now'" because doing so would lose my *use* of "now." Still, the *thought* expressed by "now" could be a thought that is about my use of "now."

In stealing any potential insights from a causal theory of reference, we are also positioned to respond to the modal issues discussed above. It does seem implausible to view names for things or kinds of things as equivalent in meaning to the most obvious definite descriptions we might associate with those terms. Just by reflecting on the meaning of "Benjamin

Franklin" I wouldn't be able to conclude that he was the inventor of bifocals. And if I discovered that bifocals weren't invented until the twentieth century, I wouldn't conclude that Benjamin Franklin didn't exist. I believe that Aristotle was the philosophy teacher of Alexander the Great, but again I couldn't reach that conclusion just by reflecting on what I *mean* by "Aristotle." And if I concluded that Alexander never actually had a philosophy teacher, I wouldn't conclude that it is not the case that Aristotle existed. I can't discover that water is H_2O just by reflecting on the meaning of "water." And if I discovered that molecular theory was all some bizarre elaborate hoax, I wouldn't conclude that water doesn't exist. All of this seems right. But, again, the causal theorist has a theory that needs to be compatible with thought experiments. And if the theory is correct then it *is* a necessary truth (knowable just by reflection on meaning) that if there was an Aristotle, then he was the person named in such a way that causally explains my use of "Aristotle."

The causal theory, I conclude, doesn't pose much of a threat to descriptivism. But what about that other idea, the idea that one can use a definite description to fix the reference of an expression, and then treat the meaning of the expression (if it has one) as whatever is denoted by the definite description? There is a sense in which I don't have much of an argument against the intelligibility of reference-fixing. The view strikes me as utterly mysterious—a truly "magical" theory. Let's consider an example. You and I are wondering what the world would be like when the first U.S. woman president is elected to office. As we mull over various possibilities, we get tired of using the expression "the first U.S. president who is a woman." Remembering our Putnam and Kripke, we agree to fix the reference of the name "Alice" with the definite description. We then start speculating about whether Alice will be a Democrat or a Republican. But if you interject: "Let's not get ahead of ourselves. Maybe Alice won't go into politics and run for office," I will be utterly confused. Given the way in which we introduced "Alice" into our language, it is simply true by definition that Alice (if she exists at all) runs for political office.

To be sure, we still have our *de re/de dicto* distinctions. We might agree that Alice (whoever she is) probably didn't have to run for office. Alice could have existed and made different life decisions. That's the *de re* reading of the modal claim (the claim about possibility). In this sense, the inventor or bifocals could have existed without having invented bifocals. But what is at issue is the *de dicto* reading of the claims about possibility. Again, I simply wouldn't understand you if you start wondering whether it might be the case that Alice isn't a future president. In the end, neither the causal theory nor the idea of reference-fixing poses a significant threat from the "direct" theories of reference.

Philosophy "from the armchair" survives the potential threat posed by an externalist account of meaning. Just as thought experiments play a critical role in evaluating views about the meaning of "meaning," so also thought experiments play a critical role in evaluating views about the meaning of other terms of philosophical interest. To illustrate further the conception of analysis I defend and how analysis informs what else falls under the purview of philosophy, I'll illustrate my view of metaphilosophy by looking at more specific meta-questions, beginning with the field of metaepistemology.

Notes

1 Subjunctive conditional, because the verbs in the "if … then …" statement take the subjunctive mood.
2 See Addis (2008) for an explanation and further defense of this idea.
3 As we shall see in Chapter 7, there is a fundamental controversy among philosophers over whether the mind is identical with the brain—whether mental states are just brain states.
4 See Fumerton and Donner (2009).
5 As we shall see, the proponent of this view should be wary of agreeing to this last way of putting their claim. It is a bit of a set up.
6 I'll talk more about this in Chapter 8.
7 Or at least they reject that idea for the vast majority of "ordinary" names for individuals and kinds of things. Some will follow Russell and allow that one might be able to use "logically proper" names to refer directly to that with which we are directly acquainted. This distinction at the level of language closely parallels the distinction we drew earlier between direct and indirect thought. On this sort of view one can refer directly only to that of which one can *think* directly.

There are a confusing set of terms philosophers use when talking about meaning and reference. Some, like Russell, will restrict the notion of reference to a term whose meaning just is the thing to which you refer. But Russell didn't think many terms do refer in this sense. As we noted he also talks about definite descriptions that have meaning. But one can also talk about the referent/*the thing denoted* by a definite description. The referent or denotation of "the world's tallest man" is that person who is taller than all other people. Predicate expressions (adjectives, or adjectives following the copula verbs) might also be thought of as having a referent—a property. But if the predicate expression itself contains a definite description the property picked out might also be thought of as denoted by the definite description. So I might describe a shirt as having my aunt's favorite color. "Having my aunt's favorite color" means having the color that my aunt likes more than any other color." That expression doesn't *mean* "red" even if red is the color that my aunt likes more than any other color. But red is denoted by the definite description embedded in "having my aunt's favorite color." Philosophers also talk about the *extension* of predicate expressions like "red." Again, the extension is just the set of all of the things that have the property of being red. Some of the debates we are discussing here are debates about whether a term can be thought of us having a referent that is distinct from its meaning. Definite descriptions seem to be like that. I can *understand* "the world's tallest person" without knowing who that person is (without knowing the denotation of the expression).

8 Kripke (1982) himself wouldn't like my characterization of the modal argument. Nevertheless, *this* is what *I* take the most plausible version of the modal argument to be. For those with a background on these issues, modal claims are potentially ambiguous between *de dicto* readings (a claim about the modal status of a proposition) and *de re* readings (a claim about whether or not some entity has a property *essentially*. So it doesn't sound that odd to say that the bachelor who lives next door could have been married (if he had been nicer to his girlfriend, for example). It sounds downright weird to suggest it might be the case that the bachelor who lives next door isn't unmarried. While there is a distinction between de dicto and *de re* reports of necessity and possibility, it is not clear at all that there are two different sorts of necessity. There are ways of trying to "translate" the *de re* readings into more complicated readings. See Fumerton (1986).

9 There is other technical terminology that enters the debate. But which I am avoiding here. The terms whose reference has been fixed by a definite description are also said to be rigid designators. In the almost poetic language of modal logicians, this means that the term (the name for an individual, property, or kind) has the same reference in all possible worlds. Names in this sense are contrasted with ordinary definite descriptions whose denotation "floats" from individual or kind across possible worlds. I think that this can all be captured with de re/de dicto distinctions; direct reference theorists like Kripke disagree. Some philosophers (Donnellan 1977) accept the rigid/non-rigid distinction but think that ordinary definite descriptions can be used in both ways.

10 See (Kornblith 2002) for an attempt to understand "knowledge" that way, and see the so-called Cornell realists (Boyd 1983; Sturgeon 1988; Brink 1989) for attempts to take a similar approach to understanding talk of value.

11 We need, for example, more information about what makes a given link in the causal chain the referent of the expression.

12 One of the funniest illustrations of the need to distinguish the use of an expression from the mentioning of an expression occurs in the movie *The Life of Brian*. Some poor guy is sentenced death to by stoning for using the name "Jehovah." The person reading the sentence tries to say just that, but the crowd eventually stones *him* to death for also using the word "Jehovah." He was right in insisting that he only mentioned the word—he didn't use it. The distinction, however, was lost on the crowd.

Chapter 5
Epistemology and Metaepistemology

We have discussed in Part I the distinction between first-level questions and meta-questions. That distinction should be made in *every* area of philosophy. Epistemological questions are those that involve the concepts of knowledge, justified belief, and other concepts defined in terms of these. When we ask whether we know or are justified in believing some *specific* proposition or some *kind* of proposition we are asking a first-level question in epistemology. When we ask what knowledge *is*, or what it *is* to have a justified belief, we are asking a meta-question. The meta-questions are certainly within the purview of philosophy. As we shall see, whether or not first-level questions should be regarded as philosophical *depends* on what the answers are to the meta-questions. Understanding how meta-positions dictate the limits of philosophy proper is the primary purpose of this and subsequent chapters.

Philosophers make distinctions, and before trying to understand what knowledge or justified belief is, we need to acknowledge that we use "know" and its cognates in different ways. We also need to recognize different senses in which a belief might be justified or supported by reasons.

5.1 Knowledge

We talk about knowing people and places, knowing how to do certain things, knowing why certain things happen, knowing when certain things happen, and knowing where certain things happen. Philosophers have traditionally been more concerned with understanding what is involved in someone's knowing *that* such and such is the case (where what is known is the kind of thing that can be true or false). This kind of knowledge is sometimes called *propositional* knowledge.

Why might one think that propositional knowledge is more important than the other sorts of knowledge? One answer is just that *qua philosophers* we are primarily curious about how the world is. We are primarily curious about *truth*. A more controversial answer is that one might be able to "translate" the statements describing other sorts of knowledge into statements describing propositional knowledge. So, for example, to know why X happened is, arguably, just to know *that* such and such is the correct explanation for X. To know when X happened is just to know that X happened at such and such a time. To know where X happened is just to know that X happened at such and such a place. To know Fred or to know Paris might involve knowing truths about Fred or knowing truths about Paris (though it might also imply something like "first-hand" knowledge of such truths). Even more controversially, one might initially suppose that knowing how to do something X involves knowing truths about what is involved in doing X.[1]

The question of how to understand propositional knowledge (knowledge *that*) was asked by Plato in the *Theaetetus*? Plato asked, "What must be added to true belief in order to get knowledge?" The question presupposes that believing what is true is at least *part* of what is involved in knowing that something is the case. It also presupposes that there is *more* to knowledge than true belief. Lucky guesses, irrational beliefs that through sheer luck turn out to be true—these are examples of true beliefs that are not knowledge.

Plato's own answer to his question is a bit vague. He seemed to suggest that in addition to a true belief, one with knowledge has an "account" of why the belief is true. Many twentieth-century philosophers articulated the "third" condition for knowledge as justification. A true belief constitutes knowledge when the belief is true and one has good reasons or justification for believing what one does. But just as there are different types of knowledge, so also, there are different kinds of reasons or justification for belief.

At least many philosophers would allow that one might have *pragmatic* reasons for believing something to be true. Consider just one example. It seems to be true sometimes that even if one suffers from an illness that is almost always fatal, one might improve slightly one's chances of surviving if one somehow gets oneself to believe that one will get better. That seems to give one a reason (in one sense of "reason") to do what one can to get oneself to be appropriately optimistic. Of course, the reason one has to believe that one will recover is compatible with the belief's being epistemically *unjustified*. Epistemic reasons or justification are supposed to make *likely* the truth of what one believes (and not by *causing* changes in the world that will make true what one believes).

In Chapter 3, I argued that philosophical analysis is fundamentally egocentric. Each of us is trying to figure out what we individually mean when we talk about knowing. And in testing a proposal we (individually) see if we can think of situations in which we could have a justified true belief without knowing, or situations in which we might describe someone as knowing even though they didn't have a justified true belief.

As I stressed earlier, in testing ideas we have about our use of "know" we consider not only our own thought experiments, but thought experiments that have been proposed by others. Or at least we consider thought experiments that we *believe* were proposed by others. But even if we misremembered a thought experiment we thought that we read, or, unbeknownst us, we dreamt having read the thought experiment, it wouldn't make the slightest bit of difference to the philosophical *relevance* of the thought experiment. Gettier convinced most epistemologists that there are justified true beliefs that wouldn't count as knowledge—at least if justification is understood in such a way that justification makes merely likely, or highly likely, the truth of what we believe. Before Gettier, Russell gave the example of a person who looks at a broken clock that just happens to indicate the correct time. Based on the appearance of the clock, the person forms a justified true belief about the time. But most would agree that the person doesn't know the time. The truth of the belief involved a kind of luck that is incompatible with knowing.[2] Or think about what would be rational to believe about a lotto ticket one buys. Rational people recognize that it is extremely likely that the ticket is a loser. It is more likely that I will die within the next 24 hours than that I will win lotto. But again, almost no one thinks that one can *know* that the ticket is a loser. Why would one buy a ticket that one *knows* is worthless?

I gave one example of a Gettier situation and talked about the lottery puzzle. There are indefinitely many Gettier counterexamples, and indefinitely many puzzles like the lottery. There are all sorts of responses to such counterexamples and puzzles. Many trees lost their lives providing paper for countless attempts to fix or, in some cases, provide radical alternatives to, the traditional account of knowledge.

One response, considered by many extreme, is to return to what is sometimes called a *Cartesian* conception of knowledge (after Descartes). In his search for secure foundations on which to build knowledge, Descartes is often interpreted as rejecting as genuine knowledge any belief whose justification doesn't preclude the possibility of error. If you can *conceive* of being wrong about something P despite having the justification or evidence you have, then you don't know that P. With this criterion in hand, Descartes quickly rejected as candidates for knowledge much of what we pre-philosophically believe. The intelligibility of dreams and evil demons bent on deceiving you should convince you that you don't know anything about the past, the future, the physical world, and other minds.[3]

The Cartesian conception of knowledge easily explains why we don't feel comfortable claiming to know the outcome of a fair lottery. We also no longer need to worry about Gettier counterexamples. The counterexamples all seem to presuppose that the justified belief in question is fallible (we can make sense of the belief's being false despite the fact that it is justified). This very strong conception of knowledge also explains another datum often pondered by philosophers. The following statement seems deeply problematic: I *know* that P but it *might* be false. Think, for example, about how strange it would be for the eyewitness on the stand to claim: I know that I saw Smith, but it might have been someone else.

However nicely the strong conception of knowledge might deal with the data I just described, it still faces the obvious concern that it would render most ordinary knowledge claims false. When you ask me if I know where my older sister was born, I wouldn't hesitate to say "Yes." And I would claim to have such knowledge despite the fact that my evidence for this belief obviously doesn't guarantee the truth of what I believe.[4] When I push myself, however, I'm not sure that I won't qualify my ordinary knowledge claims. If you ask me if I know where I'll be spending Thanksgiving, I'll probably say "Yes." When you remind me (somewhat darkly) that I might be dead long before Thanksgiving rolls around, I'll probably concede the point, and restate my knowledge claim: I know where I'll be on Thanksgiving *assuming* that I don't die before then, that the world doesn't get hit by an asteroid, that I'm not kidnapped by aliens, and so on, and so on. I might eventually acknowledge that all I *really* know is where I now *expect* to spend the holiday (or where I now *plan* to spend the holiday).

The above is hardly going to convince you to adopt strong Cartesian standards for knowledge. And there are a number of other attempts to accommodate the relevant data that many epistemologists find more plausible.[5] Here, however, I'm mainly interested in illustrating two of the claims I made in Part I. The first is the egocentric nature of philosophical analysis. It seems to me that as I reflect on what knowledge is, I am reflecting on how I would characterize (upon reflection) various hypothetical situations. To be sure, I have read (at least I believe that I have read) Descartes, Russell, Gettier, and a host of objections and responses to views about the nature of knowledge. But it doesn't matter what *caused* me to think of the relevant hypothetical situations. My investigation is guided by thinking about the relevant situations. What caused me to have these thoughts doesn't matter to what justifies me in reaching my philosophical conclusions.

Secondly, I want to illustrate the way in which our philosophical analyses might *determine* what else gets included in philosophy proper. *If* the Cartesian conception of knowledge is correct, then I can decide "from the armchair" what I do and don't know. It is precisely the thought experiments that are the stock and trade of philosophy that would be relevant to first-level questions about knowledge. On the Cartesian view, the philosophical investigation into knowledge doesn't end with our analysis of knowledge—it doesn't end with metaepistemology. Qua philosophers we are also in a position to decide what we know and don't know.

Still, I have conceded that the Cartesian analysis of knowledge is hardly the received view. What is left for epistemology if some other conception of knowledge is correct? Well, in discussing Gettier, we noted that the "traditional" view understood knowledge as justified true belief. And we haven't said anything yet about how to understand justification.

5.2 Epistemic Justification/Rationality

5.2.1 Non-epistemic Reasons to Believe

It's philosophy. So once again, we begin by making distinctions! The *epistemologist's* interest is *epistemic* justification or rationality (I'll use these two terms interchangeably). As we noted above, there are, arguably, different senses in which one might have justification or reason for believing what one does. One might, for example, have *pragmatic* reasons to believe this or that. Very roughly, pragmatic reasons to take some action X have something to do with goals or ends that one might accomplish by doing X. It is far from clear that one can treat believing itself as a kind of *action*, but one can certainly do things that might influence what one believes. Epistemic reasons/justification, by contrast, are supposed to make likely the truth of what one believes (and not by causing what one believes to be true). To the extent that one can control what one believes, it seems that one might have strong pragmatic reasons to believe something that is nevertheless epistemically irrational to believe. In the example noted above, I might discover to my dismay that I have a rare disease that is fatal 98% of the time. My doctor informs me, however, that studies indicate that if I can just get myself to believe that I will recover, my chances improve from 2% to 10%. In one sense, it seems obviously rational for me to do what I can to believe that I will get better. But this belief, while pragmatically rational, is still epistemically irrational. There is no justification I possess that makes likely the truth of what I believe.

In addition to pragmatic reasons to believe what is epistemically irrational, there might also be moral reason to believe what is epistemically irrational. At least some philosophers would argue that even if the evidence indicates that your son is guilty of some crime, you *owe* it to your child to believe in his innocence.[6] One could even imagine a dystopian state in which one has legal obligations to believe this or that (regardless of what epistemic rationality dictates). In such a nightmarish state one could suppose that new technology routinely scans the brains of citizens to monitor what is believed.

5.2.2 Propositional vs Doxastic Justification

Once we decide that the philosopher interested in truth will focus on epistemic justification, there is still one more distinction to draw. Most epistemologists will distinguish there being justification for you to believe some proposition P from your actually having a justified belief that P. The former is sometimes called propositional justification; the latter, doxastic justification. There can be justification for you to believe that P (there can be propositional justification for you to believe that P) even if you don't believe P (when you epistemically should) or when you believe P but not *on the basis* of the justification that there is for you to believe that P. You might have strong epistemic justification to believe that your son is innocent of some crime, for example, but believe in his innocence based on blind faith (rather that the epistemic justification available to you).

On one rather plausible view, your belief that P is doxastically justified when there is propositional justification for you to believe that P, you do believe that P, and you base your belief on that propositional justification. The basing relation is often construed as causal. You base your belief that P on justification J when J causes (in the right way) your belief that P.[7]

I'll address this question again when discussing issues in the philosophy of mind. But, if doxastic justification has something to do with a belief being *caused* in the right sort of way, it is not clear that questions about doxastic justification fall within the purview of philosophy proper. You can't tell through *introspection* what causes you to have the beliefs that you do. The causal explanation of belief is a contingent matter and can be settled only through empirical (presumably psychological) investigation. It is probably not an accident that most foundationalists were taught by foundationalists, most dualists were taught by dualists, most Catholics were raised by Catholics, most Democrats were raised by Democrats, and most Republicans were raised by Republicans. Noticing these facts might well lead one to be particularly careful when assessing the epistemic rationality of one's beliefs, but one obviously can't infer that there isn't *propositional* justification for you to believe that P even if you suspect that your belief isn't causally explained by the fact that you have at your disposal that propositional justification.

If what I said above is plausible, one might conclude that one shouldn't include first-level questions about *doxastic* justification as falling within the domain of philosophy proper. But that still leaves open the possibility that philosophers are competent (qua philosophers) to assess first-level questions about propositional justification.[8] Whether or not they are, I would argue, depends on metaepistemological conclusions about the nature of such justification.

5.2.3 The Internalism/Externalism Controversy in Epistemology

In the last several decades, the most important debate in metaepistemology is the debate between internalists and externalists. This internalism/externalism controversy in epistemology is different from the internalism/externalism controversy about meaning/content that we discussed in the last chapter.[9] Unfortunately, there is no agreed-upon way to define the controversy. On one understanding of the disagreement, internalists think that what one is justified in believing at a given time is entirely a function of one's internal states at that time. Externalists deny this.[10] *Access* internalists claim that the epistemic justification available to one is limited to facts to which one has direct, unproblematic access. The access in question is often understood in terms of *introspective* access.[11] Access externalists deny this claim about access.

The two versions of internalism *might* be related. Many in the history of philosophy thought that one's internal states just are one's mental states, and mental states just are states to which one has, or could have, direct, introspective access. Such a view is by no means uncontroversial. One's experiences, for example, are extraordinarily complex and it is not implausible to suppose that it requires considerable effort and skill to notice all of the details of that complexity.[12]

Why would anyone think that either version of epistemological internalism is correct? The most compelling thought experiment appeals once again to the possibility of vivid hallucination. In Chapter 2, we raised the intelligibility of skeptical scenarios when we talked about arguments for an acquaintance-based foundationalism. The internalist appeals to the same scenarios but to reach an internalist conclusion about the *nature* of epistemic justification. If we can make *sense* of being massively deceived by a powerful being capable of inducing massive, vivid, consistent hallucination, then we can also ask what the victim of such demonic machination would be justified in believing.

Following recent terminological practice (influenced by Williamson), let's call the case of massive hallucination the **bad** case. Let's call veridical perception (experiences that are caused in the way we commonsensically *think* that they are caused) the **good** case. It is enormously plausible to suggest that whatever one is justified in believing in the good case, is precisely what one is justified in believing in the bad case. Generalizing, if two people G and B are *internal* duplicates, then there is no difference in the epistemic status of any of their potential beliefs. Again, internal duplicates not only have the same sensory states, but the same apparent memories, and the same thoughts. *Access* internalists understand two people as being internal duplicates in the relevant sense when each has access to the same sorts of internal states.[13]

Externalists are not without ammunition. If the internalist succeeds in restricting the foundations of justified belief to that which is common to both the good and bad cases, it won't be easy to avoid skeptical conclusions that most philosophers find absurd. Put crudely, if all we have to rely on in reaching conclusions about a mind-independent world are premises describing the world of appearance, it is hard to see how we could ever get assurance that appearance reflects one sort of objective reality over another. In any event, we don't want to insist that epistemically justified beliefs are always true beliefs. Until very recently, almost everyone agreed that one can have a justified but false belief.[14] Still, even if we concede *that*, don't we want it to be necessarily the case that *most* justified beliefs are true beliefs? If that weren't the case, why would we even *care* about whether or not a belief is epistemically justified?[15]

If we want to tie epistemic justification to truth, certain forms of externalism might seem attractive. Consider, for example, *reliabilism*. Reliabilism is one of the most developed and dialectically attractive versions of externalism. The fundamental idea is relatively straightforward. We should understand epistemically justified beliefs in terms of their causal history. More specifically, epistemically justified beliefs are beliefs that are reliably formed. In his seminal paper developing the view, Goldman (1979) went on to make a distinction between belief-independent processes and belief-dependent processes, a distinction that allows us to recognize two ways in which reliability is relevant to epistemic justification. Belief-independent processes are "software" in the brain that take "input" that does not include beliefs; belief-dependent processes, by contrast, act on "input" that includes (perhaps among other factors) beliefs. The output beliefs of belief-independent processes are epistemically justified only if the process in question is unconditionally reliable—the beliefs produced by that way of forming beliefs are usually true. Belief-dependent processes are reliable if they produce mostly true beliefs *when* the input beliefs are also true.[16]

If you think about it, the reliabilism briefly sketched above is a version of foundationalism. It makes the strong view that the *concept* of epistemic justification is parasitic upon the concept of noninferential justification. The view makes a distinction between noninferentially justified beliefs (the beliefs that are produced by an unconditionally reliable, belief-independent process) and other inferentially justified beliefs. A belief is justified if it is noninferentially justified (i.e. it is produced by a belief-independent, unconditionally reliable process), or it can be traced via conditionally reliable belief-dependent processes to beliefs that are noninferentially justified.[17] Note that it is easier for the reliabilist to give an account of doxastic justification that it is to give an account of propositional justification. That's because if reliabilism is true, it is the causal history of the belief that determines whether or not it is justified. To understand propositional justification, the reliabilist presumably needs to talk about the *availability* of a reliable process that would have yielded mostly true beliefs if it had kicked in (whether or not it does). It is not easy to understand what makes a process available to someone if it *didn't* in fact receive the relevant input and churn out the relevant beliefs.[18]

The above is no more than a sketch of one version of externalism. And there are disagreements among reliabilists about how to understand some of the concepts that are critical to the view. The idea of reliability is tricky.

In the crude version of the view sketched above, I suggested implicitly that unconditionally reliable processes are those that produce mostly true beliefs. But a way of forming beliefs might be reliable or unreliable even if it has, in fact, only been used once (or, arguably, even if it has never been used). And we don't want such a process to be either completely reliable or completely unreliable depending on the truth or falsity of the one belief produced by the process. To avoid such a conclusion, it seems to some reliabilists better to use our old friend the subjunctive conditional: A process is unconditionally reliable when it *would* yield mostly true beliefs if it *were* used indefinitely many times. Others think that they can make sense of a process having a *propensity* to produce mostly true beliefs. Each view has its problems: the first view needs to explain what makes the relevant subjunctive true[19]; the other view needs to explain this talk of propensities.

Reliabilists also need to deal with what is sometimes called the generality problem. We can characterize a way of forming beliefs in a number of different ways, and we need a principled answer to the question of which way of forming beliefs is relevant. When I rely on apparent memory, that reliance on memory can be characterized as: (1) a person's relying on what they seem to remember; (2) a person's relying on what they seem to remember when the apparent memory is particularly vivid; (3) an old person struggling recently with unreliable memory relying on what they seem to remember; (4) a person's relying on what they seem to remember about their youth when they have also been told the story of what they did indefinitely many times by other family memories; (5) a person's relying on what they seem to remember on Tuesday, December 4, 2022 at 10 a.m.; (6) a person's relying on what they seem to remember having just awakened from a vivid dream and while not being quite sure whether they are still asleep or awake. Some of these "ways" of forming beliefs might be reliable; some might be unreliable. But we need instructions from the reliabilist on which of these ways of characterizing the belief-producing process we should use in understanding questions about the reliability of the process.[20]

Reliabilism might have the advantage of greatly expanding what is included in the foundations of justified belief. We noted earlier, that traditional foundationalists have been accused of over-intellectualizing what goes in perceptually-formed beliefs about the physical world. The critic argues that we don't normally pay attention to, and form explicit beliefs about, appearance, beliefs that give us premises from which we infer truths about the objects around us. Belief formation all seems more spontaneous than this. And for the reliabilist that would be no obstacle to the resulting beliefs being justified. Perhaps, when it comes to perception, we have evolved in such a way that we take in sensory stimuli (not *beliefs* about such stimuli) and respond in a reliable way with a torrent of beliefs about our physical environment.[21] In fact, there is no *a priori* limit on what might be an unconditionally reliable way of forming beliefs. The world *could* be such that some people are clairvoyant, some people have the capacity to "read" the minds of others, some people react in a reliable way to various stimuli to form beliefs about the existence and character of God, some people have a "Rainman" like ability[22] to look at a huge pile of toothpicks and immediately form an accurate belief about the number of toothpicks in the pile.

5.3 The Implications of the Internalism/Externalism Controversy for What Else Should Be Included in Philosophical Epistemology

So again the point of the above discussion is not to *settle* the controversy between internalists and externalists in epistemology.[23] I have a much more nuanced and extended discussion of the relevant issues elsewhere (1996). The point *here* is to illustrate yet again the way in which one's meta-positions have implications for what other first-level questions are appropriately regarded as falling within the purview of philosophy proper.

The internalist, you will recall, is convinced that what we are justified in believing is solely a function of our internal states. The epistemic justification available to our internal duplicates is precisely what is available to us. And that is true across all *possible* worlds. Put another way, the internalist thinks that we can't even *imagine* a world in which the beliefs of our internal duplicates enjoy a different epistemic status than do ours. This is a subtle point, but if you think about the internalist's position, it implies that if our internal mental states justify us in believing some proposition P, that is a *necessary* feature of those states. It couldn't be otherwise. If the internalist is correct, then epistemic principles that "license" movement from one state or set of beliefs to another set of beliefs are *necessary* truths of the sort we discussed in Part I. They are truths that we can discover just by thinking carefully about the content of those truths. They are truths that fall within the purview of philosophy. If certain versions of internalism are true, then first-level questions about what I am and am not justified in believing *can* be discovered from the armchair.

So much the worse for internalism, some philosophers might object. Why would one need scientific investigation to discover truth if we could find out what we are justified in believing just by thinking carefully in a philosophical way about our internal states and facts about what those states make likely? The answer, of course, is that we want to change our epistemic situation. In most cases we want to improve it. As I type this sentence I have forgotten the capital of Ethiopia. If I am interested in regaining that knowledge, I'll need to improve my epistemic position with respect to this geographical feature of the world. Put simply, the problem we face is that very often we can tell that we don't have any justification that bears on the answer to a given question, and we want to change our situation so that we do have such justification. A five-second google search will put me back in touch with the capital of Ethiopia.

So again, *if* internalism is true, then philosophers *qua* philosophers might be in business trying to answer first-level epistemological questions. It might not be *easy* to answer such questions. That might be in part because one wouldn't have positioned oneself well to discover the answers to first-level questions without having secured correct answers to the metaepistemological questions.

The matter is quite different if externalism is true. To be sure, one *can* know *a priori* the *conditional* reliability of *some* belief-dependent processes. Almost everyone agrees that relations of logical entailment can be known just by thinking about the content of propositions that stand in such relations. And if one's inferences follow deductively valid rules of inference, then one is forming beliefs in a way that is *conditionally* reliable. But the reliabilist, like almost everyone else, acknowledges the slogan: garbage in; garbage out. Conditional reliability gets you closer to the truth only if the input beliefs are themselves justified. The input beliefs might themselves be formed via conditionally reliable belief-forming processes, but the *source* of justification for the reliabilist will be those unconditionally reliable processes that take as their input something other than a belief. Those are the foundationally justified beliefs upon which all other justification needs to be built.

As we noted earlier, there is no limit on ways of forming belief that *might* be unconditionally or conditionally reliable. The access externalist requires no access to the reliability of a way of forming belief for the relevant output beliefs to be justified. It is enough that the belief has the right sort of history. Because access to reliability is not required for justification, one can use a method of forming belief to reach justified conclusions about that method's reliability. If I were interested in certifying the reliability of various ways of forming belief, it *might* not be all that difficult. I can certify the reliability of memory by remembering many occasions on which memory turned out to be accurate. I can certify the general reliability of relying on color appearances to reach conclusions about the color of objects by repeatedly relying on color experience to reach such conclusions, and by remembering all of my successes. At least that is so *if* relying on apparent memory to reach conclusions about the past, *and* relying on color appearance to reach conclusions about color, *and* inferring that past success will continue into the future are all reliable ways of producing true beliefs.[24]

That reliabilism allows "blind" reliability to get one justification is part of what makes the view deeply unsatisfying to those philosophers who search for a kind of epistemic justification that brings with it intellectual assurance—a kind of justification that satisfies philosophical curiosity.

And the same is true for other forms of externalism that seem to divorce justification from assurance. But the point I want to underscore here, is that the range of epistemological questions answerable by philosophy hangs in the balance.

If the *externalist* has the right metaepistemological position, then epistemology proper, the kind of epistemological questions that philosophers *qua philosophers* are competent to answer begins and *ends* with metaepistemology. Psychology, cognitive science, and neurology are the fields that study empirically the intricate workings of the brain as it receives signals and produces belief. They are, no doubt, fascinating. But they are not philosophy.

To emphasize a point made early in this book, there is no reason philosophers can't broaden their interests to study fields other than philosophy. And even if you aren't trained in a field, you can certainly read about what researchers purport to discover in other fields. Of course, you need to take into account a point made in Chapter 1. Philosophy isn't the only field in which one finds vast disagreement. One also finds it in the "softer" sciences, and I certainly include among those softer sciences cognitive science, psychology, and even neurology. These are all sciences in their "infancy."[25]

As I have emphasized before, one can also combine one's philosophical commitment to externalism with assertions of various conditionals that would be necessary truths if externalism is the correct account of justification. One doesn't have to know that a given belief-producing process is unconditionally reliable to know that if reliabilism is true and if a given way of producing beliefs is unconditionally reliable then beliefs formed in that way are noninferentially justified. Still, the conditionals get one justified belief about actual justified beliefs only if one is justified in believing the antecedents of those conditionals.

Internalists are horrified at the idea that one might be able to answer first-level epistemological questions through scientific investigation. The methods of science all *presuppose* that our "commonsense" beliefs about the legitimacy of various ways of forming belief are correct. *Internalists* should be horrified by this philosophical deference to science. But if you are going to be an externalist, be an externalist. The externalists refuse to concede that you can legitimately use a method of reasoning only if you have some independent reason to believe that that method of reasoning is legitimate.

If internalism is the correct metaepistemological position, how will we fare when it comes to satisfying intellectual curiosity? It depends. We already noted that it is an uphill battle to respond to the skeptic's challenge when one's foundations are restricted to what one knows about one's mental life. But as we noted above, at least some internalists believe that the foundations of knowledge include facts about relations of making probable. They think that if E makes probable P it is *necessarily* the case that E makes probable P.²⁶ And they further think that one can know that the relation of making probable holds just by thinking about the contents of E and P. Alternatively, if none of that is true, one might be able to figure out *a priori* that we *lack* justification for many of our "commonsense" beliefs. *Either way*, it is plausible to suppose that the internalist might be able to include in philosophy proper first-level epistemological questions.

Initially, one might suppose that it is wildly implausible to suppose that one can know without empirical evidence that one proposition or set of propositions makes probable another. The fact that litmus paper turns red in a solution might be evidence for, might make probable, that the solution is acidic. But who would think that one could discover such a truth just by thinking carefully about the content of propositions? That one has a higher than average body temperature is evidence that one has an infection. But surely this needs to be *learned*. That the barometer drops suddenly makes it very likely that there will soon be a storm, but one couldn't figure that out just by thinking carefully about barometers and storms. All that seems right, but there is a plausible response that the internalist might give:

1 Litmus paper's turning red in a solution doesn't *by itself* make likely that the solution is acidic;
2 A higher than average temperature doesn't *by itself* make likely that one has an infection;
3 A barometer's dropping suddenly doesn't *by itself* make likely that there will soon be a storm.

These claims might seem initially puzzling. But it is important to keep in mind that much of what we say in describing our reasoning is *enthymematic*. We typically don't bother to describe *all* of the premises upon which we rely in reaching a conclusion. I often use the following example. I come home, find the windows broken, and realize that valuables in my house are missing. I immediately conclude that I have been robbed. And that's precisely the evidence I would give the police in reporting the robbery. But it would only require a bit of reflection to realize that my conclusion about the robbery is reached only by relying on a host of background information. I know that windows don't often break spontaneously, that valuables don't typically disappear as a result of a window's breaking, that in our culture it isn't a perfectly acceptable custom for neighbors to break into a house to borrow valuables that they might find useful. Again, I don't bother to state these background assumptions. They are so commonly accepted that one would be viewed as decidedly pedantic if one started describing such facts as part of one's evidence. But without these background assumptions, one wouldn't be able to reach the relevant conclusion. And something similar is true of the vast majority of beliefs one forms about the world around us. I glance at a familiar face and conclude that it is my friend Lynn. But even if I am not explicitly thinking about it, I do believe that most people don't have an identical twin, that most people don't have doppelgangers, that I'm not prone to vivid hallucinations, and so on. It seems to me that there needs to be justification for me to believe all of these truths in order for me to justifiably rely on someone's appearance to identify that person.

If you find the above plausible, it won't be hard to conclude that it is only after you have *independent* empirical reason (for most of us it's no more than testimony from what we take to be experts) to believe that the color of litmus paper in a solution is a reliable indicator of the acidity of that solution. *Somebody* has to make the discovery about litmus paper without relying on testimony, but that discovery probably just involves correlations and projections from those correlations.

Summarizing the idea, we often initially describe ourselves as reasoning from E to P when in reality we are reasoning only from E together with a host of background beliefs about B to P.[27] The question of whether we can include amongst our foundationally justified beliefs, beliefs about some propositions of the form X makes probable Y is only a question about whether there are foundationally justified beliefs about the legitimacy of the inference from (E and B) to P.[28] This is a point to which we return briefly in Chapter 8 when we discuss epistemological issues as they arise in the philosophy of science.

The other factor one needs to keep in mind in trying to figure out whether it is at all plausible to suppose that there are necessary truths, knowable *a priori* about one thing's making probable another, is that even if it is true, the relation of making probable is importantly different from the relation of entailment. If E entails P, then it is absolutely impossible (metaphorically, there are no *possible* worlds) in which E is true and P is false. If you think about it, it follows from this notion of entailment that if E entails P, then (E and X) entails P (where X can be anything you like). X, after all, is just some further description of the ways things are, and if E entails P there can't be any situation (there can't be some X) where E is true and P is false.

E's making probable P, however, doesn't behave the way entailment does. From the fact that E makes probable P, it doesn't follow that (E together with X) also makes probable P. From what I know about a given lottery I just entered, it might be the case that I realize that it is very likely that the ticket I just bought will lose. But after the winning ticket announced on television matches the number on my ticket, it is no longer the case that the *totality* of my evidence makes it likely that I will lose. The fact that I seem to remember setting the alarm might make likely that I did. The fact that I seem to remember setting the alarm together with the fact that the alarm didn't go off might no longer make likely that I set the alarm. One more example: The fact that Jones is a banker together with the fact that most bankers are Republicans might make it likely that Jones is a Republican. The fact that Jones is a former Peace Corps worker together with the fact that most former Peace Corps workers are Democrats, might make it likely that Jones is a Democrat. The fact that Jones is both a banker and a former Peace Corps worker together with the fact that *that* group splits about 50/50 on party affiliation doesn't make likely that Jones is a Republican and it doesn't make likely that Jones is a Democrat. And there are countless other examples just like the above. That's just the way probability works. But again, this doesn't by itself constitute a reason for concluding that there aren't any necessary truths of the form E makes probable P. It might be necessarily the case that E makes probable P *and* necessarily the case that (E and X) makes improbable P.

I'm not arguing *here* for internalism, nor am I arguing *here* for the view that there are necessary truths describing probabilistic connections between propositions. My intent is only to argue that one's *metaepistemological* views will have implications for what *other* epistemological questions are properly viewed as philosophical.

Notes

1 *Much* more controversially. Dogs know how to swim, but I doubt that they know any truths about swimming. Professional golfers know how to hit the ball a very long way, but at least some of them have no more propositional knowledge about golfing that I do. There may just be genuine ambiguity, however. There is a sense in which I do possess propositional knowledge that counts as my knowing how to hit a long drive—propositional knowledge that might make me a good coach. There is another sense in which I can't hit the long dive—and in *that* sense don't know how to do it. See Stanley (2011) for a discussion of knowing how.
2 See Duncan Pritchard (2005) for a sustained attempt to explain the relevant notion of luck that precludes knowledge.
3 At least this is how Descartes began. He tried to "save" our common sense beliefs by arguing for the existence of a God who wouldn't allow us to be so massively deceived. It is an understatement to suggest that Descartes didn't convince many of his own solution to the skeptical challenge.
4 I'm fairly sure my parents told me where she was born. But they could have lied. They could have been in a witness protection program and have invented an elaborate fake story of their history.
5 One sort of view is called contextualism. There are lots of variation on contextualism. Painting with a very broad stroke, the idea is that standards for knowledge vary depending on context. Some contextualists think that the relevant context involves what is a *stake* if the belief in question is false (Fantl and McGrath 2009). Others think that that the context changes as others are inclined to *challenge* what you claim to know (Lewis 1996). And this just scratches the surface of the many different versions of contextualism that have been defended.
6 See Firth (1981) for a discussion of this sort of thought experiment.

7 You will recall that we discussed the problem of deviant causal chains. It might not be easy to flesh out what precisely it means to say that a doxastically justified belief is caused in the "right" sort of way by propositional justification.
8 And if questions about propositional justification fall within the purview of fundamental philosophy, one can again turn to *conditionals* to reach conclusions about what we would be justified in believing were the relevant beliefs caused in the right sort of way.
9 Although I haven't done a survey, it wouldn't surprise me if most internalists in the philosophy of mind and language are also internalists in epistemology; most externalists in the philosophy of mind and language are also externalists in epistemology. But there is no *logical* connection between the two views.
10 So on the approach I am taking, one defines externalism as the rejection of internalism. One might define the distinction taking the opposite approach. One might first define externalism and understand internalism in terms of a rejection of the externalist's position.
11 The access in question can be actual or potential. Which of the two one should emphasize can lead to an in-house debate among internalists.
12 See Ushenko (1937), Sosa (2003a and 2003b) and Markie (2009) for discussion of the idea that there might be features of experience that outstrip anyone's ability to become aware of those features. Ushenko gives the example of the experience of a speckled hen. It might be obvious to you that your visual field contains many speckles even though you wouldn't be able to tell just how many speckles occupy that field.
13 For an excellent debate on the merits of this sort of internalism, see Goldman (1999) and Conee and Feldman (2001).
14 There is now some dissent. See Littlejohn (2012) and Williamson (forthcoming).
15 Russell (1948) makes an argument like this (though I believe this represents a change from his earlier views). In a sense, Russell (1948) was a kind of proto-externalist.
16 It's a bit more complicated than this. Introspection of what we believe takes that very belief as an input, but the resulting belief that we have that belief will be justified regardless of whether the "input" belief is justified. See Wilson (2012).
17 Again, there are technical problems that require a "fix." When one engages in a series of inferences, each can be legitimate, but with each inference there can also be a slight loss of probability as one moves from premises to a conclusion. That small loss of probability can "add up" if one engages in enough reasoning, so much so that the final conclusion will no longer be likely relative to one's evidence. The idea is really no more complicated that the commonplace observation that even the best free throw shooter is likely to miss at least one of a series of thirty free throws.
18 But there are moves one could make. We talk, for example, about the tools one could have used to fix a problem even when one didn't think to use the tools at the time.
19 It would be particularly unfortunate if the only reason we think that the subjunctive is true is that we think that the belief in question is likely to be true (relative to the justification). This invites the charge of blatant circularity. Although they wouldn't agree, I think that Henderson and Horgan's (2006) *transglobal reliabilism* can ultimately only be understood in terms of relying on a *prior* understanding of probability.

20 See Conee and Feldman (1997) for their presentation of what is now called the generality problem for reliabilism.
21 Perhaps. But I have argued elsewhere that these "unreflective," "spontaneous" beliefs are formed against a vast background of beliefs that are relevant to questions about whether or not the relevant beliefs are justified.
22 The reference is to the movie *Rainman* in which the autistic character Raymond (once called by his brother "Rainman") had uncanny abilities to form correct believes about numbers.
23 Alston (1989) argues, in effect, that it is a mistake to think that one needs to "settle" these controversies. Rather, he suggests, one should recognize that we are interested in all sorts of properties that relate in one way or another to a belief's being true. Both internalists and externalists have valuable insights into which ways of forming beliefs are valuable.
24 The implausibility of supposing that one should be able to do this has come to be known as the problem of easy knowledge. See Cohen (2002). See also Sosa (2009) for a sophisticated view that attempts to deal with the charge that externalist epistemologies allow problematic "easy" knowledge.
25 See Searle (1983) for how little we actually know about what goes on in the brain as we think.
26 Again, this is the view defended by Keynes (1921). I believe that it is also a view that Russell flirted with from time to time (particularly in Russell (1967). See also Fumerton (2004).
27 See Huemer (2002) for an excellent discussion of this issue (and a penetrating criticism of some careless arguments I have made elsewhere).
28 That there are necessary truths knowable without inference about the existence of probability relations was famously argued by Keynes (1921).

Chapter 6
Ethics and Rationality/ Metaethics and Meta-rationality

There are interesting parallels among the relations between metaepistemology and applied epistemology, metarationality and applied rationality, and metaethics and applied ethics. That might not be surprising given that we use some of the same terminologies in making epistemological claims and in making claims about ethics and rationality. In epistemology, we often talk about what we *epistemically ought* to believe given our evidence; in ethics, we often talk about what we *morally ought* to do given our circumstances. And among those who distinguish morality from rationality, we also talk about what we *rationally ought* to do given our circumstances. Just as we argued that metaepistemological positions have implications for which epistemological questions fall within the purview of philosophy, so also, we will discover that metaethical positions have implications for which ethical questions fall within the purview of philosophy, and meta-rationality positions have implications for which questions about what it is rational to do fall within the purview of philosophy.

It is an open philosophical question as to precisely what the connection is between ethics and rationality. Throughout the history of philosophy, some philosophers have wondered why we ought to be moral.[1] Interpreted a certain way the question is decidedly odd. Isn't it true *by definition* that moral people do (or, at the very least try to do) what they morally ought to do? So if the "ought" in question is the moral "ought," then it should be trivially true that we ought to be moral. We morally ought to do what we morally ought to do! But the question doesn't *seem* trivial. Indeed, you have probably sometimes wondered yourself whether you ought to obey the demands of morality, particularly when such demands strongly conflict with what is in your *interest* to do. One way to recognize the relevance of the question "Why ought I be moral" is to distinguish two different "oughts"—the "ought" of morality, and the "ought" of rationality. The question then is no longer trivial. It becomes the question of whether one rationally ought to do what one morally ought to do—the question of whether the rational person will act morally.

DOI: 10.4324/9781003223566-8

6.1 Rational Action

Let's start with rational action. The question of what one rationally or pragmatically ought to do is sometimes identified with a question about how most effectively to satisfy one's subjective goals or ends.[2] We might say that X is a subjective goal or end for S when S wants or values X *for its own sake*. A great deal of what we want in life we want only as a means to furthering some other goal or end. I might want a good income, but want it only for various ways in which money will allow me to achieve other goals I have. I might want to see a doctor for an annual checkup, but want the checkup only as means of furthering my goal of staying in relatively good health. It may be that most of what I want in life I want only as a means to getting something else I want. But there must be at least some *ultimate* goals or ends that I have. There must be some things I want *for their own sake*.

The question of what I do care about for its own sake might seem to be answerable by introspection. One might suppose such truths fall squarely within the kind of philosophy that I called phenomenology or introspection. Although *you* might not be able to know directly what *I* value intrinsically, surely I can know what my ultimate goals are. That conclusion seems initially plausible, but in fact I'm not sure how easy it is for one to discover such truths about oneself. For example, I am strongly inclined to believe that I value intrinsically (for its own sake) the happiness of my children and grandchildren. But I also know that I get enormous pleasure from seeing them do well, and feel terrible when I see them suffer. So I might at least *wonder* whether it is *their* pleasure and freedom from pain that I ultimately care about or *my own*. It's not that easy to answer the question. You might think that the answer is determined by whether I would still value their happiness if I were no longer empathetically tied to them. But that's not quite right. After all, if I were the kind of person who didn't get pleasure from seeing them thrive, I might also be the kind of person who doesn't value their well-being intrinsically. So I'm not absolutely sure that philosophers can be trusted to arrive at the truth with respect to even their own fundamental goals or ends. But I'm also not convinced that any other discipline is better positioned to arrive at such truths. Perhaps one could argue that a philosopher is as well-placed as anyone else to answer the relevant questions.

Suppose I do have a clear understanding and knowledge of what makes something an ultimate goal or end for me. Knowing what one's goals are is one thing. Figuring out how to achieve one's goals is something else. One might suppose that it is pragmatically rational for me to do X just insofar as doing X will maximize the satisfaction of my ultimate goals or ends. In this context, the notion of maximizing the satisfaction of goals or ends is a technical notion. It is usually used comparatively. And it includes the idea of minimizing the frustration of goals or ends. The crude idea is this: In life one is faced with choices. Each alternative open to you might satisfy or frustrate goals or ends. Of the alternatives open to you, one will win out with respect to achieving goals. So imagine that the alternative open to you are A1, A2, A3, A4, and A5. Each of these actions has consequences. You will be completely indifferent to most of the consequences. For example, every time you move your arm you displace molecules, and almost always you are completely indifferent to the fact that as a result of your action, molecules occupy a different position. But often you value or disvalue intrinsically at least some of the consequences that would result from your actions. Most people disvalue intrinsically their own severe pain, and if one is contemplating doing something that would cause such pain, the pain counts against taking that action.[3]

In discussing such matters it is often useful to talk *as if* one can represent the consequences one values intrinsically with positive numbers, and the consequences one disvalues intrinsically with negative numbers. That to which one is intrinsically indifferent gets 0.[4] When an action brings about something that one values intrinsically, one might argue that one has *a* reason to take that action (a reason that can easily be outweighed by others). Whenever an action brings about something one disvalues intrinsically, one has *a* reason *not* to take that action (again, a reason that can easily be outweighed). What is rational to do is a function of the *net* reasons for and against taking actions. One can think of this as "summing" the intrinsic positive and negative subjective values that attach to the consequences of each of the alternatives open to one. The alternative that yields the greatest net value (that *maximizes* value) is what one rationally ought to do. It is, of course, obvious that the act that yields the greatest net value might satisfy none of one's goals or ends. Life being what it is, all of the alternatives open to you might yield nothing but negative value. But, one must make choices. *Doing nothing* is an oxymoron. It is an alternative like any other and it can have disastrous consequences. It is also obvious that there might be alternatives that "tie" when it comes to maximizing value. In that case, one could think of those alternatives as equally rational.

There are all sorts of ways in which one might criticize the above (sketch of an) account of rational action. For one thing, as we shall discuss below, many would think it almost obvious that one can rationally *assess* even one's ultimate goals or end. Many would argue that not all of one's goals are rational goals. And irrational goals shouldn't figure in one's account of rational action.[5] Here, however, the main point I want to emphasize is that *if* one understands rational action in terms of facts about would *actually* happen should we choose that action over alternatives, *then* we seem to have removed questions about what it is rational to do from philosophy proper. Questions of what causes what are often enormously complex. Think about how difficult it is to calculate what investments one rationally ought to include in one's retirement plan. Think about how difficult it is to calculate what university one ought to encourage one's child to attend. These and countless other decisions have consequences that are very difficult to discover. One certainly can't discover the consequences of such actions from the sheltered life of an academic's armchair.[6] So *if* this view of rational action were correct, then, arguably, the philosophical study of rational action begins and ends with the theory of meta-rationality.

But it is not at all obvious that one *should* understand rationality in terms of facts about the *actual* consequences that would occur from alternatives open to one. Suppose that I offer you the opportunity to enter a lottery at a cost of ten dollars. Your chance of winning the lottery is 1 in a 100, and the winner gets $1,000,000. Almost everyone reading this would agree that rationality sides with buying the lottery ticket.[7] And their conclusion would be unaltered by the knowledge that in all likelihood buying the ticket will leave one $10 poorer. Conversely, suppose that I offer you $1,000 to play one round of Russian Roulette with a six-chambered handgun. Almost everyone reading this would decline the invitation, and would do so despite their realizing that accepting the invitation would *probably* enrich them by $1,000.[8]

The obvious lesson is that rational behavior involves the assessment of risks and *potential* benefits. What one rationally ought to do is a function of the sum of subjective values of possible consequences *adjusted* for the probability of those possible consequences occurring. On one common view, one adjusts the value for the probability by taking a fraction of the value—a fraction that represents the probability. So if we represent the subjective value I attach to a possible outcome Y as a +1,000, but Y has only a 1 in a 1,000 chance of occurring, the strength of that reason I have for doing something that might lead to Y gets represented by just 1/1,000th of that +1,000 and we are down to +1. In the literature, the summed adjusted value of possible consequences is sometimes called the *expected* value of an action.

If one finds something like the above view plausible, one still needs an account of all this talk of probability. On one view the probability *p* for S that something Y will happen as a result of doing X is a function of the epistemological reasons E S has such that (E and X) makes likely to degree p that Y will happen. The emphasis on "for S" is a reminder that epistemic probability is always relative to a given body of evidence available to a person. Something might be quite likely *for me* relative to my body of evidence, while it is exceedingly unlikely *for you* relative to your body of evidence. For example, I might be a pathological liar who tells you that my name is Jones even though it isn't. Presumably, it is likely *for you* that my name is Jones, even though it is almost certain for me that it is not Jones. I might have poisoned your drink, and while it is likely *for you* that the drink will quench your thirst without any harmful side effects, it might be almost certain *for me* that your taking the drink will kill you.

After thinking about whether it is an action's actual consequences, or its possible consequences (taking into account their probabilities) that are relevant to the rationality of taking that action, one might well conclude that there are simply *ambiguities* in our thought about reasons for acting. Consider again the example of a poisoned drink. There is surely some sense in which if I know nothing of the poison, my attempt at quenching my thirst with the drink would be perfectly rational. On the other hand, suppose that *you* know that my drink has been poisoned. Noticing an anxious expression on your face, I ask you if there is any reason I shouldn't consume the drink. It would be decidedly odd for you to respond by saying "Well, there is no reason *for you* not to take the drink!" In the context of advising someone, you usually take into account your *own* epistemic situation rather that the epistemic situation of the person to whom you are giving advice. At least that is so when you believe that you have more relevant evidence than the person to whom you are giving advice. In the context of assessing praise or blame for someone, we usually take into account the evidence that person had when acting.[9] Alternatively, perhaps sometimes we do shift from talking about reasons that take into account epistemic position to reasons that are understood in terms of what is actually going to happen (compared to what would happen if alternatives were taken).

Fortunately, for our present purposes, we don't need to settle on answers to these interesting questions. Again, the whole point of this discussion is to get clear about where philosophy begins and ends with respect to the evaluation of reasons for acting. If the reasons we are talking about are defined in terms of what would *actually* happen from taking each of the alternatives open to us, then what one has the most reason to do is beyond the competence of philosophers *qua philosophers* to discover. If, however, the reasons *for me* to act take into account *my* epistemic perspective, questions about the rationality of actions in this sense may or may not fall within the purview of philosophy. It depends on what the correct *metaepistemological* view is.

As we noted in Chapter 5, the epistemological *externalist* assigns many first-level epistemological questions to the empirical sciences. It is a contingent question as to *how* such beliefs as beliefs about the past, the physical world, and other minds are formed. And it is a contingent question as to whether the processes that give rise to such beliefs are *reliable*. So if reliabilism, for example, were a correct account of epistemic justification, one should assign such questions to whatever sciences seem best equipped to study such topics. By contrast, on some versions of epistemic internalism, one has potential introspective access to the foundations of one's knowledge and justified belief, foundations that provide for one both one's ultimate premises, *and* the relations of support (probabilistic connection) that evidence provides for inferential justification. So on *that* view, in principle, one could access the extent to which various possible consequences of action are probable, and calculate from that *epistemic* perspective what one ought to do.

6.1.1 Regress

Even if from the first-person perspective one can in principle calculate both what one epistemically ought to believe, and what one ought to do (where the probability relevant to such calculations is an epistemic probability), there is an interesting regress that might threaten the philosopher's ability to satisfy intellectual curiosity on *all* questions that can arise concerning what one ought to do. Questions about what it is rational to do include questions about whether one ought to gather more evidence before choosing from among alternatives open to one.

To illustrate, suppose I had my car checked out by my mechanic a couple of months ago and it received a clean bill of health. That gives me fairly good reason to think that it is in good shape for the long car trip I'm planning. But if the trip is long enough and if I am taking my grandkids with me, I might well ask myself whether I should get another inspection before starting the grand trip. How would I decide whether or not I ought to get more evidence? Well on the view I most recently discussed, I would need to think about the probability of various possible consequences of failing to get more evidence. But when I make a decision about *that* matter, I could, of course, raise a question about whether I ought to gather more evidence that bears on the question of whether I ought to gather more evidence. And answering that question might require me eventually to think about whether I ought to gather more evidence that bears on the question of whether I ought to gather more evidence that bears on the question ... This never ends.[10]

So how should we respond to the idea that finite beings will be unable to answer *all* of the possible questions that can be raised about rational action? Perhaps with a shrug of the shoulders. It may be that we acted in a perfectly rational way when we made a decision of some kind without gathering additional evidence, even if we realize that we didn't answer all of the questions that *could* be raised concerning the decision to act without further evidence. That's the human condition. If that is so and it is our fate to always leave some possible legitimate question unanswered, *that* is also a conclusion that we can reach as philosophers reasoning *qua philosophers*.

6.2 Morality

We noted earlier that there are questions about the connection between rationality and morality. It seemed at least initially plausible to distinguish an "ought" of rationality from an "ought" of morality, if only so that we can ask a non-trivial question about whether we ought to be moral. With the two different "oughts" the question can be interpreted as one about the rationality of being moral.

In making the distinction we risk yet another regress—this time a conceptual regress. If we distinguish what one rationally ought to do from what one morally ought to do, then one must obviously come to grips with the possibility that rationality and morality might come apart. If they do, which "ought" *ought* to take precedence? It is, of course, trivially true that one rationally ought to do what one rationally ought to do, and that one morally ought to do what one morally ought to do, but what ought one do all things considered? Do we need yet another "ought" to ask *that* question? An affirmative answer would ultimately require yet a fourth ought, for the three different "oughts" we have now distinguished might all conflict and we will need to ask what we ought to do if *that* happens.

One alternative to introducing an endless array of "oughts" is to stop at some finite number of (perhaps two) fundamental "oughts" and view the choice between, say, rationality and morality as a kind of "existential" commitment.[11] The idea would be that the choice defies any sort of non-question begging assessment. Another alternative is to invoke the rhetorical strategy of arguing that a rational person will, *by definition*, act rationally. If morality and rationality come apart so, much the worse for morality.[12] And yet a third alternative is to recognize the existence of both moral reasons and reasons defined in terms of subjective goals and argue that the two sorts of reasons are fully commensurable (can be weighed against one another)—see Jeske (2008).

6.2.1 Intrinsic Value

In Section 6.1, I sketched an account of rational action, one that understands reasons for acting in terms of the actual or possible achievement of *subjective* goals or ends. I acknowledged that one source of dissatisfaction with such a view is the conviction of some that one can obviously assess not just the means to achieve various ends, but also the ends themselves. What would make a subjective goal or end appropriate or inappropriate? One answer might involve an appeal to some independent understanding of *moral* value. The moral objectivist might argue that some states of the world are intrinsically good and some are intrinsically bad.[13] The contrast here is supposed to be between things that are good or bad just in virtue of what they are, and things that are good or bad because they will (or might) lead to those states of the world that are good or bad just in virtue of what they are. One might then go on to argue that if one subjectively values for its own sake something that is intrinsically bad, that goal or end is irrational. A stronger view still is the idea that unless one subjectively values something that is intrinsically good the goal or end is irrational.[14]

How would one know that it is objectively the case that something is intrinsically good or intrinsically bad? One famous philosopher in the early twentieth century, G. E. Moore, thought that the *foundations* of knowledge include *self-evident* truths about what *kinds* of things are intrinsically good or bad. There are axioms in ethics just as there are axioms in Euclidean geometry. If Moore were right, then on the conception of philosophy for which I have argued, truths about certain kinds of things being intrinsically good or bad are among those synthetic necessary truths knowable *a priori*, and are, therefore, part of philosophy proper.

Even if the above view were true, one must be careful how one states the view. Suppose, for example, that one thought (as Moore did) that friendship is intrinsically good. It wouldn't follow that one could know of some *particular* relationship that *it* is intrinsically good. Depending on how one understands friendship, it might be difficult to tell whether the relationship is really one of friendship. So if, for example, a true friend of mine must care about me and my happiness, it might be hard to tell whether a person I *take* to be my friend has the required interests. It certainly doesn't seem plausible to me that one can know without inference what's going on in the mind of another person. Or suppose that kindness is intrinsically good. It might be difficult to know whether some particular act is one of kindness. When one disciplines a child, is that an act of kindness? When one gives a student a bad grade on a poorly written paper, is that an act of kindness? Such questions are difficult to answer and may involve empirical evidence to answer. So on a view like Moore's, one shouldn't *overstate* the extent of philosophical knowledge concerning what is intrinsically good or bad.

Moore's view of intrinsic value is hardly the only metaethical view about intrinsic value. One view that goes back to Plato and Aristotle is that almost everything has a *function* and the value of a thing is related to how effectively the thing fulfills its function. So think of an artifact like a toaster or a knife. Good toasters and good knives have features that allow the toaster and the knife to do what they are designed to do.[15] Of course, toasters and knives *are* designed *by people* to do certain things. And to many, it seems a bit odd to think of people, just as people, as having functions.[16] In any event, it is not clear how one discovers the function of something, or what it is about a thing that enables it to do what it is supposed to do.[17] Certainly, if we model discovering a thing's function on examples like discovering the function of the liver, one wouldn't expect *philosophers* to be particularly good at investigating functions. The function of a feature of a thing in this sense has something to do with the way in which the feature contributes to the survival of the thing given the circumstances in which the thing came into existence.[18]

Another approach to understanding intrinsic value reverses the order of philosophical explanation. Rather than explain the difference between rational and irrational goals in terms of the intrinsic value of the goals, one might try to explain what it is for a goal to be intrinsically good or bad in terms of the concept of rationality. Crudely, one might argue that something X is intrinsically good just when a person who is ideally rational would value X (for its own sake); a thing X is intrinsically bad just when a person who is ideally rational would disvalue X (considered as it is in itself). Such a move, however, would obviously take us right back to controversies about what makes a person rational.

There are many other views about how to understand the intrinsic value, views that have implications for whether the philosopher qua philosopher is trained to answer questions about what has intrinsic value. The examples discussed above were objectivist accounts of intrinsic value. But there is another strong tradition in the history of philosophy that rejects the idea that we can make sense of a thing's having value independently of whether it is subjectively valued. One might try to define a thing's being intrinsically valuable in terms of its being intrinsically valued by all or most people. Such accounts aren't very plausible,[19] but if they *were* correct, questions of what has intrinsic value would be beyond the purview of philosophy. It would presumably be some combination of psychology and sociology whose job it is to discover generalizations about psychological preferences. Another view, however, that is also determined to understand talk of what has value in terms of what is valued takes its cue from the theory of rational action defined in terms of a person's goals or ends. Basically, the idea is that talk about what has value is incomplete. Something X has intrinsic value *for some person S* just when S values X for its own sake. What has intrinsic value *for me* might not have intrinsic value *for you*. On such a view, I *might* be back in business qua philosopher figuring out what has intrinsic value *for me*, though I might not be particularly well positioned to discover what has intrinsic value for you.[20]

6.2.2 Right Action, Duties, Obligations, Virtues, and Supererogation

6.2.2.1 Consequentialist Accounts of Right Action

We began our discussion of metaethics and philosophy by looking at metaethical views about intrinsic value and what those views imply for whether or not first-level questions about what has intrinsic value fall within the purview of philosophy. But ethical questions are not restricted to questions about intrinsic value. Over the millennia intellectuals have raised questions about how we ought to live our lives, what duties and obligations we have, what makes a person virtuous, and whether there are acts that are noble but above and beyond the call of duty (*supererogatory* acts).

I talked about Moore's idea that there is an objective property of being intrinsically good/bad and that we have foundational (*a priori*) knowledge of what kinds of things have that property. Moore also embraced an influential view about what the connection is between ideas about what we morally ought to do and ideas about what kinds of things have an intrinsic positive or negative value. The view parallels exactly the account discussed earlier of how to understand rational action in terms of fundamental goals or ends. You get Moore's view if we just substitute talk about objective intrinsic value for all that talk about goals or ends. So the simplest view (sometimes called generic utilitarianism) is that what you morally ought to do (the right thing for you to do) in any given circumstance is whatever maximizes intrinsic value. This time, think about assigning states of the world positive or negative numbers representing how much positive or negative objective intrinsic value they have. Each alternative open to you would change the world in ways that affect how much net value is in the world. What you ought to do is whatever yields the greatest *net* value. As we noted in discussing the structurally similar view about rational action, the greatest net value that would result from an alternative might be a net negative. The world being what it is, we can find ourselves painted into a corner where every alternative open to us has horrible effects. You still need to act (doing nothing, you will recall, is an *alternative* that also has consequences). So in bad situations do what does the least moral damage. And as we also noted in discussing rational action, there might well be "ties" among alternatives with respect to the net value that results. In this sort of case, there is more than one alternative that is morally permissible.

The considerations that counted in favor of turning to possible consequences when thinking about rational action also count in favor of turning to possible consequences when trying to understand what one morally ought to do. There are moral "gambles" that make sense, and there are moral "risks" that are unacceptable. So if one is trying to understand morality in terms of maximizing objective intrinsic value, one may move to *expected* value. On that sort of view, you will recall, one adjusts the value of possible consequences for the probability of their occurring. And if there are good reasons to think that talk about rationality might involve ambiguity with respect to the epistemic perspective presupposed by a claim about what one has the most reason to do, so also there might be good reason to think that morality involves similar ambiguity.

If we understand what we morally ought to do in terms of the values of *actual* consequences, then I don't see how *philosophers* would be particularly useful at figuring out what we morally ought to do.[21] Philosophers have no *independent* way of discovering the relevant empirical facts about consequences. They can read what other people claim to have discovered, but they have no way of *checking* to see who has the correct view about the consequences of taking one alternative rather than another. When "experts" disagree with each other (as they almost always do on controversial issues) the philosopher would just need to choose based on "intuition" about whom to believe.

By contrast, as we argued earlier, if the moral value that attaches to *possible* consequences of action is summed after that value is adjusted for the *epistemic* probability of their occurring, I might be competent as a philosopher to answer first-level questions about what *I* ought to do. At least that is so *if* some version of access internalism is the correct account of epistemic justification. But also remember the possibility that we equivocate when it comes to epistemic perspective. At least sometimes when I'm trying to figure out what to do, I am interested in *improving* my epistemic position vis-à-vis evidence concerning the outcomes of alternatives open to me. In this sense, I won't think that it is appropriate to settle for conclusions reached given my current impoverished epistemic perspective.

6.2.2.2 Deontological Accounts of Morality

The "consequentialist" account of what is the right/wrong thing to do (what one ought to do) is hardly the only game in town. In fact, thought experiments convince many that one can't define what one ought to do in terms of what maximizes either value or expected value. Most of us have heard the old cliché that the ends don't justify the means. But when you think about it, the *consequentialist* should respond to the cliché with impatience: What the hell else would justify a means but an end? Why wouldn't a moral person go through life trying to make the world the best place possible?

The response to the rhetorical question is an array of thought experiments. Imagine that you *promised* me to do X, but that when it comes time to fulfill the promise you calculate that you could make the world slightly better by reneging on the promise. That wouldn't be morally permissible (the critic of consequentialism argues). Or suppose that you have a terrifying crime wave that you somehow know that you can stop if you frame and make an example of an innocent person. That wouldn't be OK, would it? Or suppose that you are a surgeon in desperate need of five organs that could save the lives of five different people.[22] The surgeon realizes that by secretly killing you and taking your organs the five lives could be saved. That's not OK, is it? Finally, ask yourself what obligation you have to vote in a presidential election given that your chance of affecting the outcome of the elections is close to zero. If we measure what you ought to do in terms of the value of possible consequences (adjusted for probability), you would make the world a better place by staying home consuming a nice bag of Doritos chased down by an ice cold beer. But that *wouldn't* be the right thing to do, would it?

I have argued elsewhere (1990) that these thought experiments don't win the day for the critic of consequentialism. But that's not what is at issue here. If one *were* moved by the thought experiments, what alternative to consequentialism might one find attractive? Within the objectivist camp, one of the more dialectically attractive alternatives is the deontology of W. D. Ross (1930). Ross denied that one can define what one ought to do in terms of facts about the intrinsic value of (actual or possible) consequences. Just as Moore thought that there was an indefinable objective property of being intrinsically good/bad, so Ross thought that there are kinds of actions that are prima facie obligatory just in virtue of the kind of actions they are. For our purposes, I'll translate talk about prima facie duty and obligation into talk of moral reasons. Put that way, we can illustrate the idea behind the view with an example. If I promise you that I will do X, then I have a moral reason to do X just in virtue of my having made the promise. Even if it is generally good that people keep their promises, I have a kind of reason to keep *my* promise that no one else has. That's why I can't get out of an obligation to keep my promise just on the grounds that I could produce a little bit more good by breaking the promise than by keeping it.

These deontological reasons to act (reasons that do not derive solely from intrinsic value that might result from the act) are still *prima facie* for Ross.[23] That's just a way of saying that they can be overridden by competing reasons. I might have a strong moral reason to keep my promise, but also a strong moral reason to protect my children from harm (in virtue of their being *my* children). And things may turn out in such a way that the only way I can keep my promise is to allow my child to be harmed. At that point, one will need to compare the strengths of competing reasons. Deontologists don't agree with each other about what features of actions generate moral reasons to take those actions. Nor do they necessarily agree on the strength of various reasons to act in various sorts of ways. Ross himself didn't think facts about consequences are irrelevant to what one ought to do all things considered. He thought one does have a reason to act so as to benefit others (he called this a duty of beneficence), and he also thought that one has a reason to avoid harming others (he called this a duty to avoid maleficence). Generally, he thought the latter sort of reason was stronger than the former. He was also skeptical that there is any neat way (any algorithm one can apply) to figure out what one ought to do all things considered.[24]

With a deontological metaethics of the sort endorsed by Ross, where would that leave philosophers qua arbiters of first-level ethical questions? Ross did think that one can know *a priori* which *kinds* of actions generate objective moral reason to act. But we must remember the point made in discussing Moore's view about intrinsic value. Philosophers *qua* philosophers may be able to discover a priori that *if* one's action is of a certain kind X *then* one will have a moral reason to take that action, but it doesn't follow that the philosopher qua philosopher will be particularly well-positioned to ascertain that the action *is* of kind X. I may have a deontic reason to help my child, but as all thoughtful parents know, it isn't easy to figure out what will actually help your children. Some think that the way to help your kid is to home school that kid. Others think that home-schooling is a sure way to stunt your kid's emotional growth. The point is even more obvious if one does include among one's *prima facie* duties Ross's duty of beneficence and his duty to avoid maleficence. Does raising corporate tax rates help or harm people? Perhaps the obvious answer is that such an act would help some people and hurt other people. But economists don't agree on what the effects of tax policy would be. They don't agree with each other about who would be hurt and who would be helped. And philosophers are hardly better positioned than economists to reach the relevant conclusions. The truth is that no one seems to be particularly well-positioned to discover the relevant truths. The policy controversies are controversial in large part just because the empirical facts are difficult to discover given the extraordinary number of variables on which the outcomes depend.

So moderate deontology faces problems very similar to those faced by the consequentialist. Both views might have to come to grips with the fact that even first-level questions about what one has *a* reason to do might easily outstrip philosophical expertise.

6.2.2.3 Virtues

We have talked about intrinsic value, right and wrong (and questions about how one ought to behave). Consequentialists take questions about intrinsic value to be more fundamental than questions about right/wrong (how one ought to behave). Deontologists don't think that one can define what one ought to do in terms of facts about consequences and their intrinsic value. But there are other concepts that are of interest to the ethical philosopher.

We certainly seem to have the idea of a virtuous person. Both consequentialists and deontologists are inclined to think that the idea of a virtue is parasitic upon other ethical concepts. One might think that a virtue is a characteristic of a person that makes it more likely that that person will do the right thing. Or one might think that a virtue is a characteristic of a person that makes it more likely that the person will have rational goals or ends. But a virtue ethicist might try to reverse the order of explanation. If one had an independent understanding of what it is to be a virtuous person, one might understand the distinction between right and wrong in terms of what a virtuous person would or wouldn't do. But that's a big "if" and I don't know of any *plausible* way of understanding virtues that doesn't presuppose an understanding of other ethical concepts. If one does need to understand virtuous character employing the concept of right action, then any attempt to discover the virtues *a priori* is no more plausible than an attempt to discover *a priori* what one ought to do.

6.2.2.4 Supererogatory Actions and Morals by Agreement

The idea of supererogatory actions is interesting. It is a way in which one might cast doubt on *both* familiar consequentialist and deontological accounts of how one ought to behave. We do sometimes seem to characterize some person as doing something that is so praiseworthy that it is "above and beyond the call of duty." Although the consequentialist and the deontologist understand moral reasons for acting in quite different ways, they both seem to understand the right action as the one favored by the preponderance of reasons to act. But then the idea of a supererogatory act wouldn't really make any sense. If there is more moral reason to do X than any alternative to X then one ought to do X—end of story. Some might argue, however, that morality is better understood in terms of rules that *constrain* our behavior. On some views, the rules are implicitly agreed upon by people committed to co-operation—perhaps because co-operation is the best way for almost everyone to achieve their individual long-term goals or ends.[25] At least some who endorse such a view argue that rational people entering into such agreements would emphasize prohibitions against certain ways of acting. Given our desire for freedom, we would be wary of agreeing to rules that require us to help one another. We might admire people who go beyond the requirements of morality even if we do not regard such behavior as mandated by the rules to which we are committed.

As with the brief discussion of other metaethical views, I am primarily interested here in the implications this view might have for whether philosophy proper includes first-level questions about morality. Any view that defines morality in terms of implicit agreements needs to flesh out the critical concept. What makes it true that there has been an implicit agreement? Who are the participants to the agreement? Are we relativizing morality to a community the members of which are party to the agreement? Is the logical limit to this a community of one (so that I can bind myself to my own morality, one that has no relevance to anyone else)? With the possible exception of this last case, it is not clear to me that a *philosopher* would be particularly well-trained to investigate the existence of implicit agreements. As with many other questions that philosophers end up discussing, it is not clear who *does* have the relevant expertise. The existence of implicit agreements among people sounds like some sociological, cultural, or psychological fact of some kind. But it wouldn't be a fact that is easy to discover. I suppose that in the limiting case where I am a community of one, I might have *introspective* access to my own "commitments" to act or refrain from acting in certain ways, though that seems to reduce to something like a resolve or an intent to act in a certain way.

6.3 Summary

My primary objective in this chapter was to illustrate the ways in which one's meta-views about rationality and ethics will have implications for what *else* should be included in philosophy *proper*. I haven't tried to convince you of any specific views about how to understand rational or moral action.[26] And it is worth emphasizing that even if the correct meta-views exclude much of applied ethics from inclusion in philosophy proper, that doesn't denigrate *at all* the importance of asking and answering first-level questions about how one rationally and morally ought to behave. Nor does it dismiss the critical role of philosophy in investigating such matters. Without a clear understanding of how to understand the questions we raise about good and bad, right and wrong, rational and irrational behavior, we will often struggle to distinguish the difference between plausible and specious reasoning.

Notes

1. This was one of the central questions raised in Plato's *Republic*. Thrasymachus and then Glaucon wondered why an ideally rational person would pay any attention to what morality requires. The "Fool" in Hobbes's *Leviathan* asked a similar question.
2. This isn't the place to argue questions of historical interpretation. Without such argument, however, I suggest that both Hobbes and Hume either explicitly or implicitly held this view.
3. Some would argue that it is true by definition that people intrinsically disvalue pain. The idea is that the only thing painful experiences have in common is the fact that we want them to stop.
4. I emphasize the "as if." While one values and disvalues intrinsically various outcomes to varying degrees, it is not clear that there is a precise "scale" one uses to measure the degree of such subjective states. It is more like the way in which the doctor will ask you to rate the degree of your pain on a scale from one to ten. One gets the general idea, and one does come up with a number, but even as one does it, one realizes that it is a bit odd to talk as if there is a scale that allows one to rank pain. When I do it, I probably just think of the worst pain I have ever experienced and think of that as a ten. I then think of one of the mildest pains I experience and assign that a one. After that, I make comparative judgments. (I have also figured out what I need to say in order to get the pain medication I want).
5. As I'll discuss below, I don't agree with this objection.
6. Every so often it is worth reminding ourselves that armchair investigation is a metaphor. One can, of course, read about empirical discoveries from the armchair. But I'm not counting that as an investigation conducted from the armchair. Whatever knowledge you acquire that way is parasitic upon research someone else has done from beyond the armchair.
7. The qualification is there because there are people in the world for whom $10 is all that stands between them and death. If you were unfortunate to be one

of those people, then the "cost/benefit" analysis one needs to do in deciding whether to place the bet is quite different.
8. Again, if one were in a position where a successful outcome to the "gamble" were the only way to save one's life or the life of a loved one, the calculation might be quite different.
9. This gets complicated. Sometimes we blame people for earlier actions that resulted in their having an impoverished evidence base. And we'll level that criticism at them even if they acted rationally given their impoverished evidence.
10. See Foley (1990) for a discussion of how best to respond to the puzzle.
11. See Sidgwick's *Methods of Ethics*.
12. I've defended this view in (Fumerton, 1990).
13. For our purposes let's say that objective intrinsic value is value that a thing has quite independently of whether the thing is subjectively valued.
14. That's a stronger view because the objectivist will concede that there are all kinds of things that are neither intrinsically good nor intrinsically bad. One might think that as a long as something isn't intrinsically bad it is OK to subjectively value it for its own sake.
15. Developing a non-circular view of this sort is difficult. One really wants to talk about how well the artifact performs its function. And how well it does is probably a matter of whether it does it better than others of its sort. But "better" is the comparative of good, and the whole account is in danger of presupposing an understanding of the very notion it is trying to explain.
16. As opposed to people in their role or job as doctors, police officers, firefighters, teachers, and so on. Of course, some theists may believe that God had a "design plan" for everything. In God's mind, perhaps we are like toasters or knives. Indeed, Plantinga (1993) endorsed a view that in some respects is like reliabilism—warranted beliefs are beliefs that are formed the way God intended believers to form beliefs (in the circumstances appropriate for forming such beliefs).
17. Plato called this property, the thing's "excellence."
18. See Hempel (1965) for what is still one of the most plausible analyses of functional explanation.
19. Consider the obvious fact that one can without contradiction criticize the values judgments of the community to which one belongs.
20. But again, as we noted when discussing questions of what one's ultimate goals or ends are, it might not be easy for me to figure out what I do value for its own sake. I might not be sure, for example, whether I value my friend's happiness for its own sake or only as a means to the happiness I get from seeing my friend happy.
21. Moore himself probably did want to understand what one ought to do in terms of what would actually happen if one choose one alternative over others. And to his credit, he basically admitted that neither philosophers nor anyone else would have much chance of figuring out which choices we ought to make. He sort of shrugged his shoulders and suggested that we should probably just rely on the accumulated wisdom of the ages with respect to what kinds of actions tend to have good consequences and bad consequences. The problem, of course, is that people don't agree on what history teaches us about such matters.
22. The example is Harman's (1977).
23. There is a much more extreme form of deontology that holds that certain kinds of actions are morally obligatory/forbidden *no matter what*. Kant (1993)

famously argued that there no circumstances in which it would be morally permissible to lie, break a promise, or kill oneself. Although Kant presented elaborate (though hardly pellucid) arguments for this view, not many are willing to follow Kant in embracing what strikes most of us as a wildly implausible view. *Really*? There are *no* circumstances in which it is morally OK to lie? Not even to save a life, ten thousand lives, a billion lives?

24 It's not clear whether he thought that it was impossible in principle or just in practice.
25 The view goes all the way back at least to Plato's *Republic*. It was a suggestion made by the character Glaucon. Hobbes (1651) famously and eloquently defends a version of the view. So does Harman (1977).
26 I've done that elsewhere (1990).

Chapter 7
Philosophy of Mind

I argued in Part I that philosophy begins with phenomenology. Indeed, *all* knowledge of *all* truths begins with a foundational knowledge of truths about phenomena with which we are directly acquainted. I believe that the facts with which we are directly acquainted include facts about our mental life. But that conclusion requires careful analysis of what it means to say of some state that it is mental.

The distinction that we discussed between metaethics and applied ethics is familiar. And by now the distinction between metaepistemology and epistemology is equally familiar. There are similar distinctions to be made within the philosophy of mind, but the terminology isn't as clear. It is harder to tell when a philosopher of mind is asking a meta-question and when that philosopher is asking a first-level "applied" question about mental states. One possible explanation is that until recently few contemporary philosophers of mind have really ever tried to answer the relevant "applied" questions.

What would be examples of first-level questions about mental states? Well, think about the *meta* vs *applied* distinction in ethics. If I ask whether we ought to give everyone a legal right to health care, I'm asking a first-level question in ethics. If I ask whether you (in particular) ought to give more to charity, I'm asking a very specific first-level question in ethics. The following are first-level ethical questions about intrinsic value (albeit questions with different levels of specificity): Is pleasure intrinsically good? Is knowledge intrinsically good? Is friendship intrinsically good? Is my friendship with Diane intrinsically good? Is my knowledge that some apples are red intrinsically good?

The analog of very specific "applied" questions in the philosophy of mind would include the following: What do I want for dinner? What is Patti thinking of right now? More general, but still first-level questions about mental states would include: Do most people fear death? Do most people believe that there is an afterlife? Do most people love their siblings? Are most people empathetic? It really does seem a bit strange to think that *philosophers* have any special sort of competence to answer *any* of the

DOI: 10.4324/9781003223566-9

above first-level questions about mental states.[1] It gets a bit more complicated when philosophers address *very* general questions about human nature. Certainly, people with a philosophical reputation have weighed in on the question of whether everyone is an egoist—whether everyone has as his or her own *ultimate* goal or end only his or her own happiness/well-being. And others have weighed in on questions relating to alleged implicit bias. But while the philosopher can offer help by way of carefully defining important distinctions,[2] the ultimate answer to such questions seems to outstrip philosophical expertise. I'm not just making the point that philosophers might have difficulty answering the relevant questions. When I talk about an investigation outstripping philosophical expertise, I'm making the point that there is nothing in a philosophical education that makes the philosopher *as philosopher* particularly qualified to answer such questions.

The analog of metaethical questions in the philosophy of mind *are* paradigmatically philosophical. They include such questions as: What is it for a person to be in a mental state?; What is it for a person to have a belief that P (fear that P, hope that P, worry that P, be anxious about P, seem to remember that P)? What is it for a person to introspect? What is it for a person to be in pain (be in a state of pleasure, have an itch, be in a state of euphoria)?

7.1 Meta-Questions in the Philosophy of Mind

We saw that the answers to metaepistemological questions have implications for what questions, if any, in applied epistemology are amenable to philosophical investigation. Similarly, we saw that the answers to questions in meta-rationality and metaethics have implications for what questions in applied rationality and ethics are amenable to philosophical investigation. It should come as no surprise that our views about the nature of mental states have implications for what other sorts of an investigation into the mind can be competently conducted by philosophers.

7.1.1 Phenomenology Again

I've argued earlier that philosophy begins with phenomenology. Without direct awareness of *something*, philosophy (and conscious beings) would be blind. I am directly aware of various sensations, emotions, and thoughts. But in characterizing the objects of direct awareness this way, I might well be accused of begging all sorts of questions. I am directly aware of a visual experience of something being red. I am directly aware of a sensation I describe as pain. That I am directly aware of *something* is, or should be, beyond dispute. But as I have noted earlier, however, we are also usually *conceptualizing* the data of which we are directly aware. I describe the sensation of which I am directly aware as *pain*. We talked earlier about the distinction between determinate properties and the many determinable (more general) properties that those determinate properties ground. There is a metaphysical controversy about whether the mind-independent world exemplifies anything other than perfectly determinate properties. And there is an epistemological controversy over whether we can be directly aware of anything other than perfectly determinate properties.

Even if the world has only perfectly determinate properties, it seems uncontroversial that when we categorize the properties of which we are aware, we *sort* them in such a way that different determinate properties fall within a given category. There are lots of different shades of red and we call all of them (I just *did*) shades of *red*. We also call the various shades of red, colors. And we are about to consider the question of whether we should recognize a distinction between phenomenal color and color as a property of physical objects. Everything said about color applies to what is given to us through other kinds of sensations. And it includes experiences such as pain. There are many different kinds of pain all of which are categorized as pain. And we are here considering the question of whether these properties of pain all fall into the category of non-physical property.

7.1.2 Substance vs Property Dualism

Arguably, one of the most fundamental controversies in the philosophy of mind is that between physicalists and dualists. But there are a number of quite different controversies that need to be distinguished within that controversy. To define clearly the relevant issues we need to settle the question of whether we are arguing about kinds of *things* or kinds of *properties*. So as we ordinarily think about the world around us, we seem to make a distinction between first-level properties and the objects that have such properties. It is complicated because first-level properties can have second-level properties, and second-level properties can have third-level properties, and so on. This apple might be red; red might be darker than pink; being darker than might be a relation that holds only between colors.

Painting with a very broad stroke, *substance* dualists believe that there are (at least) two radically different sorts of entities that have properties (entities that are not themselves properties)—physical objects and non-physical minds. *Property* dualists believe that there are (at least) two radically different kinds of *properties*, physical properties and mental properties. According to the substance dualist, I am not my body nor am I any part of my body. Because of this, the criteria for my survival through time are distinct from the criteria for the survival of my body (or any part of my body) through time. Ryle (1949) famously disparaged the dualist's conception of mind and body as the view that a person is a kind of "ghost" running the physical machine that is the body. The non-physical self "owns" the body it controls. It is affected by some changes in that body, and it, in turn, can cause changes in the body. It is I who raises my hand or who decides to walk down the street. The substance dualist may well agree that in the actual world my fate is causally tied to the fate of my body. Dip my body in a vat of acid and I'm a goner. But that's only because of a nomological (lawful) connection between my body and my self. It is at least *conceivable* that I survive the death of my body, or that I "move" from one body to another.[3]

As I indicated above, property dualists are committed only to the view that it is a mistake to identify certain paradigmatic mental properties with any physical properties. When I feel intense pain, the *immediate* cause of that pain seems to be neural activity (at least that's what we believe). One sort of physicalist thinks that being in pain is the very same thing as the brain undergoing a neural change. While we certainly talk as if pain has various locations in the body (I have a pain in my foot, in my knee, in my back), one prominent physicalist view is that these kinds of pain are all really identifiable with properties of the brain. The knee pain and the back pain must be in *some* sense different, but that difference is supposed to be compatible with both being neural states.

While the "mind/brain" identity theory was once probably the dominant version of physicalism, just as many self-proclaimed physicalists now embrace a version of *functionalism*. On at least one form of functionalism, psychological properties are identified with functional properties. When we attribute a functional property to a thing, we are making an assertion about the thing having a property that itself has certain properties. Consider, for example, a functionalist account of pain. A *crude* version of a functionalist account of pain will identify a creature's being in pain with it being in a state that typically results from damage to the organism and typically produces behavior that is conducive to the repair of such damage.[4] Note that in saying that a creature is in such a state I don't characterize the state in any way other than by describing its causal role. Put in terminology I introduced in Chapter 2, my thought of the property that plays the functional role is often indirect. I think of that property as *whatever* it is that plays a certain role in a causal chain. Some will identify the pain as the property playing the causal role, but that seems to me to be a sloppy way for the functionalist to talk.[5] If the view were plausible (it's not very plausible), one should identify being in pain as being in the state that typically has the relevant cause and typically results in the relevant behavior. But there is nothing to stop the functionalist from introducing a *technical* expression to pick out the state playing the causal role. Often such a state is called the *realizer* of the functional property.

Consider one more analogy that might be useful in explaining the view. Think about your understanding of what your computer is doing when it spell checks a document. If you are anything like I am, you have very little idea of what exactly is happening in the hard drive of the computer as it spell checks a document. Nor do you have much of an idea of how the software is designed to respond to a spell check command. However, you do understand what it is for your computer to be spell checking a document—it's doing whatever it is that results from the spell check command (or from the default setting) and that in turn highlights in some fashion misspelled words. Put another way, you probably *do* understand spell checking in functional terms.

In Chapter 4, we considered and rejected another philosophical take on the use of expressions like "spell check." There we considered the externalist about meaning who would allow that we use something like a functional definite description to pick out the spell-checking process that then becomes the referent of "spell-checking" (a referent that is the meaning of the term, a meaning that is untethered to the definite description that introduced it). Because we argued against this sort of view earlier, I won't repeat the arguments here.

7.1.3 Applying Our Conception of Philosophy to the Philosophy of Mind

In a familiar refrain now, I emphasize that my concern here is not to settle issues in the philosophy of mind. It is rather to underscore what the philosophical questions are, and understand how the answers to those questions will impact the boundary between the philosophical study of the mind and the scientific study of the mind.

7.1.3.1 Conceptual Analysis

We shouldn't even wade into controversies among physicalists and dualists without careful analysis of the concepts invoked in stating the views. Before drawing lines in the sand, both physicalists and their critics obviously need to understand clearly what makes a thing or a property physical. When we are entering a debate about whether all substances (understood as kinds of things that are not properties but that have properties) are physical, the task might not seem that formidable. A thing is physical if it occupies space—if it has a spatial location and stands in spatial relation to other things that similarly occupy space. If I am not physical then I do not occupy space. At least I do not occupy space in the same way that my body occupies space. Putting the distinction *that* way might seem to allow us to dismiss rather easily substance dualism. It seems obvious that when I use the expression "I" to refer to myself I don't hesitate to ascribe spatial location to my self. I'm typing this sentence in my office. I'm in Iowa right now. I was in Mexico a month ago, I traveled quite a bit during the pandemic, and so on. So that settles that. I have spatial properties—I move through space. But, of course, these facts about how we speak and think don't settle much of anything. The substance dualist is going to acknowledge that when I think of myself I think of a complex that includes both a mental self and a body. We can separate the two, and still think that it is odd to attribute spatial location to the mental self.

How do we separate the "two?" Well, one very controversial approach begins again with the phenomenology that is so important to my conception of philosophy. Descartes observed, at least initially, that he could doubt the existence of a great many things. He could make sense of merely dreaming that he is before a fire. He could make sense of being deceived by a very powerful but malevolent being. These hypotheses seemed to him (at least initially) *consistent* with his available evidence. But, he decided, he couldn't coherently doubt his own existence.

Such considerations might give you reason to think that you might not be where you think you are. But that doesn't imply, by itself, that you might not be *anywhere*. Doesn't visual experience, even the experiences of a dream or hallucination bring with it something like a *perspective*, a perspective replete with objects given to one as standing in spatial relations to one another. Still, the "space" in which all of this takes place doesn't have to be "objective" physical space, or so the dualist might argue. The dualist's thesis might be revised to posit a core self whose existence doesn't require occupying any *objective* physical space.

The above issues in the philosophy of mind obviously take one immediately to issues in the philosophy of space and time. We'll now need to think carefully about how we understand what it is to be in space and time. Through the cinematic wonders of Disney, *Marvel* movies and television series have adolescents trying to make sense of a reality that contains many spaces as opposed to just one; many timelines as opposed to just one; many universes as opposed to just one. The need for conceptual analysis takes us from thinking of one kind of thing to thinking of many others. That's the nature of philosophy.

However difficult it is to define a clear distinction between a thing that is physical and a thing that is not, it is even more difficult to define a clear distinction between a property that is physical and a property that is not. One could, of course, define a physical property as one that characterizes a thing that is physical. But the whole point of turning to property dualism is to allow that the very same thing might have both physical and non-physical properties. So the above proposal would hardly be useful. Alternatively, some have tried to define physical properties as those that are recognized by physics—either current physics or some idealized "completed" physics of the future.[6] Attempts to understand the physical in terms of what is recognized by *current* physics seem hopeless. I won't try to predict the development of physics but I would bet a great deal that a hundred, a thousand, or a million years from now the commitments of physics won't look very much like the commitments of contemporary physics. For all I know the physics of the future will be a physics that embraces some form of dualism (consider some of the truly weird hypotheses entertained by contemporary theoretical physics).

In the final analysis, one might well conclude that the debate over whether certain properties are physical or not is not well defined (see Fumerton 2013). But that doesn't mean there aren't genuine philosophical disagreements that need to be resolved. Property "dualists" are perhaps best understood as philosophers who reject various attempts to identify paradigmatic mental properties with properties that self-proclaimed physicalists take to be philosophically unproblematic. We talked above about the mind-brain identity theorist who takes one's being in pain as one's having a brain that is in a certain state. In the "old" days of this discussion, the place-holder for the relevant neural state was "c-fibers firing." But in support of the view that the debate really isn't about the empirical discoveries of current neurological science, *philosophers* never really cared that much about what the relevant brain state is supposed to be. Their rejection of the mind/brain identity theorist's claim was based on the idea of direct acquaintance to which I have already appealed on a number of occasions. We are directly acquainted with the *intrinsic* character of pain. We are not directly acquainted with the intrinsic character of any neural states. Pain isn't a neural state.

To my way of thinking the debate on the mind-brain identity theory hasn't really made much progress since the seminal discussion of the issue by J. J. C. Smart (1959). Smart makes a few remarks about how much less mysterious the world would be if when giving accounts of persons and their mental life we didn't need to posit anything other than complicated biological organisms with brains that have very complicated structures. Physicalists don't need to posit causal connections among radically different sorts of phenomena and their worldview is obviously simpler than is the picture of the world defended by critics of the identity theory. He then pivots quickly to objections to the mind-brain identity theory and offers his replies to those objections. Again, Smart's discussion of these objections is still one of the most comprehensive and sophisticated.

It is interesting that most of Smart's responses to his opponent's objections concede quickly that the *meaning* of terms like "pain" is not equivalent to the meaning of expressions like "c-fibers firing." Because, he thinks, the terms don't have the same meaning, it also follows that the *logic* and *epistemology* of claims about the mind will be different from the logic and epistemology of claims about the brain. But those concessions, he argues, are perfectly compatible with the relevant identity claims. To use one of his own examples, "lightning" doesn't mean "electrical discharge," but, for all that, we can discover that lightning is nothing more than a certain sort of electrical discharge in the sky. "Water" doesn't mean "stuff with molecular structure H_2O," but science tells us that water isn't anything other than hydrogen and oxygen molecules arranged in a certain pattern. And for those more comfortable with the world of D. C. comics, in the story, "Clark Kent" didn't mean the same thing as "Superman" even though, unbeknownst to almost everyone Clark Kent was *identical* with Superman.

As I noted above, we have already had occasion to critically evaluate the *externalist* accounts of meaning and reference that purport to offer one explanation of how there can be informative identity claims of the sort given as examples above. Putnam and Kripke's theories postdated Smart's discussion of the issue, but Smart does seem to rely on something like the distinction we drew earlier between direct and indirect thought. There is one objection to the mind-brain identity theory that Smart clearly thinks is potentially stronger than the others. Here's a paraphrase of the objection Smart considers to his idea that one can identify a yellow after image with a neural state.

> If [someone] S discovers only a posteriori [through experience] that x = y that must be because S "picks out" x via a property x uniquely exemplifies, a property which is different from the property S employs in "picking out" y.
>
> So, if S picks out an after-image X and a brain state Y and doesn't know that the after image X and brain state Y are identical, it's because S has employed a property of the after-image (let's call it a *phenomenal* property P) which is different from the property or properties B employed to single out the brain state. But then while it will make perfectly good sense to identify the after-image X with the brain state Y, we are left with distinct identifying properties A and B (we are left with property dualism). (148–159)

Smart responds to the argument by suggesting that our grasp of the intrinsic character of the yellow after-image, despite what one might initially think, is also indirect. Our understanding of what it is to experience a yellow afterimage, Smart argues, is actually *parasitic* upon our understanding of what it is to experience a yellow object. We think of having a yellow afterimage as being in the sort of state that one is in when a normal person is looking at something yellow. And a state described *that* way might be a neural state. The dualist's response, of course, is that we know perfectly well what *kind* of state that is, and we know what kind of state that is, quite independently of any knowledge we might acquire concerning what is happening in the brain.

Strangely, physicalists today find more plausible the functionalist accounts of at least some mental/psychological states. The direct refutation of functionalism relies again on the idea that at least some mental states are event-like states that have an intrinsic character—*an intrinsic character that makes them the kind of mental states that they are*. And we can know that we are in such states in a way that we can't know complex causal truths— truths, for example, about the causal role something (typically) plays in the survival of an organism. The philosophical debate over functionalism can also be framed as a debate over the plausibility of a functionalist analysis of what it is to be in a mental state. But understood that way, functionalism was never any more plausible than the cruder form of behaviorism that preceded it.

Crude behaviorism (sometimes called logical behaviorism) was a view about how to *understand* claims about mental states. A really crude behaviorist analysis of pain, for example, might suggest that being in pain is just grimacing. But you don't need to be a philosopher to realize that when we say that someone is in pain we are not just saying that they are grimacing. It's not that hard to *disguise* the fact that you are in pain. Professional athletes often make a point of smiling at their opponents after having been victimized by a vicious hit. And what is true of grimacing is true of every other outward manifestation of pain. More sophisticated versions of behaviorism turn to dispositions. One is in pain just when one *would* grimace if one weren't *trying* to disguise the fact that one is in pain and one would respond to the question "Did that hurt?" with "Yes," provided that one *understood* the question and one *wanted* to reveal one's pain. The italicized words emphasize the problem any such view faces. If one's project is to *translate* all talk about mental/psychological state talk into talk about such dispositions one will need to eliminate from one's "translation" all of the terms that are themselves descriptions of "inner" mental life.

In any event when we become aware of some sudden, excruciating pain it is *wildly* implausible to suggest that we become aware of a complex disposition to behave in certain ways. It isn't really any more plausible to suppose that when we become aware of sudden, excruciating pain, we are merely coming to the conclusion that we are responding to some input in a way that results in a certain behavioral output.[7]

I picked pain as my example, precisely because it is so resistant to both behavioral and functionalist analyses. To be clear, I'm not denying that pain *has* a function. It probably plays an important role in our survival. But it is one thing to say that pain *has* a function; quite another to say that it *is* a functional state. The view that the dualist rejects is the view that pain can be *understood* as a functional state. Pain is hardly the only example of a sensation that is very "event-like." Visual, tactile, olfactory, gustatory, auditory, and kinesthetic sensations are all "event-like." They are states that often have a noticeable beginning and end, and where there is also something that it is like to be in the state—a given quality that makes it the state that it is.

As I'll discuss in more detail in the next section, not all of our mental life is like that. Some of our mental life seems to resist any sort of unproblematic introspective access. And some of our more complex mental life might seem to be conceptually entangled with our behavior or dispositions to behave. Think about what is involved in loving someone, being jealous of someone, hating someone, or being annoyed by someone. Even states like belief and desire are sometimes understood in such a way that it seems dubious that we have unproblematic introspective to them. When my wife and I go out for dinner, she spends a *very* long time trying to figure out what she wants to order. And she wouldn't be amused if I impatiently suggest that she just introspect to get the answer she seeks. Many of the plots of a book or movie turn on the slow and difficult discoveries that people make about their emotional love. Scarlet took a very long time (as it turns out *too* long) to realize that she loved, and *had* loved for some time, Rhett.[8] Many people who are intensely jealous of others never do figure out that they are. And when I am asked what I believe about various philosophical matters, it often takes me quite a while to figure out how to accurately describe my view, a description that is often highly fallible.

Are states that resist introspective access more amenable to behavioral or functional analysis? Probably not. They *are* more amenable to treatment as dispositions. Arguably, you only love someone when you would react in various ways to that person under various conditions. You would miss them if they were absent for a long time, you would be upset if they were upset (or you thought they were upset), you would be happy if they were happy (or you thought they were happy), and so on. But the critical dispositions are at least partly dispositions to respond in certain ways to various beliefs with other *mental* states, states that themselves resist behavioral or functional analyses.

Again, my intention here is not to settle longstanding controversies about the correct analyses of mental states. *If* some version of functionalism were correct, it would be an empirical question as to what features of a person realize the relevant functional states. *If* the content externalism discussed in Chapter 4 were correct, it would be an empirical question as to what we are talking about when we describe the mental states of people. My point here is only to apply my criteria for what counts as philosophy proper to the philosophy of mind. If property dualism is correct, we cannot define paradigmatic occurrent mental states. And if more complex mental states involve dispositions to be in certain paradigmatic occurrent mental states, the philosophical project ends with the analysis of the relevant dispositions.

On the view I take to be correct, is there any role for neurology, cognitive science, or psychology to play in the philosophy of mind? Not much of a role. I suppose one might think that certain versions of the mind/brain identity theory could be *falsified* by empirical research. If a physicalist can't even find a kind of neural state that is the constant correlate of pain, for example, that physicalist might start worrying about identifying being in pain with being in a certain kind of neural state.[9] That's one of the reasons some physicalists moved to a version of functionalism. But it isn't really an empirical worry that motivated the move. It was thought experiments that are the stock and trade of philosophical argument. Lewis (1980) talked to us about the *possibility* of Martian pain. He asked us to imagine a creature who didn't have the kind of brain we have—a brain that responds to tissue damage and initiates pain-averse—but who nevertheless felt pain. He was confident that you could make sense of such a creature and that this should convince you that the traditional sort of physicalism that identifies pain with a brain state has a problem. Lewis was pushing for a version of functionalism. If one identifies being in pain with being in a kind of state that plays a certain functional role, we can imagine that what plays the causal role varies from creature to creature (perhaps even varies among individuals within a species). The dualist is fully on board with the intelligibility of Martian pain, but that is because the dualist thinks pain is a certain kind of sensation, a sensation that might be caused in different ways in different creatures.

It should go without saying that one won't assign to the philosopher the task of figuring out what *causes* pain. Nor is it within the province of philosophy to figure out how creatures capable of feeling pain evolved. These are fascinating questions. But on my view, they aren't philosophical questions.

7.2 Inappropriate Philosophical Intrusion into Empirical Matters

Throughout this book, I have been emphasizing the need to guard against misplaced intrusion by the empirical sciences into debates that are philosophical. This might be a place to acknowledge that the intrusions go both ways. I'll talk a bit more about this in the next chapter. But in the philosophical tradition, it does seem to me that philosophers have sometimes been overly ambitious when it comes to the scope of truths that can be discovered employing philosophical method.

I have suggested a number of times now that philosophy begins with phenomenology. There simply is no alternative to adopting a first-person perspective on all knowledge of everything. I have further argued that the foundations of knowledge include what can be discovered through introspection. But one might well argue that in the history of philosophy many have been overly sanguine about the scope of truths discoverable through introspection.

Above I made a distinction between occurrent "event-like" mental states that are the most plausible candidates for truth-makers with which we are directly acquainted. I also acknowledge that there are psychological states that involve complex dispositions to behave in various ways and to respond in various ways to situations in which one finds oneself. Although the precise understanding of dispositions is difficult, and an important part of philosophy proper, knowledge of truths describing dispositions often outstrips the competence of philosophers. Consider some simple examples. Our psychological makeup includes what are sometimes described as character traits. We describe some people as kind, cowardly, courageous, perceptive, generous, selfless, narcissistic, jealous, humble, unassuming, and also as having or lacking self-knowledge. Given the epistemology I have defended, it should come as no surprise that I don't see why philosophers would be particularly good at discovering which of these traits *other* people have. We certainly don't have direct access to the inner psychological life of others. But do we even have direct, introspective access to our own psychological character? Probably not.

Am I courageous? I hope so, but I don't really know. I'm one of those privileged, lucky people who have lived a life in which I never faced any dangers that called for anything like heroic action. I have never fought in a war. I have never faced someone trying to use force to rob me. I have never had to defend a loved one from an aggressor. I might still be brave in the sense that I *would* respond in the right sort of way to these challenges, but that is hardly something that can be settled through introspection.[10] To be sure I can imagine myself in various situations and fantasize about how I might respond. But it is not clear what evidential force one's fantasy life has.

I gave what I take to be a particularly plausible example that illustrates the point I'm trying to make. But most of the character traits on the list above seem to me quite like courage. Am I kind? The words of Frank Baum's Wizard of Oz strike me as containing more than a grain of truth: A heart is not judged by how much you love, but by how much you are loved by others. Am I sometimes jealous of the achievements of others? I don't *think* so, but, again, I'm inclined to concede that people are probably capable of great self-deception. I would bet a lot of money that certain people I know *are* jealous of others in various ways, but I'm also fairly sure that they don't believe that they are. If others are capable of self-deception, shouldn't I allow that I can be as well? I won't say much about the other negative character traits on the list and my beliefs about which of those I do or don't exhibit—it's probably not a good idea for others to get too much insight into my character (even if my views about that character are fallible).

There are other psychological states that aren't as obviously dispositional, but which might still resist introspective discovery. In discussing direct acquaintance, I pointed out that the ability to notice aspects of one's sensory experience might be a skill, one that is difficult to acquire.

I argued that painters *develop* the ability to notice the subtly different shades and hues of color that change with the time of day and the place of an object relative to the light. But the same is true of *every* sense modality. We are bombarded with an enormously complex range of sensation every moment of our lives, and while it might be *possible* to develop the ability to become directly acquainted with the complex intrinsic character of that experience, it is not as simple as engaging in "casual" introspection.

I talked about my wife and the agonizing decision-making that is almost always part of her deciding what to order from the restaurant's menu. But we are all like that in various respects. Many traditional philosophers have been far too sanguine in supposing that we have direct, unproblematic access to what we *want* in life. But in part that's because desires, wants, and values, at least in *one* sense, lend themselves to dispositional analysis. At least sometimes when we ask ourselves if we want X, we are asking ourselves if getting X would please us or make us happy. And introspection by itself isn't going to give you the answer to that question.

Philosophers have also sometimes supposed that each of us has unproblematic introspective access to what we believe. Here again the issue is complicated. As I noted earlier, it certainly seems to me that if I am asked what I believe about some complex matter, it takes me a while to figure out the correct answer. And I don't believe that I'm always just thinking about the best way to *describe* my belief. It does sometimes *seem* that we are at least in a special sort of "authoritative" position with respect to our belief states. After I decide that I do believe that P, doesn't that settle the issue? Perhaps. But in conversations with others, I often find myself saying (perhaps somewhat obnoxiously) "You don't really believe that." And I usually try to follow up the comment with some consequence of what the person professed to believe that they obviously don't accept, a realization that I expect will alter their assessment of what they believe.[11]

The above issue is complicated by the distinction we discussed in Chapter 2 between *occurrent* beliefs from *unconscious* or *dispositional* beliefs. The expression "dispositional" belief is also potentially confusing. Those who think that there are dispositional beliefs will often distinguish a dispositional belief from a disposition to believe. You have a disposition to believe something x (in one sense) just when you would believe x were you to consider it.[12] But as we had occasion to note earlier, we will also attribute beliefs to people who are not currently considering the claim about which they are supposed to have beliefs. My colleague Greg believes that logicism is true. My colleague Diane believes that Moore was right about intrinsic value. My colleague Asha believes that we need to reform the way in which we care for others in our society. I assert all of these claims about my colleagues' beliefs, but I know that it is very unlikely that any of those colleagues are currently (at this *very* moment) considering the relevant issues about which I say they have beliefs.

It is not clear to me what an unconscious belief is, but we *might* go full Freudian and consider the idea that unconscious beliefs are just like occurrent beliefs (assent to claims as you are considering them), but they are *unconscious*. They exist, but they aren't before consciousness—we are not directly aware of them. To exist don't they at least need to have been before consciousness at one time or another? Maybe. But it is not clear to me that even this is so. Nor is it clear to me that it will be easy to get an unconscious belief before consciousness. Such beliefs might be a bit like that tune you are searching for—the tune that is "stored" somewhere in memory but that is currently eluding your attempts to get it before mind even when it is "on the tip of your tongue."

If we do allow for occurrent but unconscious beliefs, we should obviously do the same for other "intentional" attitudes. Again, *intentional* attitudes are states of mind that are "directed" at some "object." You can't just believe—you must believe *that something is the case*. You can't just desire, you must desire *something* or *that something has been, is, of will be the case*. You can't just fear, you must fear *something*. You can't just be jealous, there must be something of which you are jealous. Again, it may make perfectly good sense to suppose that these sorts of psychological states exist in me even when it is very difficult for me to discover their existence through introspection.[13] If the above is true (it might not be), we would need to embrace the appropriate philosophical modesty. Our rich psychological life might outstrip our ability qua philosopher to access that life through introspection.

Kornblith (2014) has criticized "armchair" philosophical theorizing by claiming that we have empirical evidence from fields such as cognitive science that cast doubt on the reliability of such reasoning. Epistemologists, he argued, have always been interested in discovering what we know and what we justifiably believe. But as we noted in discussing epistemological matters, the question of whether we have justified beliefs in some propositions is often understood in such a way that the answer depends on what we base the relevant belief. There might be perfectly good evidence available to me to reach a given conclusion which, nevertheless, I don't embrace. Or if I do believe the conclusion, I might not believe the conclusion *because* I appreciate the strong evidence that there is in support of the conclusion.

According to Kornblith, there is evidence from psychology and cognitive science that we are largely ignorant of the many influences that causally affect our beliefs. Philosophers have theories about such matters, but the theories tend to be false. We just aren't particularly good at figuring out upon what we base our conclusions. And that's a problem for the epistemologist trying to figure out from the armchair what we are justified in believing.

It seems to me that Kornblith is probably right about the limitations of armchair theorizing as a way of discovering what *causally* contributes to our beliefs. I acknowledged this earlier in this book. Because I think that he is right, I would argue that *qua* philosophers we shouldn't worry about what we know or justifiably believe. In the first instance, we should try to answer for ourselves the metaepistemological questions: What is knowledge? What is justified belief? What is legitimate inferential reasoning?, and so on. If certain forms of internalism are correct, we can then turn to the question of whether there is *propositional* justification for us to believe this or that kind of proposition. Answering that question doesn't have anything to do with the causal influences on our beliefs. After we figure out whether we have or lack justification for believing P, we shouldn't worry anymore, *qua* philosophers, about whether our actual beliefs are caused by our appreciation of the relevant propositional justification. To emphasize a point made earlier, we can, of course, make conditional claims about what we are justified in believing. Once we decide there is propositional justification to believe P, and we settle on an account of basing, we can claim that if we base our belief that P appropriately on the propositional justification there is to believe P, then we would have a justified belief that P.

Kornblith's criticism of armchair philosophy isn't confined to the issues discussed above. More generally, he is skeptical about the armchair philosopher's ability to figure out (from the armchair) the answers to metaquestions. And that's because introspection doesn't tell us all that much about the nature of our concepts. He gives as one example the suggestion that it was a discovery of psychology/cognitive science that prototype theory gives us a better story that does traditional philosophy about the ordinary concepts we deploy. Very crudely prototype theory rejects as naïve the traditional philosophers search for conditions that are individually necessary and jointly sufficient for the application of a concept. The correct theory of concept possession is much more complicated. There are various features of a thing that count toward the thing falling under a concept. There are features of the thing that tell against it falling under the concept. The things that count for concept application, however, come in varying degrees of strength. Something counting strongly *for* this being an X can outweigh a number of "weaker" considerations *against* the thing's being X. And the absence of that strong condition in favor of the thing's being X can be compensated for by the presence of a great many weaker considerations that also count for the thing's being X.

Prototype theory has a great deal of plausibility. Kornblith describes it as an empirical discovery of cognitive science, but it is not clear to me that a philosopher who embraces my conception of philosophical analysis couldn't have arrived at precisely the conclusion under consideration. Wittgenstein convinced many that the meaning of many, or even most, terms should be understood in terms of the metaphor of family resemblance. What do all games have in common, he famously asked? Hard to say. Competition? Perhaps, if understood broadly enough, but solitaire is a very odd sort of competition. Activity designed to bring about pleasure? No that obviously won't do. Sex can sometimes involve playing games, but it needn't. And golf is a game even though many golfers are nearly driven to madness by the way in which it defies mastery. But just as the large family contains members who resemble each other (albeit in different ways), so also the things we call games resemble each other in various ways.

It's also not clear that one couldn't put prototype theory in the language of necessary and sufficient conditions. One might try something with the form: a is X just when either a is F, G, H, and I, or when it is not-F, but G, H, I, J, and K, or when it is .... And one goes on as long as one pleases. The fact that I end with ..., however, might be an implicit concession that the concept is, in Wittgensteinian language "open textured." I might understand that there will always be borderline cases of a sort I haven't considered where the question of whether that thing is X will seem more like a *decision* than a discovery.

Much more would need to be said about the similarities and differences among "traditional" understanding of concept possession and "prototypical" understanding of concept possession. My intent here is only to say enough that it becomes plausible that whatever insights are contained in prototype theory are precisely the sorts of insights that can be discovered through the thought experiments that are the stock and trade of armchair philosophy.

7.3 Summary

We sorted through a number of questions that arise in the philosophy of mind. Our point, once again, was not to decide those controversies, but to sort questions into those that fall within philosophy proper, and those that do not. A common theme in Part II of this book is that it is only after one settles various meta-controversies that we are in a position to decide what other questions fall within the purview of philosophy to answer.

Notes

1 Philosophers might have introspective access to their own mental states, but that access doesn't distinguish philosophers from anyone else.
2 So, for example, in thinking about egoistic conceptions of human nature we need to think about what it means to say of someone that he or she has X as an ultimate goal or end. If we define that in terms of what one desires as an end, we'll end up in philosophy of mind trying to answer philosophical questions about what it is to desire something.
3 Grist for the plots of many television shows and movies. And, of course, many a religion is built around the possibility of a life after the death of the body.
4 See Lewis (1980) for one clear and colorful presentation of the view.
5 See Kim (1998) for careful distinctions among the different versions of functionalism.

6 See Hempel (1969) for an argument that such an attempt isn't plausible.
7 The functionalist can certainly argue that there is a state that plays the functional role, and that that state is introspectively accessible. But to know that one is in pain one would need to know that the state one introspects does, in fact, play the functional role. And that is something one couldn't introspect.
8 As everyone my age knows, the reference is to *Gone with the Wind*.
9 So Bickle (1992) seems to think that the fate of an identity theory lies with finding a kind of physical activity that is common to all of the organisms to which we attribute pain. The fact that such a search seems Quixotic is one of the reasons many physicalists turned to functionalism.
10 See Dummett's (1978) discussion of this issue.
11 The alternative is to suppose that I am just trying to get you to accept a conclusion about what you *should* believe.
12 There is a technical problem with this. If you are in a deep coma, this definition might suggest that you have a disposition to believe that you are not in a deep coma! After all, if you were to consider the question of whether you are in a deep coma (something you won't do if you are in a deep coma), you would believe that you are not in a deep coma.
13 There is a serious problem concerning the philosophical analysis of such states. For one thing the "object" of some intentional states might be something that doesn't exist, and many philosophers are loathe to admit that there *are* objects that don't *exist*. I might fear hell even if there is no hell; I might want world peace even if there is no world peace, I might be jealous of my sister's being more successful than I am even if she isn't. I have discussed such matters in considerable detail elsewhere (2013).

Chapter 8

Philosophy of Science and Metaphysics

It takes a lot of nerve to suggest that philosophy of mind can be done through introspection, armchair conceptual analysis, and *a priori* discovery of synthetic necessary connections. But it takes even more nerve to suggest that philosophy of science and metaphysics is conceptually distinct from empirical investigation.

As I pointed out in the introduction to this book, early philosophers didn't seem to think that philosophy was distinct from at least theoretical science. The ancient philosophers' search for the types of things that make up all other things often looked very much like the theoretical physicist's search for the ultimate categories of entities out of which the universe is built.

Still, it is worth noting that even when philosophers were suggesting that the simple constituents of reality were water, earth, heat, and cold they did describe what they were doing as **meta**physics. But this understanding of philosophy as "above" or "about" physics might have been a way of distinguishing very theoretical empirical questions in physics from more applied questions in physics, a distinction physicists still make today.

In what follows I'll start with questions that arise in the philosophy of science. I'll then briefly discuss the way in which philosophy of science inevitably merges with epistemology and more general metaphysics.

8.1 Philosophy of Science—An Older Paradigm

So what are paradigmatic philosophical questions that arise in the philosophy of science? Not surprisingly, it depends on whom you ask. There has been a significant shift in the focus of the field in the last century or two. In the analytic tradition, the older, and I believe the more *philosophical*, questions in the philosophy of science include the following:

What is science?
What is causation?
What are the conditions of adequacy for a correct scientific explanation?

What is the relationship between being able to explain and being able to predict?

What is a law of nature? More generally, what *are* lawful regularities (universal or statistical)?

What is time? Or, perhaps better, what is it for one state of the world to be before, concurrent with, or after another state of the world?

What is space? Or, perhaps better, what is it for one object to stand in a spatial relationship to another?

Is there an important metaphysical distinction between theoretical entities and observational entities?

This last question is but one in a host of epistemological questions closely related to it.

What counts as evidence in support of the claim that one thing causes another?

What counts as evidence in support of the claim that E is the best explanation of O?

What counts as evidence that some generalization describes a universal or probabilistic law?

How do we know truths about temporal or spatial relations?

If there is an important distinction between theoretical claims and observational claims, how do the latter support the former?

8.2 Causation and Explanation

Again, it may sound a bit strange to suggest, but it seems to me that answering the *above* questions requires very little background in *science*. To be sure, a philosopher trying to figure out what makes it the case that one thing causes another will often start by thinking about *examples* of causation. When Newtonian physics was on a high, it was natural enough that such examples would involve action and reaction. Hume often thought about one billiard ball's striking another and causing it to move. In considering such examples it might also be natural to wonder, as Hume did, whether spatial and temporal contiguity (one thing's coming into physical contact with another and occurring just before the other) are necessary conditions for causation. But Newtonians were already worried about gravitational attraction and how to accommodate *that* sort of causal connection—a kind of causal connection that doesn't *obviously* involve spatial contiguity. And since many philosophers of science were also dualists, the idea of causal connection didn't easily come together with the idea of physical contact. Indeed, the paradigm of causal connection for many of the early modern philosophers was the *mind* controlling the motions of the body.[1] But in any event, attempts to get clear about the *concept* of causation don't stand or fall only on *actual* examples of causal connection. If one can make *sense* of telekinetic power one realizes that one doesn't require spatial contiguity for causal connection.

Thought experiments might also cast doubt on the idea that X is the direct cause of Y only if X occurred just prior to Y.[2] We *seem* to be able to make sense of time travel and in *some* sense of time the time traveler's actions in the present cause that person to appear in the past.[3] All sorts of fiction (think of the witches in *Macbeth* or the boy in *The Rocking Horse Winner*) seem to rely on our ability to understand premonition. And the most natural understanding of veridical premonition seems to involve a future state of the world causing a present experience (the premonition). It's not clear how stable our thought experiments are on such matters, but their *apparent* intelligibility is enough to cast initial doubt on philosophical analyses of causation that require a cause to be prior to its effects.

On one very natural understanding of *explanation*, one explains some phenomenon Y by identifying the *cause* of X.[4] On this sort of view, understanding explanation takes us right back to understanding causation. One of the most famous models of scientific explanation was Hempel's *Deductive-Nomological* model of explanation. Roughly, when offering an explanation, one begins by describing some phenomenon C (the *explanandum*) that one is trying to explain. A correct *complete* explanation consists of statements describing *antecedent* conditions A and *laws of nature* L such that (A and L) entails C.[5] There is the following potential connection between the D-N model of explanation and the idea that to find an explanation is to find the cause of what one is trying to explain.

One of Hume's most dramatic contributions to philosophy was his regularity theory of causation. Struggling to find relations among *particular* events with which he could plausibly identify the causal relation, Hume finally decided that causation is nothing over and above certain regularities in nature.[6]

While the idea behind Hume's regularity theory was attractive to many empiricists,[7] the devil is always in the details. At least some regularities don't seem to be the right *sort* of regularities to back a *causal* claim. Let us suppose that from now until the end of time it will be true that whenever a match is struck someone dies somewhere shortly thereafter. We don't want to conclude on that basis alone that a match's being struck is the cause of that person's dying. Or to use a well-worn example, it might be true that whenever a barometer falls dramatically there will be a storm shortly thereafter. Again, it doesn't follow that the barometer's falling *caused* the storm. The example involving matches suggests that we need to make a distinction between lawful regularities and regularities that are mere accidents of history (to use the terminology developed by philosophers of science). The example involving the fall of the barometer and the storm isn't one of an "accidental" regularity, but it suggests that even among non-accidental regularities we will need to make a distinction between *causal* lawful regularities and other sorts of non-accidental regularities. But at this point, we might well wonder whether we need a *prior* understanding of causal connection in order to get an understanding of a causal law.[8]

In thinking about causation and explanation, it is important to distinguish Humean *regularity* theories from what we might call *generality* theories. On Hempel's Deductive-Nomological model of explanation, we can't offer a *complete* explanation of anything without an appeal to general laws. While Hempel himself was sympathetic to the general idea that we can understand laws in terms of regularities, a philosopher who rejects that idea might still be sympathetic with the claim that explanations involve both an appeal to antecedent conditions and an appeal to lawful regularities. Again, as we saw above, we will probably need to find a way to distinguish causal laws from other sorts of lawful regularities.

Hempel, of course, was well aware that ordinary (commonplace) explanations fall short of what he called complete explanations. He acknowledged that often (perhaps almost always) we succeed only in identifying some *part* of the cause of the phenomenon we are trying to explain.[9] Mackie (1965) offered a quite technical account of the idea. On his view, X causes Y when X is an INUS condition for Y. X is an INUS condition for Y when X is by itself lawfully Insufficient for Y but is a Necessary part of some complex condition C which, though Unnecessary for Y, is lawfully Sufficient for Y. The view needs further qualifications to deal with counterexamples (see Fumerton and Kress 2001), but the basic idea seems more or less right. The storm caused the power in my house to go off. It is not a law that whenever there is a storm there is a loss of power in my house, but the storm is presumably a part of some (very complex) set of conditions that is lawfully connected to the relevant loss of power. Historical explanations (of revolutions, inflation, the stock market going up, the stock market going down, etc.) are even more obvious examples of explanations that *at best* find some part of the complete causal explanation of the relevant explananda.[10]

There are a huge number of INUS conditions for everything that happens and there are many rough and ready criteria we employ in our decisions about what we call *the* or, even, *a* cause of something that happens. We emphasize change rather than standing conditions—though both are causally relevant to the outcome, we say that the striking of the match causes the match to light; we don't say that the presence of oxygen is the cause. In legal contexts, evaluative judgments seem to seep into our causal judgments.[11] But for the parents of the murderer, the murderer wouldn't have existed, but for his existence, the murder wouldn't have taken place, but as we ordinarily talk we wouldn't identify the fact that the parents decided to have a kid as the cause of the murder. On the other hand, if the parents tortured the kid until he became insane, we might well point to the parents' behavior as a remote cause of the murder.

The point of this very brief discussion of causation is not to settle long-standing controversies about the nature of causation and explanation. The above discussion no more than scratches the surface of interesting questions that arise concerning causation and explanation. Our point is rather to illustrate the kind of questions in the philosophy of science that admit of philosophical analysis—the kind of questions that philosophers can answer. On most views, one has no *a priori* or introspective access to what causes what, or to the correctness of scientific explanations. On the view of philosophy I defend, these latter questions do not fall within the purview of philosophy. By contrast, *modal* questions about causation and explanation *are* philosophical questions. Once I get clear about what causation and explanation are, I can ask and answer the philosophical question of whether it is conceptually *necessary* that everything has a cause or that everything has an explanation. That *is* a philosophical question. If I ask whether it is conceptually *possible* for matter and energy to pop into existence through a "big bang," I am asking a philosophical question. If I ask whether it is conceptually *possible* for a sequence of sounds made by a cat to destroy the universe, I am asking a philosophical question.

Conceptual necessity and possibility are, of course, quite distinct from lawful necessity and possibility, and those in turn are distinct from a much vaguer kind of modality that presupposes all sorts of background conditions. So it is conceptually possible (I think) for something to pop into existence without a cause. Something is lawfully possible, in one sense, if it is consistent with the laws of nature. Something is lawfully possible, in *another* sense, if it is consistent with the laws of nature and a complete description of antecedent conditions. By contrast, there are claims about what is *epistemically* necessary and *epistemically* possible. On a first try, we might say that something is epistemically necessary if it is entailed by what we know, and epistemically possible if it is not epistemically necessary. That's not quite right, at least if we want to allow that I can think without contradiction that certain necessary falsehoods are epistemically possible *for me* (they might be too complicated for me to realize that they are necessarily false). A necessary falsehood is (trivially) inconsistent with anything I know.

As we noted earlier, it is not universally admitted that we lack epistemologically direct access to causal connections. Some of the early modern philosophers thought that a paradigm of causation is the control our mind exercises over bodily motion, and that we can be directly aware of our exercising such control. C. J. Ducasse apparently tried to convince his students that they were directly aware of causation by smashing a vase with a hammer.[12] As they saw the vase break, he asked rhetorically if they were not immediately aware of the hammer's breaking the vase (where breaking just is the exercise of a causal power). Generality theorists would be unimpressed. With Hume they would argue that the "sense" of an inevitable breaking of the vase is just the habituation of the mind to project outcomes based on past experience. Certainly, it seems that we can *conceive* of the vase not breaking when it was struck. We can imagine living in a world in which objects about to be struck vanish into thin air only to reappear after the danger of destruction passed. But again, the point here is not to settle this controversy. It is, rather, to note that if there were causal connections or causal laws that could be discovered through introspection or direct awareness, then there would be some causal and explanatory claims that fall within the purview of philosophy. By contrast, if such views are false, philosophers (qua philosophers) aren't in the business of discovering causal explanations.

8.3 Space and Time

In our passing comment about time travel, we had occasion to note that there may be more than one concept of time. An old-fashioned relational theory of time (sometimes called the B-theory of time) holds that our concept of time is built up out of our ideas of temporal *relations*. We seem to have the idea of *simultaneity*, and of one thing happening *before* or *after* another thing. The simple idea of temporal relations might have its source in our direct awareness of two experiences being simultaneous, or in one experience occurring before or after another experience.[13] In any event, however, we got the ideas, the relational theory argues that those ideas are the conceptual building blocks of all concepts of time. When we try to make sense of something like time travel, we are thinking of the time traveler's experiences "in the past" to which he traveled as still experiences that *in some sense* followed the pre-time-travel experiences. But because it's supposed to be time *travel*, we are also thinking of the traveler as moving to a temporal part of the world that existed before the events of entering the time machine.

The task of analyzing all temporal concepts into complex claims about temporal relations is more than a bit intimidating. The American Civil War began in 1860. It is not exactly easy to translate that assertion into propositions describing nothing but temporal relations among various events. And remember that I can know what the relevant date is even if I don't know much about American history.

The idea of a relational theory of space follows the alleged insight of a relational theory of time. We can think of spatial relations and we might hope that we can build our understanding of space out of these ideas of spatial relations. But again the devil is in the details, and it is more than a bit difficult to carry out the "translation."

If we embrace relational theories of time and space, we still need to get as clear as we can be about the relata of the relevant relations. To be sure, we can talk about one event taking place before or after another event, but on this approach, we still need to get clear about what an event is. Easy enough? Not really. To take a well-worn example, is Oedipus's killing the king of Thebes the same or a different event from Oedipus's killing his father (in the myth his father was the king)? Is my playing the piano yesterday the same or a different event from my playing "As Time Goes By" on the piano yesterday (when that's the tune I played)? And are the aforementioned events the same or different events from my waking up the neighbor (by playing the piano too loudly)?[14]

A relational theory of time is usually thought of as an alternative to a so-called *absolutist* theory of time. Crudely, the absolutist thinks of time as a kind of container in which events occur. But on this view of time, one might think that there are temporal points (along a temporal continuum) analogous to the spatial points along the continuum that constitutes a line. And these temporal points might be thought of as existing before or after other temporal points. One might suppose that one should build all conceptions of time out of the simple notions of one point in time being prior to or after another point in time.

Exactly analogous distinctions can be made with respect to relational theories of space. Any such theory needs an account of the relata of spatial relations. An absolutist about space also thinks of space as a "container" that can be empty or occupied by various fields and objects. But the absolutist might also allow that the most primitive spatial idea is the idea of one point in space standing in various spatial relations to other points in space. With that concept of a point, one can, perhaps, understand lines, intersecting lines, angles, enclosed space, and synthetic necessary connections among spatial relationships (essentially the truths of geometry).

The above are nothing but sketches of the *kind* of philosophical analyses one might explore about the *meaning* of claims about time and space. But this way of approaching philosophical questions about space and time is probably viewed as hopelessly out of date. Many would argue that empirical research has shown that space and time are not independent of one another. Other research has shown that space is not "Euclidian" and that the "necessary" truths postulated or proved by Euclid are neither necessary nor even true. Even more provocatively, others have argued that empirical research casts doubt on classical logic. Subatomic particles, it is argued, can both be and not be at a given location. The arguments for these views get far too technical to address in this context. The most I can do here is make suggestions about how to push back on this sort of "intrusion" by empirical science into matters philosophical and geometrical.

The more provocative claims about science and logic often seem to rest on a very strong form of verificationism that is wildly implausible. Put crudely, verificationism is a view about the meaning of meaning. The strongest form of verificationism identifies the meaning of a claim about the world with the conditions that would *conclusively* verify it. But it is not clear what could conclusively verify universal claims like the claim that all crows are black. No matter how many crows one observes being black, there is always the possibility that the next crow one runs across will be some other color. In light of this and many other examples, verificationists moved to the slightly weaker claim that meaningful statements should be understood in terms of conditions that would either conclusively verify or conclusively *falsify* the statement. And it became obvious that this in turn needed to be modified in such a way that it applied only to simple statements (statements that were not made by combining those statements with connectives (like "and" or "or").[15] Still weaker forms of verificationism require only that meaningful statements allow for the possibility of *some* degree of confirmation or disconfirmation.

As I suggested, strong verificationist faces all sorts of puzzles. It is an unsurprising fact that the way in which you try to study certain sorts of phenomena affect the very phenomena you are studying. Anthropologists understood this long before theoretical physicists became frustrated by the realization that the way in which they try to measure the location of certain sorts of particles interferes with other aspects of the same particles that they are studying. As I said, anthropologists understood quickly that people you are studying might not behave the way that they usually do when there is someone standing around watching their behavior. (I imagine the phenomenon is even more obvious in "reality" TV that attempts to portray people as they "naturally" behave).

When it comes to so-called alternative geometries, the most obvious question is whether the respective geometries are employing the same concepts—concepts such as straight line or point. Although the issue is much more complicated than I'm making it sound here, it *might* turn out that it is *lawfully* impossible for anything to travel in a Euclidean straight line. Light, for example, might always travel in a Euclidean curved line. If that were true and you were in the grips of a primitive form of verificationism, you might start toying with the idea that space itself is "curved" (from a Euclidean point of view). You might also start talking as if Euclidean geometry doesn't "apply" to our world.

No one has a monopoly on how one can use language. And for certain purposes, it may be useful to redefine such expressions as "straight line." But if one does, one shouldn't suppose that the geometry one constructs using these redefined expressions is inconsistent with Euclidean geometry. Alternative geometries are geometries that understand the fundamental expressions of geometry differently from the way in which Euclid understood those expressions.

8.4 Epistemology and the Philosophy of Science

The questions we discussed above in this chapter have been *metaphysical* questions in the philosophy of science. They take the form: What is

X? (What is causation?; What is lawful connection; What is an explanation?; What is space?; and What is time?)

There is another kind of metaphysical question that has played a prominent role in the history of philosophy of science, but it is a metaphysical question that arises out of *epistemological* controversies. At least some philosophers of science draw a contrast between what is *observable* and what is *theoretical*. Once that distinction is in place, questions arise concerning how to *understand* theoretical claims in science. But before we turn to those questions we need to think more carefully about this distinction between the observable and the theoretical.

8.4.1 Is There a Distinction between the Observable and the Theoretical?

I have already discussed some of the main philosophical questions that define epistemology. One of those questions concerns the structure of justification. I argued that one can understand that controversy as one concerning the correct *analysis* of justification. The dominant view in the history of philosophy was foundationalism. On that view, we *understand* inferential justification in terms of noninferential justification. The basic idea is that a belief is justified when it is either noninferentially justified or can be legitimately inferred from what is noninferentially justified.

While philosophers of science were always interested in epistemological issues as they relate to *scientific* hypotheses, many of them were not that interested in *traditional* epistemological problems. In the context of science, they took as relatively unproblematic knowledge about ordinary physical objects based on sense experience. I can observe that there is a rectangular object in front of me, that there is a tree in my backyard, and that there is a car in my driveway. This knowledge based on observation was often contrasted with claims about micro-entities, fields, and forces—the kind of claims that might be inferable from what can be observed, but were not themselves directly observable.

Not surprisingly, when the distinction is drawn *that* way, at least some prominent philosophers of science argued against the existence of any *sharp* distinction between the observable and the theoretical. In what is still a classic attempt to reject the distinction, Maxwell (1962) described hypothetical situations in which what was first taken to be theoretical was later observed. He correctly pointed out that seeing with the naked eye, seeing with the aid of glasses, seeing through a microscope or telescope, seeing with the aid of an electron microscope, and seeing with the aid of a cloud chamber, all seem to fall along a continuum. It would surely be more than a bit capricious to deny observable knowledge of physical objects to those whose vision is aided by contact lenses.

In the same spirit as Maxwell's critique of the observation/theoretical distinction, many philosophers of science embraced a *holistic* view of justification.[16] But that view is essentially just a coherence theory of justification. The famous Quine/Duhem thesis[17] became almost unchallenged. That view is that any hypothesis can be saved if one is willing to make enough adjustments to one's auxiliary hypotheses. I think that there is a tree in my yard. Why? Because I seem to see one. But if I don't want to accept the hypothesis that the tree is there, I can adjust my "background" beliefs. I can reject the presupposition that I am sane, that I am awake, that I am not suffering alien-induced hallucination. My "innocent" tree hypotheses are starting to look a bit more like scientific theories that are always held against a vast array of background presuppositions, presuppositions that can be modified in the light of what would otherwise be unproblematic observational evidence.

In a *footnote* to his attempt to dismantle the observation/theoretical distinction, Maxwell does interestingly concede that it might actually be easier to defend a sharp line between *direct* knowledge of subjective appearance (or sense data) and *indirect* knowledge of all other empirical truths. But in that same footnote, he suggested that such a view is so divorced from commonsense that few would take it seriously. It would put on the *theoretical* side of the distinction, rocks, trees, toasters, and mountains.[18] Certainly, this way of talking would have little connection to the way in which *philosophers of science* worried about the problem of theoretical entities. Later in his career, however, Maxwell (1978) decided that the possibility briefly suggested in his footnote was actually the right view. And in that, I think, he was completely correct. But to *defend* that conclusion one needs to answer fundamental philosophical questions in epistemology.

Science is often contrasted with religion, gossip, fantasy, and wishful thinking (to list just a few spurious ways of forming beliefs). Though the conclusion might sound a bit strange, I would argue that in most meta-epistemological theories, there is nothing special about scientific reasoning.[19] The kinds of inference that needs to be employed in reaching justified beliefs about God, afterlives, electrons, quarks, black holes, and the behavior of light, are precisely the same kinds of reasoning needed to form justified beliefs about trees, the color and shape of objects, and facts about world history. Does that imply that those without a scientific background are just as well-positioned to adjudicate scientific theories as those who have the relevant background? Of course not. But the difference lies in the evidence base available to those pursuing scientific theories. That is not to suggest that there is no distinction between fallacious and legitimate reasoning. Nor is it to ignore the critical distinction between reasoning from true premises and reasoning from false premises. But scientists sometimes reason badly and often rely on premises that turn out to be false.

The above claim is often obscured by the fact that it is easy to confuse the nature of one's *reasoning* with the nature of one's *evidence*. So one might initially suppose that through scientific knowledge one discovers the legitimacy of inferences not available to the ordinary person. The vast majority of people are unable to infer the acidity of a solution from the fact that litmus paper turned red in the solution. The vast majority of people are unable to infer that someone has pneumonia from streaks that appear on an x-ray of that person's lungs. Most are unable to infer the existence of quarks from data generated by "smashing" atoms. But on one plausible *metaepistemological* view, it is simply a mistake to suppose that there is any legitimate reasoning that takes one from a premise describing the color of the litmus paper to a conclusion about the acidity of the solution. But as we noted earlier in our discussion of epistemology, the *inference* is from what we know about the color of the litmus paper *together with a huge body of background information* to a conclusion about the acidity of the solution. And the same is true of the other examples sketched above.

Put another way, descriptions of our reasoning are almost always enthymematic. Consider again, the example I have used earlier. I come home, see that the lock on my door is broken, and discover that a great many of my valuables are missing. I conclude that I have been robbed. But even with an example this simple, it is clear that I rely on complex (but unsated) background information to reach my conclusion. I know that valuables don't periodically disappear *in nihilo*, that it isn't an accepted custom around here for neighbors to borrow my stuff by breaking into my house when I am not there, and so on.

None of this is an argument for a coherence theory of justification—it is rather an argument that our conscious and unconscious thought processes are enormously complex. Indeed, it takes a great deal of philosophical work to uncover the premises needed to infer justifiably a given conclusion. And that work is potentially extremely important, for it is often only after that work is done that we are in a *position* to assess whether our reasoning is legitimate or not. Experts in a field of inquiry almost always have at their disposal premises that non-experts lack. But that is, of course, consistent with my claim that there is nothing special about the *reasoning* employed in scientific research.

8.4.2 *How to Understand the Theoretical*

Philosophers who drew a distinction between the observable and the theoretical also engaged in a considerable debate about how to understand theoretical claims. Some (*reductionists*) argued that with enough ingenuity one could simply translate claims about theoretical entities into complex claims about observable entities and the way in which they would behave under certain observable conditions. On such a view, the supposition that A exercises gravitational pull upon B would be understood as a supposition about how B would move in the presence of A (holding constant a wide range of other factors). Others (*fictionalists*) argue that at least some talk about theoretical entities is best understood as a kind of convenient fiction that helps us make predictions (think about the tinker toy displays of molecular structures that you probably had hanging from your high-school science classroom ceiling). Still others (*scientific realists*) thought that you should take the sentences employed in making theoretical claims at face value. If the statements are true then the subject terms of such statements refer, and the predicate expressions pick out properties that are attributed to the subject. To be sure, the kinds of things and their properties might only be inferable from what can be known directly, and the realist then faces the epistemological task of explaining what the relevant inferences are and why they are legitimate.

8.5 From Philosophy of Science to Traditional Metaphysics

As we noted above, if traditional foundationalism is correct, and all we ultimately have as available foundational evidence is what we know about subjective experience, then the theoretical includes commonplace claims about physical objects. And sure enough, all of the positions in the philosophy of science referred to above have counterparts outside of what is normally called philosophy of science. So worried about how to "bridge" the gap between subjective appearance and mind-independent objective reality, idealists and phenomenalists tried to reduce thought about the physical world to complex thought about sensations.[20] Fictionalists took claims about physical objects to be convenient ways of pretending that objects continue to exist unexperienced. And the most common view is realism, the view that thought about physical objects is to be taken at face value—thought about entities that exist and whose character must be inferred somehow from what we know about the appearances they are taken to cause.

I haven't argued for any specific view here. But I have argued that to address important questions in the philosophy of science, one needs to address more fundamental questions in epistemology and metaphysics.[21] To decide whether there is a sharp line between what can be observed directly and what is theoretical one needs to decide *classic* controversies in metaepistemology. One also needs to answer those questions in order to figure out where the line is most plausibly drawn.

Depending on where the line is drawn we may discover that there isn't really such a gulf between the exotic theoretical posits of theoretical physics and the mundane objects we take to be relatively unproblematic. The difference might lie in the fact that we are all familiar with the appearances we associate with ordinary objects. By contrast, many are unfamiliar with the various appearances that result from the use of exotic instruments employed in the study of science. On one way of thinking, this is precisely what gives rise to Eddington's famous puzzle about the "two" tables. About these tables Eddington begins his (1929) book by saying:

> One of them has been familiar to me from earliest years. It is a commonplace object of that environment which I call the world. How shall I describe it? It has extension; it is comparatively permanent; it is coloured; above all it is *substantial*. By substantial I do not merely mean that it does not collapse when I lean upon it; I mean that it is constituted of "substance" and by that word I am trying to convey to you some conception of its intrinsic nature. It is a *thing*; not like space, which is a mere negation; nor like time, which is — Heaven knows what! But that will not help you to my meaning because it is the distinctive characteristic of a "thing" to have this substantiality, and I do not think substantiality can be described better than by saying that it is the kind of nature exemplified by an ordinary table. And so we go round in circles. After all if you are a plain commonsense man, not too much worried with scientific scruples, you will be confident that you understand the nature of an ordinary table. I have even heard of plain men who had the idea that they could better understand the mystery of their own nature if scientists would discover a way of explaining it in terms of the easily comprehensible nature of a table.
>
> Table no. 2 is my scientific table. It is a more recent acquaintance and I do not feel so familiar with it. It does not belong to the world previously mentioned—that world which spontaneously appears around me when I open my eyes, though how much of it is objective and how much subjective I do not here consider. It is part of a world that in more devious ways has forced itself on my attention. My scientific table is mostly emptiness. Sparsely scattered in that emptiness are numerous electric charges rushing about with great speed, but their combined bulk amounts to less than a billionth of the bulk of the table itself. Notwithstanding its strange construction, it turns out to be an entirely efficient table. It supports my writing paper as satisfactorily as table No. 1; for when I lay the paper on it the little electric particles with their headlong speed keep on hitting the underside, so that the paper is maintained in shuttlecock fashion at a nearly steady level. If I lean upon this table I shall not go through; or, to be strictly accurate, the chance of my scientific elbow going through my scientific table is so excessively small that it can be neglected in practical life. Reviewing their properties one by one, there seems to be nothing to choose between the two tables for ordinary purposes; but when abnormal circumstances befall, then my scientific table shows to advantage. If the house catches fire my scientific table will dissolve quite naturally into scientific

smoke, whereas my familiar table undergoes a metamorphosis of its substantial nature which I can only regard as miraculous.

There is nothing *substantial* about my second table. It is nearly all empty space ...

Eddington's puzzle recognizes what should be the obvious fact that we think of the causes of various appearances in quite different ways. That same mind-independent cause of the appearances we associate with objects that are solid, still, smooth-surfaced, and colored seems to be capable of playing a causal role in producing experiences of a radically different sort, experiences as of tiny particles, spatially separated, and in rapid motion. Some philosophers seem to want to know (or at least form a justified belief) about what those objects are like in terms of their *intrinsic* nature. *Whether* one can discover such truths, or even *think* of properties other than those associated with appearances has been and will always remain a matter of considerable philosophical dispute. Hume poetically suggested the limitations of thought in the following famous passage from his *Treatise* (1888, Book I, Part 2, Sec. 6):

> Let us fix our attention out of ourselves as much as possible; let us chace our imagination to the heavens or the utmost limits of the universe; we never really advance a step beyond ourselves nor can conceive of any kind of existence but those perceptions, that have appeared in that narrow compass.

In trying to get clear about thoughts fundamental to the philosophy of science we are led inexorably to more fundamental questions in metaphysics. But the points of contact between philosophy of science and general metaphysics go far beyond epistemological and metaphysical controversies concerning the distinction between what is observational and what is theoretical. One of the most ancient controversies in metaphysics concerns the existence and nature of properties. One can develop the relevant questions in a number of different ways. One can start with the linguistic distinction between subject terms and predicate expressions. I single something out and say of it that it is red. Indeed, I say (and think) of a number of different things that they are red. What do these different things have in common in virtue of which it is appropriate to describe all of them as red?

We are not about to answer that question here. There are all sorts of different answers proposed by philosophers. The least plausible (almost comically ineffective) answer to the question is called *linguistic nominalism*. The simplest version of that view is that what makes red things red is that we use the word "red" to describe such things. Of course, given the egocentric conception of philosophy I am defending, I would need to put the view in terms of the idea that what the red things have in common is just that *I* use the word "red" to describe just those things. But no one would stop with this linguistic data (even if that is where we *start*). I'd want to figure out in virtue of what I call the red things "red." The linguistic disposition is hardly capricious. We need to figure out what grounds the relevant linguistic dispositions.

So some version of mind-independent reality about properties seems inescapable. Realists (as the term has come to be used) think that there is some entity—the universal *redness*—that all the red things have in common in virtue of which they are red.[22] Property nominalists hope that they can distinguish *this* redness (e.g. the redness of that balloon) from *that* redness (the redness of that apple), but try to give some account of what these different instances of red all have in common in virtue of which that they are instances of *redness*. Some think in terms of relations of similarity between different "particular" properties or between the different properties and some paradigm, or, alternatively, some common relation that the different instances of red have to some paradigmatic *thought* of redness. All such accounts are left with the question of how to understand similarity, or how to understand the relevant "fit" between a thought and these mind-independent features of reality.[23]

But why would someone interested in the fundamental questions that arise in the philosophy of science be driven to explore metaphysical questions about the nature of properties? One reason is that plausible views about the nature of causation and the nature of lawful connection force one to think about properties. If we are trying to understand causation, we need to think about the relata of causal connection. In developing his then revolutionary regularity theory of causation Hume sometimes talked about "objects" standing in causal connection. But he made clear (1888, Book I, Part III, sec. xv) that on his view it is really something's having a property that causes that thing or another thing to have a different property. But as we saw earlier, it will be critical for anyone trying to understand causation in terms of regularity to distinguish lawful regularities from other regularities. As we also discussed, even within the class of lawful regularities it might also be necessary to distinguish causal laws from other laws. Armstrong (1983) famously argued that one should try to understand lawful regularities in terms of relations between properties, and he correctly concluded that to explore such a view he needed a satisfactory account of properties.[24] If one embraces realism about properties, one might also have a solution to the problem of what would make true laws that seem to have no instances. Newton asserts that bodies in motion on which no forces are acting will continue in motion. But it is not clear that there are any bodies on which no forces are acting. Physicists will also talk about what would happen to a body whose body temperature reaches absolute zero. But it is not clear that there are any such objects. Still, one can wonder whether the relevant laws might be made true by relations among properties—at least one can consider such a view if one becomes convinced that properties can exist even if nothing ever has the relevant properties.

8.6 Summary

I haven't argued for very many specific *answers* to questions that define the philosophy of science. I gave examples of what I take the relevant questions to be, and I have argued that one can't evaluate questions that arise in the philosophy of science without also addressing classic philosophical questions that arise in both metaphysics and epistemology.

The question about whether there is a sharp clear line between what is observable and what is theoretical, for example, is really best understood as the traditional epistemological controversy over whether foundationalism is true If some things can be known directly, while others are knowable only through inference, then *that* is where to law the pivotal epistemological line about which philosophers of science were arguing. If one defines foundational knowledge in such a way that it ends up restricted to the world of the mind and abstract entities like properties, we might quickly reach the (perhaps surprising) conclusion that the familiar objects about which we talk and think *all* fall on the side of the theoretical. It is no easy task to understand such claims in such a way that one will be able to avoid skepticism.

It is worth reminding ourselves here of the conclusions we reached in Chapter 4. I argued against the direct reference theory of names for individuals and kinds. But I did leave open the possibility of "Russelling" such theories. It may well be that my grasp of a technical expression from science is radically indirect. I may mean by "quark" only "that kind of thing called 'quark' by somebody else whose use of that expression is ultimately responsible for my own." But it is also important to stress that the person to whom I defer when I use the term might also have thought about quarks only indirectly. That person who introduced the term into the language might have done so using definite descriptions, albeit not definite descriptions that describe the use of language by others. That would make my use of the term *doubly* indirect. I indirectly think of quarks by thinking about the use of language by others who are also thinking of quarks only indirectly.

Qua philosopher I can uncover the above truths through thought experiments. I can't figure out from the armchair who got the linguistic ball rolling. Nor can I figure out what description that person used in an attempt to introduce a technical term into our vocabulary. Even more obviously, I can't figure out from the armchair what kind of thing, if any, was originally picked out in that attempt at reference. It is entirely possible that no one will ever be in a position to discover the *intrinsic* character of anything to which one has only indirect access. What counts as the discovery that a certain kind of thing exists might be only the discovery that there is a common potential cause of vastly many appearances many of which the scientist produces in the context of scientific experimentation.

I'm at best quasi-literate with respect to science. It should go without saying that I can't begin any sort of philosophizing concerning the meaning of terms of which I am wholly ignorant. There are all kinds of expressions introduced in technical sciences with which I am completely unfamiliar. Trivially, I can't even "Russell" *those* expressions—I don't know what they are. But I do know how to go about "Russelling" their meaning for me once I run across them. Still, deferring to the use of a term by others presupposes that somewhere down the line somebody successfully introduced a term into the language. There is the question of what the terms mean as used by those people and there are questions concerning whether or not that term successfully refers. Unless one knows how the term was introduced one isn't in a position to answer either of those questions. In that sense, there are questions about meanings that a philosopher of science can raise only if that philosopher knows science. But that doesn't suggest that there are *kinds* of expressions that arise in philosophy of science that have a *kind* of meaning that we haven't already addressed. It is precisely for that reason that I'm inclined to stand by my claim that to do philosophy of science proper one doesn't need to know much about science.

Notes

1 Berkeley (1713) went so far as to take it as axiomatic that matter (stuff that isn't mind) is causally inert. The irony is that the paradigm eventually shifted from one in which mental causation is understood best to one in which mental causation was "mysterious" and needed to be explained in terms of physical phenomena.
2 It is important to emphasize the "direct." Certainly, as we ordinarily talk, the cause of something's happening might lie in the more distant past. It's not easy to define precisely the relevant notion of priority. On one view, X is just prior to Y when the last moment of X is immediately followed by the first moment of Y (with no moments in between). But it is also tempting to think that time is infinitely divisible and the idea of two successive moments in time with no moments in between might be problematic.
3 This all gets complicated. Perhaps to understand time travel we need to distinguish at least two concepts of time—objective time (in which the time traveler moves backward) and subjective time (in which each of the time traveler's experiences follow an earlier experience). See Lewis (1976). For a clear, accessible, and interesting argument against the intelligibility of time travel, see Huemer's blog on *Fake Nous*, June, 2022.
4 See Scriven (1962).
5 Hempel (1965) always insisted that there was an intimate connection between being able to explain and being able to predict—his symmetry thesis. Certainly, when has the complete explanation of some phenomenon E, had one possessed the relevant knowledge in advance one would have been able to

predict that E would occur. For reasons discussed below, it doesn't seem that the connection goes in the other direction. The behavior of the barometer allows us to predict the storm, but the change in the barometer doesn't explain the storm. Hempel also applies his model of explanation to the explanation of laws. One explains laws at one level of generality by deducing those laws from laws at a more abstract level (often together with descriptions of facts). So Kepler's laws can be deduced from Newton's laws (together with very complex descriptions of the sun, the planets, and relations between them).

6 It's actually a bit more complicated than this. Hume seemed to offer his readers a choice between the regularity theory of causation and a few that defines causal claims as describing the "determination" of the mind to expect certain things to happen when it has certain experiences. He doesn't really like either definition acknowledging that the regularity theory will seem to leave out an idea of necessary connection that people associate with causation, and that the psychological theory will have the absurd consequence that the existence of causal connection is dependent on conscious beings. The two definitions are as follows:

   1 An object precedent and contiguous to another, and where all objects resembling the former are placed in like relations of precedence and contiguity to objects resembling the latter.
   2 An object precedent and contiguous to another, and so united with it that the idea of the one determines the mind to form the idea of the other, and the impression of the one to form a more lively idea of the other (1888, 31).

7 Mill (1906) was clearly influenced by Hume.
8 See again Davidson (1967).
9 He also allowed for probabilistic explanation. Such explanations differ from D-N explanations in virtue of the fact that the laws to which one appeals are probabilistic, and the relation between the explanans and explanandum is one of making probable.
10 At best. The experts' "explanations" of daily fluctuations in the stock market seem almost comically ad hoc (e.g. today "people" are worried about inflation; tomorrow "they" aren't so worried any more). Anscombe (1993) argued that we can make perfectly good sense of causation in an indeterministic universe and that it is a mistake to suppose that causation presupposes underlying *general* laws.
11 So, this discussion of causation is critical to understanding the notion of proximate cause that is so important to assigning responsibility, particularly in civil law. Some (see Moore 2009) try to avoid the idea that the relevant notion of proximate cause is heavily laden with value judgments.
12 See Ducasse (1969). See also Madden and Harre (1973).
13 Again, this would presuppose that direct awareness can have as its object an expanse of time.
14 There is an enormous literature on the nature of events. I would recommend Kim (1976) and Chisholm (1970). An excellent anthology on events is Casati and Varsi (1996).
15 Consider the obviously intelligible claim that the number of people alive today is even while it is also true that no one has had, has now, or ever will have any reason to believe that this claim is true. See Geach (1957).
16 See Fodor and Lepore (1992) for a sympathetic discussion of holism.
17 See Quine (1969), 80–81.

18 See Stoljar (2001) for a sophisticated discussion of the ways in which we might think of claims about the physical world.
19 See Fumerton (2017).
20 Berkeley (1713) was one of the most famous idealists. In his more swashbuckling moments, he seemed to suggest that we can identify physical objects with "congeries" of sensations (he called them ideas). In his more careful moments, he seemed to identify objects that are independent of the experiences of finite beings either as "archetypical" ideas in the mind of God or as hypothetical facts about what sensations a being would have were they to have others. This last view is the basic idea behind phenomenalism. Mill (1874) identified physical objects with what he called "permanent possibilities of sensations." In the twentieth century, Ayer (1952) sketched a similar view. C. I. Lewis (1946) developed what I still think is the most careful statement of the view. Chisholm (1948) gave what some take to be a devastating argument against phenomenalism, and there aren't very many self-proclaimed phenomenalists left. Both C. I. Lewis (1948) and Firth (1950), however, try to respond to Chisholm's argument.
21 It is important to stress that I am not arguing that to do science (e.g. to discover causal explanations and lawful regularity) one needs to address fundamental questions in epistemology and metaphysics. The claim is one about the philosophy of science. Scientists, at least scientists dealing with more practical issues, don't need to do philosophy of science, metaphysics or epistemology any more than plumbers need to grapple with fundamental issues in metaphysics or epistemology. More theoretical physics, on the other hand, tends to bring one into close contact with fundamental issues in philosophy.
22 Some realists believe that the relevant universal exists whether or not anything actually is red. As we note below, properties understood that way might be particularly useful for those who need to find truthmakers for uninstantiated laws (e.g. laws governing the behavior of bodies on which no other forces are acting; laws governing the behavior of bodies at absolute zero.
23 See Russell (1967) and Fumerton (2002 and 2006a) for two quite different attempts to explain the notion of "fit."
24 Armstrong (1978 and 1989) was a realist about properties. He thought that were universals, but he denied that universal could exist if it never had, has, or will be exemplified. So, he still has work to do when it comes to finding truthmakers for laws that have no instances.

Chapter 9

The Relevance of Philosophy Proper

In Part I of this book, I tried to explain how I think of philosophy *proper*. Many will find the account I give far too restrictive. Some will describe my view as a not very subtle attempt to justify a conception of philosophy that allows me to ask the questions I want to ask and to answer the questions the way I want to answer them. I did carve out the history of philosophy as an important part of philosophy, but one that is distinct from philosophy proper. And I distinguished philosophy proper from all sorts of applied philosophy—philosophical questions that require empirical input to answer. *I have stressed that one can always turn a question that seems to require empirical input to answer into one that doesn't by embedding the empirical claims in the antecedent of a conditional.*

Knowing conditional truths is, of course, potentially valuable.[1] Once one knows that if P then Q, one is *in a position* to know that Q provided that one can discover that P. The conditionals that one can discover in fields like ethics and political philosophy, for example, are decidedly complex, but realizing that is important. It is a way of avoiding corrosive dogmatism when it comes to taking positions on the ethical and political debates that divide people in this country. Most controversies are controversies precisely because it is really *hard* to figure out the truth. Understanding how complex many questions are should lead to a healthy epistemic modesty.

In characterizing philosophy proper, I have in *no way* denigrated what we might call applied philosophy. As I have tried to make clear throughout, and as I will summarize below, the meta-questions that define philosophy proper are important to address when coming to grips with the applied questions that in many cases are the questions we are most interested in answering. But just because you want the answer to a given question doesn't mean that you qua philosopher will be positioned to get that answer. Indeed, it doesn't mean that anyone is particularly well positioned to get the relevant answer.

In what follows I'll try to address a number of goals one might try to achieve by engaging in philosophy of proper.

DOI: 10.4324/9781003223566-11

9.1 Intellectual Curiosity

Why would someone be interested in doing the kind of philosophy I have characterized in this book? Well, why do *I* find the questions that define philosophy proper interesting? The most obvious answer is that I am trying to satisfy intellectual curiosity. One certainly doesn't need to ask or answer philosophical questions. Even if *ideal* inquiry into other subjects requires one to answer philosophical questions, one doesn't need to engage in what I am calling ideal inquiry.

I acknowledged in Chapter 1 that it is not obvious that one needs to answer meta-questions in order to navigate the world. I think that there are genuine and fascinating questions about the nature of perception and the ontological and epistemic relations a conscious being can have to a mind-independent physical world, the nature of causation, and the nature or rationality and morality (to take a few examples). But it would be almost comical to suggest that I should carefully screen the plumbers, carpenters, electricians, and automobile mechanics that I hire for their philosophical acumen. Paraphrasing an earlier quote, Hume might well be right when he speculated that with respect to successfully navigating the world, "nature" has thought the matter far too important to let success depend on figuring out the answers to philosophical questions. Put in more contemporary terms, we have probably evolved in such a way that we react to a host of conscious and unconscious stimuli with beliefs and behavior that are advantageous to our survival. The beliefs don't need to satisfy a philosopher's conception of being rational to accomplish the goal. They don't even need to be true.[2]

We are animals among other animals. But we are also obviously creatures who have a very special ability to wonder about how to make sense of the world about which we think and talk. Consider again something as simple as the way in which we think about color. Color terms are among the first units of language we started to use. Big Bird taught little kids the differences among various colors. But Big Bird didn't comment much about the fact that our idea of color is obviously compatible with the apparent color of a thing changing *dramatically* depending on the subjects who have such experiences and their environment. Indeed, it is obvious *upon reflection* that someone doesn't understand color expressions the way I do unless they do grasp the way in which appearance varies in such ways. Once I think about such matters, it might well occur to me to wonder what the "real" color of an object is. I might start wondering how I could ever know what the real color of a physical object is. I might even start to wonder whether physical objects have color at all. Read Berkeley's *Three Dialogues Between Hylas and Philonous* and the kinds of questions you raise about color will also emerge when you think about other properties that we attribute to physical objects. It's not just the nature of color experience that varies dramatically depending on circumstances.

So when I think about these matters I might be confused. I don't like being confused. I want to get clear about just how I understand the way in which I describe the world around me. I casually throw into the discussion a distinction between how things are in themselves and how they appear, but when I start thinking about that distinction, I might well get more confused. And I might get even more confused when I try to get clear about the way in which I distinguish a thing from its properties. I can turn my attention away from the questions I start to ask. Again, I don't *need* to do philosophy. But if I can't get myself to stop asking the questions, I'll stay confused until I figure out the answer to such questions, figure out that there is something wrong with the way in which I am asking the questions, or, perhaps, figure out why I'll never be able to get an answer to the questions. Again, I don't like being confused. So I do philosophy.[3]

I illustrated the kind of intellectual curiosity I want satisfied by looking at the problems associated with perception and the physical world. But similar questions give rise to philosophical puzzlement in all of the major areas of philosophy. I start thinking about questions about how to explain some phenomenon I find interesting. I ask about what causes what and I realize that if the world is at all as I think it is, causally relevant states of the world proliferate both at and through time. Now I'm puzzled about what I might be looking for when I look for *the* cause of something I'm trying to explain. I start thinking about the great, often bitter, debates about the morality and rationality of various actions and I try to understand why it is often so very difficult to figure out what I ought to do. That will inevitably lead an intellectually curious person to think about the content of such thought—I'll need to think about what I'm asking when I ask whether I ought to take this action rather than that.

9.2 Positioning Oneself Better to Answer Applied Questions

I talked about how easily intellectual curiosity might lead one to address fundamental philosophical questions from the first-person perspective. But I worry that I am making philosophy sound too much like a crossword puzzle or today's wordle puzzle. If you are interested in these sorts of puzzles you can get addicted to solving them as well. You look forward to the next puzzle and won't give up until you figure out how to solve the puzzle. It would certainly be nice if philosophy had more to offer than a cure for puzzlement. And it does—far more.

Above, I emphasized some of the grander, more abstract philosophical questions which might grab one's attention. I acknowledged that one can probably get through life successfully without addressing many of those questions. But I'm still convinced that one cannot approach in an ideal way many of the more practical questions that concern us unless one comes equipped with an answer to the "What is ..." questions that partially define philosophy.

As I write this chapter, the always simmering controversies about abortion are back on the front burner. The U.S. Supreme Court has just overturned *Roe v Wade* and individual states are going to be arguing strenuously about what their laws concerning abortion should be. But group decisions are defined in terms of some facts about individual decisions.[4] My first conclusion should be about what policies I ought to support. As I indicated earlier, asking that question will lead me to think about the nature of rationality and morality. But there are a host of other *philosophical* questions that really should be addressed before one even considers arguments for or against various laws. If one even glances at the heated rhetorical exchanges on social media, one realizes that one better think long and hard about what it means to be a person if one is going to address the pro-life stance that abortion involves the killing of a person. One probably needs to think about the fascinating fundamental questions concerning the survival of a person through time.

Upon reflection, it seems obvious to me that *neither* side is going to get anywhere by starting with premises asserting either that a fetus is or that a fetus is not a person. As we noted earlier in this book, there are a host of terms that are disguised normative or legal expressions. To repeat an earlier example, the distinction between killing a living thing and murdering that thing is surely a distinction about whether the killing was morally or legally permissible. The question about moral permissibility seems much more fundamental than the question about legal permissibility given that most of us will describe wrongful killing as murder (say the heinous killing of Jews by Nazis) whether or not the law permitted such killing. But the term "person" carries with it similar implications. In describing some being as a person, I am probably asserting that the being deserves considerations of a sort that other beings don't. If I conclude that artificial intelligence becomes so sophisticated that it makes choices, is capable of evaluating actions, understands what it is doing, and so on, I'll give that entity the status of a person.[5] But given that "person" is used with evaluative meaning, one begs fundamental questions when one says of a fetus (at any stage of development) that it is or isn't a person. Whatever the principles are about which the two sides of the debate disagree, it isn't the principle that one should treat fetuses the way fetuses should be treated![6]

Consider another example of a contemporary controversy. There are a number of questions that arise concerning what rights transgender people ought to have. Some of those controversies, for example, concern the rights such people have to compete in various sports. It should go without saying that one needs to define clearly the terms of such debates in order to discuss sensibly the relevant issues. And it isn't easy to define the relevant notion of gender. Without a clear understanding of the content of various views, one gets the feeling that participants to the debate are just thrashing around often talking at cross purposes. I may not mean the same thing as someone else by "gender," but I can't even formulate clearly my own thoughts about the controversies without getting clear in my own mind about how I understand the relevant terms.

Ethical and legal controversies concerning if, when, and how wars should be fought, if, when, and how torture should be used to extract information, if when and how humans should be given or denied extraordinary measures to preserve their lives, all really do benefit from careful thought about the underlying questions concerning how to understand claims about rights and obligations. Philosophy is, in a sense, dangerous. Once you start asking philosophical questions you run the risk of coming up with the wrong answers. And those incorrect philosophical positions can lead to false conclusions about what we ought to do. Deontologists in ethics think that consequentialists have false views about what makes right actions right. A consequentialist will have a very difficult time avoiding the conclusion that there are *circumstances* in which one ought to steal, torture, kill innocent people, or let people drown—in short engage in all sorts of choices that may initially shock most people. By contrast, at least some deontologists are willing to allow no end of mayhem to occur in order to live by exceptionless moral principles. Although the underlying philosophical positions are usually not articulated clearly by people without a philosophical background, you can see traces of those views emerge in the arguments we have with each other about various critical controversies. And I can't help but think that we would be better off if we brought the underlying philosophical views to the fore. In any event, I know that once *I* start thinking about the controversies, I can't think clearly about them until I get clear in my own mind about the terms of the debate. I also often soon come to the conclusion that the issues are controversial precisely because once the questions are understood clearly it becomes obvious that there is no obvious answer to them. Answering the questions involves empirical information that just isn't available to me (or, for that matter, to anyone else).

In Chapter 4, I argued that it may well be true that from the first-person perspective my understanding of some terms is in terms of definite descriptions that attempt to make reference to the successful use of the term by others. I also noted that it can't be the case that all meaning is "parasitic" in this way. If there is any successful reference, *someone* needs to language in a way that doesn't require the successful use of language by others. It doesn't seem to me that my use of expressions describing my experience and the ordinary objects around me has built into it the sort of indirectness that involves "borrowing" meanings from others. As I argued earlier in the book, even if I am not "taking" meaningful terms from others, I might still think of a host of things only in terms of whatever it is that affects me in certain ways, and I did characterize that thought as indirect. But it isn't indirect in the sense that it employs descriptions of others and how they use expressions. Philosophical puzzles arise concerning the meaning of familiar expressions like "red," "round," "belief," "pain," "perception" (and the various verbs that describe the different modes of perception), "good," "right," "cause," "obligation," "is" (the "is" we use to make assertions about the identity of things at and through time), and a host of other expressions I use (usually) without any philosophical reflection. But as I argued, the meaningful use of such expressions is entirely compatible with my not being clear about just how I am using the terms (about what the semantic rules are that I'm following when using the expressions).

If all that is true of the commonplace terms we all use unreflectively, how much more likely is it to be true of those technical terms professionals introduce in their fields of study? I can speak with knowledge about philosophy. Someone who hasn't studied philosophy is unlikely to be familiar with philosophical terms of art such as "verificationism," "empiricism," "rationalism," "nomological generalization," "content internalism," "epistemic internalism," "property realism," "nominalism," "naturalism," "functionalism," "non-cognitivism," "representative realism," "naïve realism," "direct realism," "phenomenalism" "utilitarianism," and "deontology" (to name just a few expressions). One might suppose that because such expressions are often introduced to make precise the terms of various debates that such expressions would typically be clearly understood by those who make free use of them. But that isn't true. As we saw earlier, self-proclaimed functionalists end up arguing with each other about how to understand the meaning of the term they have introduced. Self-proclaimed naturalists struggle long and hard to explain what they mean by "naturalism." As we noted earlier, it is notoriously difficult to even define the debate between property dualists and property monists—it is not at all easy to get clear, even in one's own mind, about what it might mean to describe a property as physical.

A good philosopher soon realizes how difficult it is to define in a clear, meaningful way philosophical questions. It is often even more difficult trying to answer the questions once they are clearly defined. Is there any reason to suppose that things are better in the more theoretical parts of fields like physics, biology, psychology, history, sociology, economics, political science, and law. I know enough about law to know that concepts fundamental to legal claims are used in ways that are not easy to define. In Chapter 7 I called attention to the crucial role that the concept of proximate cause plays in assigning legal responsibility for harm. One needs an understanding of that concept if one wants to arrive at reasoned verdicts in civil cases. I know enough about political science and economics to know that in those fields it is critical that one has a clear understanding of causation and explanation. And I know just enough about most of the other disciplines I mentioned to realize that it isn't easy to *define* the controversies about which those in the disciplines argue. Without a clear understanding of what is at dispute, people will often be talking at cross-purposes.

I've written more about metaepistemology than any other field in philosophy. There is certainly a sense in which almost all disputes lead to epistemology. If one makes any sort of claim, particularly a claim that is controversial, the discussion will quickly lead to the question of what reason one can offer in support of one's claim. And if I'm right, that question will ultimately lead to fundamental questions about what counts as evidence for what. Questions about the legitimacy of various forms of reasoning will in turn lead to metaepistemological questions concerning the very concept of epistemic rationality. The internalism/externalism controversies in epistemology are not just abstract philosophical debates about how to understand justified belief and knowledge. They raise questions that need to be answered if we are to position ourselves well to address disagreement about what counts as evidence for what. Again, it *may* be that when we understand clearly the metaepistemological questions we might find that we can't find an intellectually satisfying answer to those questions. But even if that turned out to be true, that is still a kind of progress.

9.3 For *Whom* Is This Book Written

In Part I of this book I defended a radically egocentric approach to how to understand fundamental philosophical questions. I realize that throughout the book I acknowledge the arguments of others, I talk about the historical influences of important figures in the history of philosophy, and I talk about what *we* would say about this and that. I could have written the entire book in the style of a Cartesian meditation. I could have carefully qualified all references only to what I seem to remember people saying, or what I believe people would agree to if there are other people. But that style of writing would get tiresome quickly. I do take for granted without argument all sorts of commonplace assumptions about the world, the past, and other people. In arguing that my philosophical conclusions are compatible with even very radical skeptical scenarios (fantastic worlds in which there is no physical world, there is no distant past, there are no other minds) I should emphasize one last time that I am not operating on the assumption that we *are* in any of the skeptical scenarios.

Thinking about skeptical scenarios is just a way of trying to isolate what is essential to satisfying philosophical curiosity. I'm not crazy[7]—I don't believe that I have consciously or unconsciously created in my imagination a complex world of other philosophers with whom I have interacted. I am subjectively confident that I have learned a great deal from others, that I have influenced others, and that the way in which I use language is not idiosyncratic. If I were a genuine solipsist—if I really thought that I was the only conscious being, I might still write (or seem to write) a book like this as a way of getting clear about what I think. I suppose, however, I wouldn't worry that much about getting it published.

I said above that I am subjectively confident that other people use language the same way that I do. If I figure out the semantic rules I follow when using the expressions that puzzle me, I think that others might be persuaded that that's how they understand the critical terms as well. But I don't want to overstate this presupposition. If the world is as I think it is there is the obvious fact that there is apparent widespread disagreement among philosophers on almost all of the fundamental issues that interest philosophers. And there is a really interesting literature on the epistemic significance of the existence of such disagreement. In that literature, it is usually stipulated that the philosophers with whom we disagree are just as smart as we are, have read the same research, are unbiased (or if they are biased are no more biased than others). They are our epistemic peers.

The epistemic significance of disagreement is not, of course, a subject that is limited to the field of philosophy. There is widespread disagreement on the more theoretical issues that arise in virtually every academic field of inquiry. This is not the place to address the question of what you should infer from the fact that intelligent and informed people seem to disagree with you. But I do want to stress the fact that there is literally no alternative to investigating truth from the first-person perspective. It is obviously not the mere existence of disagreement that would be relevant to what I am justified in believing. It is only the *justification* I have for thinking (correctly or incorrectly) that there are peers who disagree with me.

I've taken the extreme position that I can find answers to the fundamental philosophical questions that interest me even if I were in one of the skeptical scenarios that fascinated epistemologists for so long. There is a closely related view that many would find more plausible. That is the view that I can be justified in believing that I have correct answers to the philosophical questions that interest me even if I were in one of those skeptical scenarios. This view is no less (and no more) plausible than is epistemic internalism. The internalist, you will recall, is committed to the view that all of the justification available to one at a given time supervenes (depends solely) on one's internal (mental) life at that time. On this view, I could still embrace a number of metaphilosophical views that I have previously rejected in this book. I could even think that a claim about what knowledge is, for example, is a claim about how most people use the word "know." Or I could think a claim about what knowledge is is an empirical claim about what is denoted by some "reference-fixing" definite description. In my attempt to arrive at answers to questions understood that way, I could still "from the armchair" (or from the position of a brain in a vat, or of a victim of demonic machination) arrive at justified answers. To repeat, if epistemic internalism and content internalism are true, the justification for all of my beliefs depends solely on mental states that would exist even were the skeptical scenarios true.

Again, this is not my view. I argue for the more extreme position that my philosophical conclusions can be not only justified, but be true even were I in the skeptical scenarios discussed. Ask yourself the following conditional question. Would you be able to continue your attempt to answer philosophical questions even if you were to become convinced that you were in one of the skeptical scenarios? Would you be able to "live the examined life" that is the philosophical life even if you were to come to the conclusion that you are the only conscious being to exist? Some might scoff at the idea that one can reach a conclusion about what is possible in hypothetical situations so bizarre. I don't. The philosophical issues that interest me are controversies that I can explore even if I were to become a solipsist—even if I were to reach the decidedly odd conclusion that I am the only person alive.[8]

Notes

1. It should be acknowledged that to be valuable the conditionals shouldn't be *trivial*. It is true that if P then P. But knowing that isn't going to help anyone discover that P. It is true that if P and Q then P. And knowing that isn't going to help anyone discover that P. The more trivial and more obvious the connection is between the antecedent (the part following the "if") and the consequent (the part following the "then,") the less interesting the conditional will be.
2. To take a familiar example, most people respond with fear to snakes. Arguably, they have an instinctive belief that they are dangerous. Most snakes aren't dangerous, but some are very dangerous. It is probably better for human survival that we react the way we do.
3. I'm not suggesting that doing philosophy will end disquieting confusion. Philosophy is hard and one question tends to lead to another. But if one wants to satisfy philosophical curiosity there is no alternative to continuing the philosophical search.
4. So a state decides to do X just when, for example, a majority of its citizens, or a majority of its representatives, or some defined percentage of its individuals decides to do X.
5. Think about the dramatic trial at the end of the movie *Millennial Man*—the point of which was to settle whether the robot had become sophisticated enough to be considered a person. As Locke (1690) pointed out, we may still want to distinguish persons from humans. We can imagine aliens who get the legal status of persons but who might not be humans.
6. As a reviewer pointed out to me, Judy Thompson's (1971) classic defense of abortion is rare in that she *grants* for the sake of argument that a fetus is a person. Nevertheless, she argues, the personhood of a fetus wouldn't preclude a mother's having the moral *right* to kill the fetus if the pregnancy was unplanned (whether or not she *should* exercise that right). Her argument relies on a deontological approach to rights of a sort we discussed earlier in this book.
7. I realize that this is something genuinely crazy people often say.
8. One might think that it would be easier to make the point by asking the reader to consider the somewhat less bizarre possible world in which one is the only surviving conscious being. You could more easily imagine some horrible deadly virus that takes the lives of everyone but you. Could you not while a way your lonely days by continuing to work on philosophical puzzles? The problem is that one could still think that one's philosophical musings are about what the people who used to exist *would* say about this and that. Oddly, ordinary language philosophy of a sort could still be done even if you are the last surviving linguist.

References

Addis, Laird. 1989. *Natural Signs: A Theory of Intentionality.* Philadelphia: Temple University Press.
Addis, Laird. 2008. "Dispositions, Explanations, and Behavior." *Inquiry* 24, no. 1, 205–227.
Alston, William, and Richard Brandt. 1967. *The Problems of Philosophy.* London: Allyn and Bacon.
Alston, William. 1989. *Epistemic Justification.* Ithaca: Cornell University Press.
Anscombe, Elizabeth. 1993. "Causality and Determination." In Ernest Sosa and Michael Tooley, eds., *Causation.* Oxford: Oxford University Press, 88–104.
Armstrong, David. 1963. "Is Introspective Knowledge Incorrigible?" *Philosophical Review* 72, 417–432.
Armstrong, David. 1968. *A Materialist Theory of Mind.* New York: Routledge.
Armstrong, David. 1978. *A Theory of Universals, Volume II.* Cambridge: Cambridge University Press.
Armstrong, David. 1983. *What Is a Law of Nature?* Cambridge: Cambridge University Press.
Armstrong, David. 1989. *Universals: An Opinionated Introduction.* Boulder, CO: Westview Press.
Ayer, A, J. 1952. *Language, Truth and Logic.* New York: Dover.
Bergmann, Gustav. 1964. *Logic and Reality.* Madison: University of Wisconsin Press.
Bergmann, Gustav. 1967. *Realism: A Critique of Brentano and Meinong.* Madison: University of Wisconsin Press.
Berkeley, George. 1713. "Three Dialogues between Hylas and Philonous." In M. R. Ayers, ed., *Philosophical Works: Including the Works on Vision.* Totowa, NJ: Rowman and Littlefield, 1975, 129–207.
Bickle, John. 1992. "Multiple Realizability and Psychophysical Reduction." *Behavior and Philosophy* 20, no. 1, Spring/Summer, 47–58.
Bigelow, John, and Robert Pargetter. 1990. "Acquaintance with Qualia." *Theoria* 61, 129–147.
Boyd, Richard. 1983. "How to Be a Moral Realist." In Geoffrey Sayre-McCord, ed., *Essays on Moral Realism.* Ithaca, NY: Cornell University Press.
Brentano, Franz. 1874. *Psychology from an Empirical Standpoint.* Translated by T. Rancurello, D. Terrell, and L. McAllister. (English translation published by New York: Routledge Press, 1973).

Brink, David. 1989. *Moral Realism and the Foundations of Ethics*. New York: Cambridge University Press.
Broad, C. D. 1925. *The Mind and Its Place in Nature*. London: Routledge & Kegan Paul LTD.
Butchvarov, Panayot. 1982. "That Simple, Indefinable, Nonnatural Property Good." *Review of Metaphysics* 36, 41–75.
Casati, R., and A. C. Varzi, eds. 1996. *Events*. Dartmouth: Aldershot.
Chalmers, David. 1995. "Facing Up to the Problem of Consciousness." *Journal of Consciousness Studies* 2, 200–219.
Chalmers, David. 1996. *The Conscious Mind*. Oxford: Oxford University Press.
Chalmers, David. 2003. "The Matrix as Metaphysics." *Matrix* website (https://consc.net/papers/matrix.html)
Chalmers, David. 2004. "Phenomenal Concepts and the Knowledge Argument." In Peter Ludlow, Yujin Nagasawa, and Daniel Stoljar, eds., *There's Something about Mary: Essays on Phenomenal Consciousness and Frank Jackson's Knowledge Argument*. Denver: Bradford Books, 269–298.
Chisholm, Roderick. 1942. "The Problem of the Speckled Hen." *Mind* 51, 368–373.
Chisholm, Roderick. 1948. "The Problem of Empiricism." *The Journal of Philosophy*, 45, 512–517.
Chisholm, Roderick. 1957. *Perceiving*. Ithaca, NY: Cornell University Press.
Chisholm, Roderick. 1970. "Events and Propositions." *Nous* 4, 15–24.
Chomsky, Noam. 1975. *Aspects of the Theory of Syntax*. Boston, MA: MIT Press.
Churchland, Paul, 1989. "Knowing Qualia: A Reply to Jackson." In *A Neurocomputational Perspective*. Cambridge, MA: MIT Press, 67–76. Reprinted in Peter Ludlow, Yugin Nagasawa, and David Stoljar, eds., *There's Something about Mary*, 163–178. Cambridge, MA: MIT Press.
Cohen, Stewart. 2002. "Basic Knowledge and the Problem of Easy Knowledge." *Philosophy and Phenomenological Research* 65, 309–321.
Conee, Earl. 1994. "Phenomenal Knowledge." *Australasian Journal of Philosophy* 72, 136–150. Reprinted in Peter Ludlow, Yujin Nagasawa, and Daniel Stoljar, eds., *There's Something about Mary: Essays on Phenomenal Consciousness and Frank Jackson's Knowledge Argument*. Cambridge, MA: MIT Press, 2004, 197–215.
Conee, Earl, and Richard Feldman. 1997. "The Generality Problem for Reliabilism." *Philosophical Studies* 89, 1–29.
Conee, Earl, and Richard Feldman. 2001. "Internalism Defended." *American Philosophical Quarterly* 3, no. 1, 1–18.
Cunning, David. 2010. *Argument and Persuasion in Descartes' Meditations*. London: Oxford University Press.
Davidson, Donald. 1967. "Causal Relations." *Journal of Philosophy* 64, no. 21, 691–703.
Dennett, Daniel. 1991. *Consciousness Explained*. New York: Little, Brown.
Donnellan, K. S. 1977. "The Contingent A Priori and Rigid Designators." *Midwest Studies in Philosophy* 2, 12–27.
Dowell, J. L. 2006. "The Physical: Empirical not Metaphysical." *Philosophical Studies* 131(1), 25–60.
Ducasse, C. J. 1969. *Causation and the Types of Necessity*. New York: Dover.

Duerlinger, James. 2013. *Refutation of the Self in Indian Buddhism: Candrakīrti on the Selflessness of Persons*. New York: Routledge.

Dummett, Michael. 1978. *Truth and Other Enigmas*. Cambridge, MA: Harvard University Press.

Eddington, Arthur. 1929. *The Nature of the Physical World*. New York: Macmillan.

Fantl, Jeremy, and Matthew McGrath. 2009. *Knowledge in an Uncertain World*. Oxford: Oxford University Press.

Feldman, Richard. 2004. "The Justification of Introspective Belief." In Earl Conee and Richard Feldman, eds., *Evidentialism*. Oxford: Oxford University Press, 199–218.

Feldman, Richard, and Ted Warfield, eds. 2010. *Disagreement*. Oxford: Oxford University Press.

Firth, Roderick. 1950. "Radical Empiricism and Perceptual Relativity." *Philosophical Review* 59, 164–183.

Firth, Roderick. 1981. "Epistemic Merit, Intrinsic and Instrumental." *The Proceedings and Addresses of The American Philosophical Association* 55, 5–23.

Fodor, Jerry, and Ernest Lepore. 1992. *Holism*. Oxford: Blackwell.

Foley, Richard. 1990. "Fumerton's Puzzle." *Journal of Philosophical Research* 15, 109–113.

Frege, Gottlieb. 1892. "On Sense and Reference." *Zeitschrift fur Philosophie und Philosophische Kritik* 100, 25–50.

Fumerton, Richard. 1983. "The Paradox of Analysis." *Philosophy and Phenomenological Research* 43, 477–497.

Fumerton, Richard. 1985. *Metaphysical and Epistemological Problems of Perception*. Lincoln and London: University of Nebraska Press.

Fumerton, Richard. 1986. "Essential Properties and De Re Necessity." *Minnesota Studies in the Philosophy of Science* 11(1), 281–294.

Fumerton, Richard. 1989. "Russelling Causal Theories of Reference." In C. Wade Savage and C. Anthony Anderson, eds., *Rereading Russell*. Minneapolis: University of Minnesota Press, 108–118.

Fumerton, Richard. 1990. *Reason and Morality: A Defense of the Egocentric Perspective*. Ithaca, NY: Cornell University Press.

Fumerton, Richard. 1992 "Skepticism and Reasoning to the Best Explanation." In Enrique Villaneueva, ed., *Philosophical Issues*. Atascadero CA: Ridgeview Publishing Co., vol. 2, 149–169.

Fumerton, Richard. 1996. *Metaepistemology and Skepticism*. Boston, MA: Rowman and Littlefield.

Fumerton, Richard, and Ken Kress. 2001. "Causation and the Law." *Law and Contemporary Problems* 64, no. 4, 83–106.

Fumerton, Richard. 2002. *Realism and the Correspondence Theory of Truth*. Boston, MA: Rowman and Littlefield.

Fumerton, Richard. 2003. "Introspection and Internalism." In Susana Nuccetelli, ed., *New Essays on Semantic Externalism, and Self-Knowledge*. Cambridge, MA: MIT Press, 257–276.

Fumerton, Richard. 2004. "Epistemic Probability." *Philosophical Perspectives* 19, 121–139.

Fumerton, Richard. 2006a. *Epistemology*. Malden: Blackwell.
Fumerton, Richard. 2006b. "Direct Realism, Introspection, and Cognitive Science." *Philosophy and Phenomenological Research* 73, no. 3, November, 680–695.
Fumerton, Richard. 2007. "Open Questions and the Nature of Philosophical Analysis." In Susana Nuccetelli and Gary Seay, eds., *Themes from G. E. Moore*. Oxford: Oxford University Press, 227–243.
Fumerton, Richard, and Wendy Donner. 2009. *Mill*. Oxford: Wiley-Blackwell.
Fumerton, Richard. 2010. "You Can't Trust a Philosopher." In Feldman and Warfield eds., *Disagreement*. Oxford: Oxford University Press, 91–110.
Fumerton, Richard. 2013, *Knowledge, Thought and the Case for Dualism*. Cambridge: Cambridge University Press.
Fumerton, Richard. 2017. "Epistemology and Science: Some Metaphysical Reflections." *Philosophical Topics* 45(1), 1–16.
Geach, Peter. 1957. *Mental Acts: Their Content and Their Objects*. London: Routledge & Kegan Paul.
Gertler, Brie. 2011. *Self-Knowledge*. London and New York: Routledge.
Gettier, Edmund. 1963. "Is Knowledge Justified True Belief?" *Analysis* 23, 121–123.
Goldman, Alvin. 1979. "What Is Justified Belief?" In George Pappas, ed., *Justification and Knowledge*. Dordrecht: D. Reidel, 1–23.
Goldman, Alvin. 1999. "Internalism Exposed." *The Journal of Philosophy* 96, no. 6, 271–293.
Harman, Gilbert. 1977. *The Nature of Morality: An Introduction to Ethics*. New York: Oxford University Press.
Harre, Rom, and Edward Madden. 1973. *Causal Powers: A Theory of Natural Necessity*. Lanham, MD: Rowman and Littlefield.
Hempel, Carl. 1965. *Aspects of Scientific Explanation and Other Essays in the Philosophy of Science*. New York: Free Press.
Hempel, Carl. 1969. "Reduction: Ontological and Linguistic Facets." In Suppes Morgenbesser and White, eds., *Philosophy, Science and Method*. New York: St. Martin's Press, 179–199.
Henderson, David, and Terence Horgan. 2006. "Transglobal Reliabilism." *Croatian Journal of Philosophy*, 6(2), 171–195.
Hobbes, Thomas. 1651. *Leviathan*. London: Printed for Andrew Crooke.
Huemer, Michael. 2002. "Fumerton's Principle of Inferential Justification." *Journal of Philosophical Research* 27, 329–340.
Hume, David. 1888. *A Treatise of Human Nature*. Edited by L. A. Selby-Bigge. Oxford: Oxford University Press.
Jackson, Frank. 1982. "Epiphenomenal Qualia." *Philosophical Quarterly* 32, 126–136.
Jackson, Frank. 2004. "Mind and Illusion." In Peter Ludlow, Yujin Nagasawa, and Daniel Stoljar, eds., *There's Something about Mary*. Boston, MA: MIT, 421–442.
Jeske, Diane. 2008. *Rationality and Moral Theory*. New York: Routledge.
Johnston, Mark. 2004. "The Obscure Object of Hallucination." *Philosophical Studies* 103, 113–183.

Kant, Immanuel. 1929. *Critique of Pure Reason*. Translated by Norman Kemp Smith. London: Palgrave Macmillan.

Kant, Immanuel. 1993 [1785]. *Groundwork of the Metaphysics of Morals*. Translated by James Ellington. Indianapolis, IN: Hackett.

Keynes, John Meynard. 1921. *A Treatise on Probability*. London: Macmillan.

Kim, Jaegwon. 1976. "Events as Property Exemplifications." In M. Brand and D. Walton, eds., *Action Theory*. Dordrecht: D. Reidel, 310–326.

Kim, Jaegwon. 1998. *Mind in a Physical World*. Cambridge, MA: MIT Press.

Kornblith, Hillary. 2002. *Knowledge and Its Place in Nature*. New York: Oxford University Press.

Kornblith, Hillary. 2014. "Is There Room for Armchair Theorizing in Epistemology?" In Mathew Haug, ed., *The Armchair or the Laboratory?* New York: Routledge, 195–216.

Kripke, Saul. 1982. *Naming and Necessity*. Cambridge, MA: Harvard University Press.

Langford. C. H. 1942. "The Notion of Analysis in G. E. Moore Philosophy." In Paul Schilpp, ed., *The Philosophy of G.E. Moore*. Evanston, IL: Northwestern University Press, 319–342.

Leibniz. Gottfried *Monadology*. Section 17. 1714. Translated by Paul Schrecher and Anne Martin Schrecher. Indianapolis, IN: Bobbs-Merrill, 1965.

Lewis, David. 1976. "The Paradoxes of Time Travel." *American Philosophical Quarterly* 13, 145–152.

Lewis, David. 1980. "Mad Pain and Martian Pain." In Ned Block, ed., *Readings in the Philosophy of Psychology*. Cambridge, MA: Harvard University Press, 216–222.

Lewis, David. 1996. "Elusive Knowledge." *Australasian Journal of Philosophy* 5, 49–67.

Lewis, David. 2004. "*What Experiences Teaches*." In In Peter Ludlow, Yujin Nagasawa, and Daniel Stoljar eds., *There's Something about Mary*. Boston, MA: MIT, 77–103.

Lewis, C. I. 1946. *An Analysis of Knowledge and Valuation*. Lasalle, IL: Open Court.

Lewis, C. I. 1948. "Professor Chisholm and Empiricism." *Journal of Philosophy* 45, 517–524.

Littlejohn, Clayton. 2012. *Justification and the Truth-Connection*. Oxford: Oxford University Press.

Locke, John. 1690. *An Enquiry Concerning Human Understanding*. London: Thomas Bartlett.

Ludlow, Peter, and Noah Martin, eds. 1998. *Externalism and Self-Knowledge*. Stanford, CA: CSLI Publications.

Ludlow, Peter, Yujin Nagasawa, and Daniel Stoljar, eds. 2004. *There Is Something about Mary*. Boston, MA: MIT Press.

Mackie, J. L. 1965. "Causes and Conditions." *American Philosophical Quarterly* 2, no. 4, 245–264.

Madden, E. H., and R. Harre. 1973. "Natural Powers and Powerful Natures." *Philosophy* 48, 209–230.

Markie, Peter. 2009. "Classical Foundationalism and Speckled Hens." *Philosophy and Phenomenological Research* 79, no. 1, 190–206.

Maxwell, Grover. 1962. "The Ontological Status of Theoretical Entities." In Herbert Feigl and Grover Maxwell, eds., *Scientific Explanation, Space, and Time: Minnesota Studies in the Philosophy of Science*. Minneapolis: University of Minnesota Press, 181–192.

Maxwell, Grover. 1978. "Rigid Designators and Mind-Brain Identity." In C. W. Savage, ed., *Perception and Cognition. Issues in the Foundations of Psychology*. Minneapolis: University of Minnesota Press, 365–405.

Melynk, Andrew. 2003. *A Physicalist Manifesto*. Cambridge: Cambridge University Press.

Mill, John Stuart. 1874. An *Examination of Sir William Hamilton's Philosophy, and of the Principal Philosophical Questions Discussed in His Writings*. New York: Henry Holt and Company.

Mill, John Stuart. 1906. *System of Logic*. New York: Longmans, Green, and Co.

Moore, G. E. 1903. *Principia Ethica*. Cambridge: Cambridge University Press.

Moore, Michael. 2009. *Causation and Responsibility*. Oxford: Oxford University Press.

Nagasawa, Yujin, and Daniel Stoljar. 2004. "Introduction." In Peter Ludlow, Yujin Nagasawa, and Daniel Stoljar, eds., *There's Something about Mary*. Cambridge, MA: MIT Press, 1–36.

Nagel, Thomas. 1974. "What Is It Like to Be a Bat?" *Philosophical Review* 83, 435–450.

Nemirow, Lawrence. 1990. "Physicalism and the Cognitive Role of Acquaintance." In William Lycan, ed., *Mind and Cognition: A Reader*. Oxford: Blackwell, 490–499.

Nemirow, Lawrence. 2007. "So This Is What It's Like: A Defense of the Ability Hypothesis." In Torin Alter and Sven Walter, eds., *Phenomenal Concepts and Phenomenal Knowledge: New Essays on Consciousness and Physicalism*. Oxford: Oxford University Press, 32–51.

Nida-Rümelin, Martine. 2004. "What Mary Couldn't Know: Belief about Phenomenal States." In P. Ludlow, Y. Nagasawa, and D. Stoljar, eds., *There's Something about Mary*. Cambridge, MA: MIT Press, 241–265.

Nuccetelli, Susanna, ed. 2003. *New Essays on Semantic Externalism and Self-Knowledge*. Cambridge, MA: MIT Press.

Plantinga, Alvin. 1993. *Warrant and Proper Function*. New York: Oxford University Press.

Pritchard, Duncan. 2005. *Epistemic Luck*. Oxford: Oxford University Press.

Putnam, Hilary. 1975. "The Meaning of 'Meaning.'" *Minnesota Studies in the Philosophy of Science* 7, 131–193.

Putnam, Hilary. 1981. *Reason, Truth and History*. Cambridge: Cambridge University Press.

Quine, W. V. O. 1951. "Two Dogmas of Empiricism." *Philosophical Review* 60, 20–43.

Quine. W. V. O. 1969. *Ontological Relativity and Other Essays*. New York: Columbia Press.

Ramsey, F. P. 1929. "Theories." In R. B. Braithwaite, ed., *The Foundations of Mathematics and Other Logical Essays*. Paterson, NJ: Littlefield and Adams, 212–236.

Reed, Baron. 2006. "Shelter for the Cognitively Homeless." *Synthese* 148, 303–308.
Ross, W. D. 1930. *The Right and the Good*. Oxford: Clarendon Press.
Russell, Bertrand. 1905. "On Denoting." *Mind* 14, no. 56, 479–493.
Russell, Bertrand. 1910. "Knowledge by Acquaintance and Knowledge by Description." *Proceedings of the Aristotelian Society* 11, 108–128.
Russell, Bertrand. 1948. *Human Knowledge: Its Scope and Limits*. New York: Simon and Schuster.
Russell, Bertrand. 1967. *The Problems of Philosophy*. Oxford: Oxford University Press.
Ryle, Gilbert. 1949. *The Concept of Mind*. Chicago: University of Chicago Press.
Scriven, Michael. 1962. "Explanations, Predictions, and Laws." In Herbert Feigl and Grover Maxwell, eds., *Scientific Explanation, Space, and Time*. Minneapolis: University of Minnesota Press, 170–230.
Searle, John. 1983. *Intentionality: An Essay in the Philosophy of Mind*. Cambridge: Cambridge University Press.
Sellars, Wilfrid. 1956. "Empiricism and the Philosophy of Mind." *Minnesota Studies in the Philosophy of Science* 1, 253–329.
Sidgwick, Henry. 1874. *The Methods of Ethics*. London: Macmillan.
Smart, J. J. C. 1959. "Sensations and Brain Processes." *Philosophical Review* 68, 141–156.
Sosa, E. 2003a. "Privileged Access." In Q. Smith and A. Jokic, eds., *Consciousness: New Philosophical Perspectives*. Oxford: Oxford University Press, 273–292.
Sosa, E. 2003b. "Beyond Internal Foundations to External Virtues." In Laurence BonJour and Ernest Sosa, eds., *Epistemic Justification*. Malden, MA: Blackwell, 99–170.
Sosa, E. 2009. *Reflective Knowledge*, volume II. Oxford: Oxford University Press.
Stanley, Jason. 2011. "Knowing (How)." *Nous* 45, no. 2, 207–238.
Stoljar, Daniel. 2001. "Two Conceptions of the Physical." *Philosophical and Phenomenological Research* 62, no. 2, 253–281.
Strawson, Peter. 1959. *Individuals: An Essay in Descriptive Metaphysics*. London: Methuen.
Stevenson, C. L. 1937. "The Emotive Meaning of Ethical Terms," *Mind* 46, no. 181, January, 14–31.
Sturgeon, Nicholas. 1988. "Moral Explanations." In Geoffrey Sayre-McCord, ed., *Essays on Moral Realism*. Ithaca, NY: Cornell University Press, 229–255.
Thompson, Judith Jarvis. 1971. "A Defense of Abortion." *Philosophy and Public Affairs* 1, no. 1, 47–66.
Ushenko, Andrew Paul. 1937. *The Philosophy of Relativity*. London: G. Allen and Unwin Ltd.
Weinberg, Jonathan, Nicholas Shaun, and Stephen Stich. 2001. "Normativity and Epistemic Intuitions." *Philosophical Topics* 29, 429–460.
Williamson, Timothy. 2000. *Knowledge and Its Limits*. Oxford: Oxford University Press.
Williamson, Timothy. 2007. *The Philosophy of Philosophy*. Malden, MA: Blackwell.

Williamson, Timothy. Forthcoming. "Justification, Excuses, and Sceptical Scenarios." In Fabian Dorsch and Julien Dutant, eds., *The New Evil Demon*. Oxford: Oxford University Press.

Wilson, Jennifer. 2012. "Rethinking the A Priori/A Posteriori Distinction." *Logos & Episteme* 3(2), 261–277.

Wittengstein, Ludwig. 1953 Philosophical Investigations. London: Macmillan

Index

Note: Page numbers followed by "n" denote endnotes.

absolutist theory of time 137
access internalists 86
Addis, Laird 22n13, 22n14, 78n2
agricultural ethics 4
Alexander the Great 77
Alston, William 9, 96n23
alternative geometries 138
American Philosophical Association Meeting 4
analysis: conceptual 118–124; linguistic 26–27; phenomenology and 58–61; property 25
analytic philosophy 13
Anscombe, Elizabeth 147n10
applied epistemology 7–8
applied ethics 6–8, 22n6, 30, 97, 111, 114
applied philosophy 150
applied questions 4, 5, 114, 152–156
Aristophanes 31
Aristotle 3–4, 5, 75, 76, 104
"armchair" philosophical theorizing 127–128
Armstrong, David 22n10, 65n24, 145, 149n24
atoms 14; conceptual 15, 43; philosophical 13–14
attitudes: intentional 127
Austin, J. L. 17, 48, 49, 50
Ayer, A. J. 8, 9, 48, 149n20; *Language, Truth and Logic* 33n7

baptism 19
Baum, Frank 125
begging questions: doing metaphilosophy without 20–21
behaviorism: crude 122; logical 122
belief-independent processes 87

beliefs: dispositional 126; forming 88, 90; justified 80, 87; justified true 82; knowledge 63n1; occurrent 126; unconscious 126–127
Bergmann, Gustav 4, 21n2, 65n14
Berkeley, George 3, 5, 151, 147n1, 149n20
bias, implicit 115
Bickle, John 130n9
Bigelow, John 22n10
"blind" reliability 90
Brandt, Richard 9
Brentano, Franz 39, 65n14
Broad, C. D. 22n12, 23n16
business ethics 4, 30
Butchvarov, Panayot 33n3

Cartesian conception of knowledge 82–83
Cartesian meditation 156
Casati, R. 148n14
causal theories 71, 75
causation 132–136
Chalmers, David 22n16
Chisholm, Roderick 38, 40, 49, 64n11, 148n14, 149n20
Chomsky, Noam 22n9
Churchland, Paul 22n10, 22n16
The Clouds (Aristophanes) 31
Cohen, Stewart 96n24
coherence theory of justification 140, 141
Columbus, Christopher 54, 55
"common denominator" 26, 49, 54, 66n30
conceptual analysis 118–124; philosophy 15–16
conceptual atoms 15

Index

conditional reliability 90
Conee, Earl 22n10, 22n16, 95n13, 96n20
consequentialism 107–108; and intrinsic value 109
content externalism 18–20
content internalism 73–75, 157; and philosophy 73–75
contextualism 94n5
crude behaviorism 122
Cunning, David 64n12

Davidson, Donald 25, 148n8
Deductive-Nomological model of explanation 133–134
definite description 19, 23n24, 71–77, 78n7, 118, 146, 154, 157
Dennett, Daniel 22n16
deontological accounts of morality 107–109
Descartes, René 3, 5, 9, 22n11, 28, 29, 39, 62, 64n12
descriptive metaphysical analysis 20
determinate and determinable properties 44–45
direct acquaintance 37–38, 41, 120, 125
dispositional beliefs 126
Donner, Wendy 78n4
Dowell, J. L. 22n10
doxastic justification: defined 84–85; *vs.* propositional justification 84–85
dualism 22n11; plausibility of 12; property 116–118; substance 116–118
Ducasse, C. J. 135, 148n12
Duerlinger, James 23n17
Dummett, Michael 130n9

Eddington, Arthur 143–144
empirical knowledge 55
empirical question 12, 74; about inferences 4; abstract 61; theoretical 131
empirical reality 24, 40
empirical sciences 5, 8, 11, 21, 32, 101, 124
enthymematic reasoning 92
environmental ethics 30
epistemic internalism 101, 155, 157
epistemic justification/rationality 84–89, 101; non-epistemic reasons to believe 84; propositional *vs.* doxastic justification 84–85
epistemology 4, 13, 80–94, 114; applied 7–8; defined 80; epistemic justification 84–89; internalism/externalism controversy in 85–89; and knowledge 80–84; metaepistemology 78; and philosophy of science 138–142; social 30; technical language in 50
ethics 4, 5–7; agricultural 4; applied 6–8, 22n6, 30, 97, 111, 114; axioms in 104; business 4, 30; environmental 30; feminist 4, 30; metaethics 6–7, 16; meta *vs.* applied distinction in 114; military 4; normative 22n6; and rationality 97
Euclidean geometry 138
"existential" commitment 103
expected value of action 100, 106
experimental philosophy (X-Phi) 23n21
explanation 132–136
externalism 73–75; about meaning 69–73; controversy (*see* internalism/externalism controversy); defined 95n10; and philosophy 73–75; rejecting 75–78
externalists 86–87, 91; epistemological 101

Fales, Evan 23n24
Feldman, Richard 22n10, 32n1, 95n13, 96n20
feminist ethics 4, 30
first-level question 21n4, 21n5, 80, 83, 105, 107, 109, 111; about doxastic justification 85; about knowledge 83; about mental states 114–115; about morality 110; about propositional justification 85
first-person perspective 40, 69
Firth, Roderick 94n6, 149n20
Fodor, Jerry 148n16
Foley, Richard 112n10
forming beliefs 88
foundationalism and phenomenology 35–45
Franklin, Benjamin 73, 76, 77
Frege, Gottlieb 22n7
Fumerton, Richard 22n10, 32n2, 65n19, 78n4, 79n8, 96n26, 149n22
functionalism 117, 121–124

Geach, Peter 148n15
generality problem 88
generic utilitarianism 106
Gertler, Brie 22n10
Gettier, Edmund 17, 46, 55, 56, 82–83
Gettier thought experiments 23n21
Glaucon 111n1
Goldman, Alvin 87, 95n13
goodness 15–16; instrumental 16; intrinsic 16, 27
Grice, Paul 17

hallucination 28, 29; alien-induced 140; consistent 86; evil demons inducing 38; massive 29, 37, 86; radical 49; vivid 29, 49–50, 64n7, 86, 93
Harman, Gilbert 112n22, 113n25
Harre, R. 148n12
Hempel, Carl 133–134, 112n18, 130n6, 147n5
Henderson, David 95n19
hieroglyphics 70
higher-level meta-questions 8
Hobbes, Thomas 3, 111n1, 113n25
Horgan, Terence 95n19
Hudson, Henry 50
Huemer, Michael 96n26, 147n3
human psychology 3
Hume, David 3, 5, 21n1, 23n17, 25, 33n3, 41, 42, 46, 133, 144, 148n6, 151

ideal political theories 48
identity theory 130n9
implicit bias 115
inferential justification 36, 64n3, 102, 139
instrumental goodness 16
intellectual curiosity 151–152
intentional attitudes 127
intentional states 32, 39–40, 64n13, 130n13
internalism 89–91; content 73–75, 157; epistemic 101, 155, 157
internalism/externalism controversy 36, 48, 73–75; in epistemology 85–89; and philosophical epistemology 89–94
internalists 89, 91
internal relations 58–61
intrinsic character 15, 120–122, 126, 146

intrinsic goodness 16, 27
intrinsic value 103–105; and consequentialists 109; of goals 105; metaethical view 104
introspection 98
Investigations (Wittgenstein) 57

Jackson, Frank 22–23n16, 42
justification: coherence theory of 140, 141; doxastic 84–85; epistemic 84–89, 101; propositional (*see* propositional justification)
justified beliefs 80, 87
justified true beliefs 82

Kant, Immanuel 5, 34n14, 65n19, 112n23
Keynes, John Meynard 96n26
Kim, Jaegwon 129n5, 148n14
knowledge 80–84; Cartesian conception of 82–83; empirical 55; foundations of 124; propositional 80–81; as true belief 63n1
Kornblith, Hillary 127–128
Kripke, Saul 61, 70, 71, 73, 77, 79n8, 79n9

Langford. C. H. 28
language: philosophy of 69–78; technical 50
Language, Truth and Logic (Ayer) 8, 33n7
Leibniz, Gottfried 5, 22–23n16
Lepore, Ernest 148n16
Lewis, C. I. 149n20
Lewis, David 22n16, 124, 129n4, 147n3
lexicographer 16
The Life of Brian 79n12
linguistic community 51
linguistic nominalism 144
linguistic turn 16–18; second 18–20
linguists 17, 27
Littlejohn, Clayton 95n14
Locke, John 158n5
logical behaviorism 122
Ludlow, Peter 22n10, 23n16

Madden, E. H. 148n12
Markie, Peter 95n12
Martin, Noah 22n10
master argument 28–32
Maxwell, Grover 139–140
meaning: externalism about 69–73

Index

Meinong, Alexius 39, 65n14
metaepistemology 78, 80–94, 114; and internalism/externalism controversy 89–94; reliabilism 87–88
metaethical controversies 18
metaethical non-cognitivism 7
metaethical questions 16
metaethics 6–7, 16, 97, 105, 108, 114–115
metaphilosophical questions 8, 20
metaphilosophical view 13, 31, 63, 157
metaphilosophy 8–9; doing without begging questions 20–21; thought experiments 53–56
metaphysical analysis: descriptive 20; prescriptive 20
metaphysics 4, 5, 29, 41; traditional 142–146
meta-questions 6; epistemology 7–8; ethics 5–7; within fields of philosophy 5–9; higher-level 8; metaphilosophy 8–9
meta-rationality 97, 100, 115
methodological solipsism 28; and master argument 28–32
military ethics 4
Mill, John Stuart 5, 70, 148n7, 149n20
"mind/brain" identity theory 117, 120–121
modal claim 73, 77, 79n8
Moore, G. E. 15, 16, 17, 25, 27–28, 33n3, 63, 104, 106, 112n21
morality 102–111; deontological accounts of 107–109; intrinsic value 103–105; and rationality 102–103
morals by agreement 110–111
moral value 103, 107

Nagasawa, Yujin 23n16
Nagel, Thomas 22n10, 23n16
naturalism 155
Newtonian physics 132
Nida-Rümelin, Martine 22n16
non-cognitivism 7, 155
non-epistemic reasons to believe 84
non-ideal political theories 48
noninferentially justified: defined 87
non-physical objects 116–117
normative ethics 22n6

object 9–10, 22n14, 28–31, 37–40, 46, 119

occurrent beliefs 126
"ought" of morality 92, 102–103, 106
"ought" of rationality 92, 102–103

paradigmatic philosophical questions 8, 9–13
paradox of analysis 24–28
Pargetter, Robert 22n10
Peace Corps 94
Perceiving (Chisholm) 38
phenomenology 40, 58, 63, 98, 115–116, 124; and analysis 58–61; foundationalism and 35–45; as starting point of all philosophical reflection 40–45
philosophers 10, 11, 14, 15, 17, 21n5, 24, 54
philosophical analysis 45–58; beyond stipulation 51–53; "internal" relations among properties 58–61; stipulative definition 47–51; thought experiments 53–56; Wittgenstein and private language argument 56–58
philosophical epistemology: and internalism/externalism controversy 89–94
philosophical intrusion: inappropriate, into empirical matters 124–129
philosophical questions 13
philosophy 8, 9, 14, 15, 17, 20, 21, 24, 30, 31, 40, 45, 53, 58, 60, 61; analytic 13; conceptual analysis 15–16; content externalism 18–20; content internalism/externalism controversy 73–75; different conceptions of 13–20; as a distinct field 3–5; linguistic turn 16–18; meta-questions within fields of 5–9; political 3–4, 48, 150; as search for fundamental categories of reality 14–15; second linguistic turn 18–20
philosophy of language 69–78; content internalism/externalism controversy 73–75; externalism about meaning 69–73; rejecting externalism 75–78
philosophy of mind 114–129; and conception of philosophy 118–124; dualism 116–118; meta-questions in 115–124
philosophy of science 131–147; causation and explanation 132–136; and epistemology 138–142; older

paradigm 131–132; space and time
  136–138
philosophy proper 150–158; answering
  applied questions 152–156;
  intellectual curiosity 151–152
physicalism 117
physical objects 116
Plantinga, Alvin 112n16
Plato 3–4, 5, 14, 15, 31, 81, 104, 111n1,
  113n25
plausibility of dualism 12
political philosophy 3–4, 48, 150
prescriptive metaphysical analysis 20
Price, H. H. 48
prima facie obligatory 7, 22n6, 22n8,
  108, 109
Principia Ethica (Moore) 15, 63

Pritchard, Duncan 94n2
private language argument 56–58
problem of easy knowledge 96n24
property dualism 116–118; non-
  physical objects 116; physical
  objects 116
property dualists 116–117,
  120, 155
propositional justification 95n8,
  128; defined 84–85; *vs.* doxastic
  justification 84–85
propositional knowledge 33n4, 80–81,
  94n1
prototype theory 128–129
pseudo-questions 11
Putnam, Hilary 61, 65n15, 69, 70,
  71, 77

Quine, W. V. O. 5, 66n35, 148n17

Ramsey, F. P. 65n19
rational action 98–102
rationality: epistemic justification/
  rationality 84–89; and ethics 97; and
  morality 102–103; "ought" of 92,
  102–103
rational reconstruction 21n3
realists 145, 149n22
reality: empirical 24, 40; philosophy as
  search for fundamental categories of
  14–15
realizer of functional property 117
Reed, Baron 22n10
regress 102, 103; conceptual 103

regularity theory of causation 46,
  65n24, 133, 145, 148n6
relational theory of space
  136–137
reliabilism 87–88, 101, 96n20;
  transglobal 95n19
reliabilists 88
reliability: "blind" 90; conditional 90
The Republic (Plato) 15, 31, 111n1,
  113n25
right action 105–107
Roe v Wade 153
Ross, Bob 56
Ross, W. D. 108
Russell, Bertrand 3, 5, 23n18, 36, 55,
  65n18, 78n7
Ryle, Gilbert 17

second-level questions 21n5
Searle, John 22n14, 96n25
Sellars, Wilfrid 48, 65n27
skeptical scenarios 156–158
skepticism 21n1, 29, 36, 39, 47, 51
Smart, J. J. C. 23n25, 65n27,
  120–121
social epistemology 30
Socrates 31
Sosa, E. 95n12, 96n24
space 136–138
speaker's meaning 47, 69
Stanley, Jason 94n1
Stevenson, C. L. 20–21, 33n5
stipulation: beyond 51–53; philosophical
  analysis 51–53
Stoljar, Daniel 23n16, 149n18
Strawson, Peter 20
substance dualism 116–118
supererogatory actions 110–111
supererogatory acts 105
surface grammar 7, 18, 22n9

Theatetus (Plato) 15
Thompson, Judith Jarvis 158n6
Thompson, Judy 158n6
thought experiments 53–56, 133
Thrasymachus 111n1
*Three Dialogues Between Hylas and
  Philonous* (Berkeley) 151
time 136–138
transglobal reliabilism 95n19
A Treatise of Human Nature (Hume) 41
truth 80

unconscious beliefs 126–127
Ushenko, Andrew Paul 95n12

Varzi, A. C. 148n14
verificationism 137–138
virtues 109–110

Warfield, Ted 32n1

Washington, George 35, 43
Wayne, John 66n34
Williamson, Timothy 53–56, 63n1, 86, 95n14
Wilson, Jennifer 95n16
Wittgenstein, Ludwig 5, 17, 33n5, 57, 58; *Investigations* 57; and private language argument 56–58

For Product Safety Concerns and Information please contact our EU
representative GPSR@taylorandfrancis.com
Taylor & Francis Verlag GmbH, Kaufingerstraße 24, 80331 München, Germany

www.ingramcontent.com/pod-product-compliance
Lightning Source LLC
Chambersburg PA
CBHW050302010526
44108CB00040B/2084